Water Resources:
Process and M

V:

College

Dr Robert Prosser

Lecturer, CURS, University of Birmingham

Collins Educational
An imprint of HarperCollins*Publishers*

Contents

Skills matrix
(distribution of numbered tasks)

Chapter	Understanding of text/ newspaper extracts and classification	Graphical/mapping methods and annotated diagrams	Analysis of data from tables, graphs and diagrams	Analysis of photographs	Analysis of maps	Statistical analysis/methods	Values enquiry	Project work based on library/ fieldwork/research/ data collection	Writing: essays, rep…
1	1		1, 2						
2	7, 10, 11, 14	1	2, 3, 8, 9, 10, 11, 13, 18, 21	7	1, 6, 15, 16, 17	4, 5, 6		20	12, 19, 22
3	2, 3, 14, 23, 32	1a, 4, 6, 7, 8, 15, 21, 27	1b, 2, 3, 5, 9, 10, 11, 13, 18, 20, 22, 24, 25, 26, 29, 30, 31, 32, 33, 34, 35	15	9, 10, 11, 17,18, 19, 21				12, 16, 28
4	5c, 21, 24d, 26, 27, 30 37a, 38, 40	4, 5a, 6, 17 18a, 24b, 25c, 36, 43	7, 8, 10, 11, 12, 13, 14, 15, 19, 20, 21, 22, 23b, 24c, 25b, 28, 29, 33, 34, 35, 37b, 39, 41, 42, 44	1	2, 3, 4, 5b, 13, 16, 18b, 26, 28, 37b	9, 23a, 24a, 25a	40		31, 45
5	13, 15	4, 10, 15, 16	7, 8, 9, 11, 12, 14, 17, 18, 19, 20, 21		4, 5	1, 2, 3, 6			22
6	1, 4, 11, 14, 19	3, 7, 9, 10, 21, 27, 34	4, 5, 8, 12, 13, 16, 17, 18, 20, 22, 23, 24, 25, 28, 29, 31, 32, 33, 35		2, 11, 15		6		26, 30, 36, 37, 38
7	1, 11, 14, 15, 16, 17, 18, 22, 30, 32a, 35	3, 5, 23, 25	2, 7, 8, 9, 10 12, 13, 19, 20, 21, 26, 27b, 33, 34	12	4, 6a, 24, 28, 29, 31		6, 27b, 32b		
8	6, 8, 9, 10, 11, 14, 15, 18, 19, 20, 21, 22, 23, 24b	1, 3, 10b, 16, 18, 24a	5, 7a, 12, 13, 17, 23		2, 4	7b			
9	1, 9, 10, 13, 14	3a, 5b, 6a, 11	2, 3b–d, 4, 5c,d, 6b, 7, 8, 12			5a,b, 6, 11	8d, 9d, 14c		11
10	1, 3, 4, 5, 9, 10, 11, 14, 20	1a, 4a, 8	2, 6, 12, 13, 15, 16, 17, 18, 19, 21				1b,c, 5d, 7, 9c	15	
11	2, 8, 11, 12, 17, 18	3, 5, 6, 7, 9, 10	1, 4, 11, 15, 16		1, 6		13		14

To the student

This book examines how water behaves on and beneath the earth's surface. The oceans are not included, and so the focus is upon the 'fresh' water component of the hydrosphere. You will follow the journey of fresh water from its arrival as precipitation, i.e. rain, snow and hail, until its departure back to the atmosphere or into the oceans. This journey involves interactions with the lithosphere – the physical skin of landmasses – and with the biosphere – the realm of living organisms. The journey may last a few minutes or thousands of years. There are several routes and stopping places, and many things happen along the way.

To help you make sense of the complex details, the materials throughout the book are presented within the simple framework of a model. This model is built from a set of pathways along which water moves, and stores where it is retained for varying lengths of time. As the water moves or is stored, a variety of processes act upon it. This structure of pathways, stores and processes is known as a system, and this book adopts a systems approach. Through the fluvial system, water and sediment are moved by the vital ingredient of energy. Water which contains energy can do work, e.g. erode, transport and deposit material.

Water is an essential part of all human societies, and there are few rivers or groundwater stores which are unaffected by our activities. Consequently, in this book we view water as a precious resource. We show that fluvial systems impact upon human activities, particularly with flood events, but also that human activity can have a strong influence upon fluvial systems. In early chapters you will study natural systems at work, but as the chapters proceed you will become more aware of the human element. None the less, you need not follow the chapters in sequence, although Chapter 1 is intended as an introduction, and the final chapter is a review which is most effective when you have covered the other materials.

Throughout the book we have illustrated key hydrological and fluvial terms and concepts with case studies. Learning these terms and concepts as you use the chapters will develop your knowledge and understanding. You will progress to higher-level skills, such as evaluation and justification, which are important in 'A' level studies today. In addition, geographical skills and techniques are used to develop your analysis and interpretation of geographical data. These techniques can be used in other areas of geography and for your individual studies or other coursework. People and fluvial system interactions are a topic in nearly all areas which you could consider for your project work.

The interaction between people and fluvial systems is continuous and changing. We hope that this book will increase your interest in this subject. Watch the news on television and read quality newspapers to keep up to date with events such as floods and developments in water management. Try to apply the concepts you learn in this book to new situations as they arise, and evaluate the human responses as an informed geographer.

Victoria Bishop and Robert Prosser

1 Water: a global resource

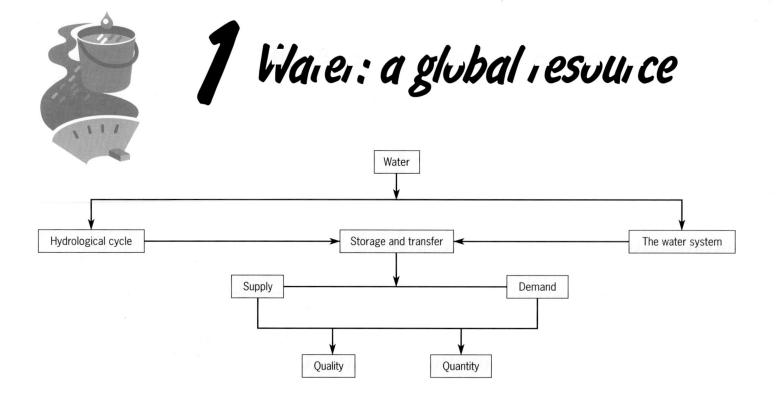

```
                           Water
                             |
        +--------------------+--------------------+
        |                    |                    |
  Hydrological cycle ---> Storage and transfer <--- The water system
                             |
                +------------+------------+
                |                         |
             Supply                    Demand
                |                         |
                +------------+------------+
                |                         |
             Quality                   Quantity
```

1.1 A resource for life

'Water is the foundation of life on earth: without it there would be no plants, no animals, no living things' (Bellamy and Quayle, 1986). This opening statement sums up the importance of the theme of this book: water is a fundamental resource for all life. To ensure that humans and other species will survive and thrive in the future, we must understand how water works in the global environment. We can develop this understanding through the framework of the **hydrological cycle**. Water moves through this cycle in all its three forms – liquid, solid, gas. This book explores those parts of the hydrological cycle tinted pale green on Figure 1.4.

1.2 Global water supplies

In terms of total volume, planet earth has plenty of water (Figs 1.1 and 1.2). However, less than 8 per cent of it is readily accessible. The rest is stored in saline oceans, or deep below the land surface, or in the polar ice caps. So, humans and organisms other than oceanic species must compete for the small percentage that is available.

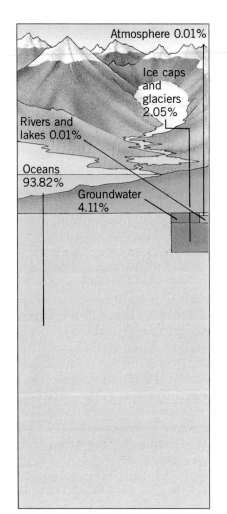

Figure 1.1 Distribution of the world's water

Figure 1.2 The earth's water

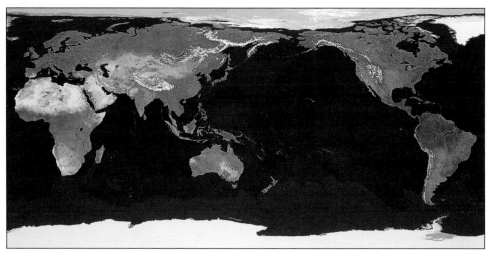

Water is, therefore, a scarce resource. Questions are raised throughout this book concerning this scarcity and the competition for water:

- How much water is there? (Quantity)
- Where and when? (Distribution and frequency)
- How much is needed? (Demand-supply relationships)
- Whose is it? (Ownership)

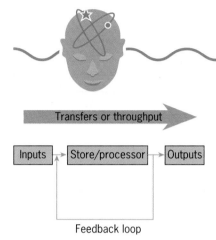

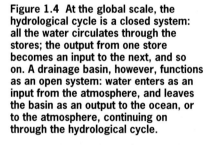

Figure 1.3 The basic system

A systems approach

Geographers often take a systems approach for their study of aspects of the environment. A system has a form or structure, built around a set of stores and pathways within an identifiable boundary. It also has a function, consisting of inputs, throughputs and outputs of energy and matter (Fig. 1.3).

All environmental systems, including rivers and **drainage basins**, possess the ability to adjust to change. For example, if the rainfall input increases, a river may respond by enlarging its channel to cope with the extra water. This response is represented on Figure 1.3 as **negative feedback**, processes which work to sustain or restore balance in the way a system works.

There is a limit to the ability of a system to adjust to change, i.e. a tolerance limit. If inputs of energy and/or material change too severely or too suddenly the system may be overwhelmed. Then, **positive feedback**, or the 'runaway mechanism of progressive change', takes over. When the system settles down once more, it may have quite a different form. For example, a catastrophic flood may result in a river taking a new course. Human activity can cause such fundamental change, e.g. building and operating a **dam** will permanently alter a river's flow **regime** downstream.

Figure 1.4 At the global scale, the hydrological cycle is a closed system: all the water circulates through the stores; the output from one store becomes an input to the next, and so on. A drainage basin, however, functions as an open system: water enters as an input from the atmosphere, and leaves the basin as an output to the ocean, or to the atmosphere, continuing on through the hydrological cycle.

?

1 Study Figure 1.4. For each of the three environmental stores, lithosphere, hydrosphere and biosphere, suggest two ways in which human activities might affect the way the store works.

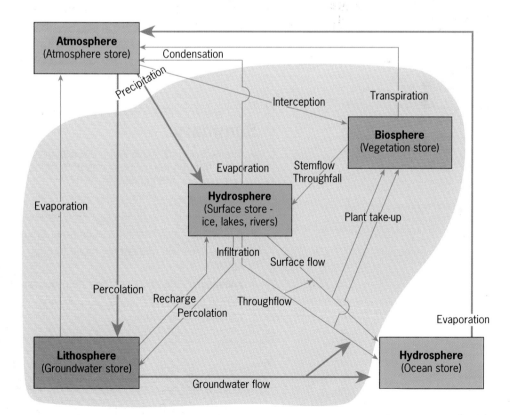

Table 1.1 Internal renewable freshwater resources of selected countries, 1990 (*Source:* UNEP, 1993)

Country	Total (km³/y)	Per person (000 m³/y)
United Kingdom	120	2.14
Norway	405	97.10
Cameroon	208	18.84
Egypt	2	0.04
Canada	2901	109.51
Mexico	357	4.11
Brazil	5190	35.21
Peru	40	1.84
Laos	270	59.51
Pakistan	298	2.72
Australia	343	20.78
New Zealand	397	115.57

Note: These figures are for internal resources which are renewable. Many countries rely on sources outside their boundaries, e.g. Egypt.

2 From Table 1.1:
a List the characteristics of the freshwater resources shown.
b Select two countries showing different characteristics. Suggest reasons to explain their features.

Water availability

Countries vary enormously in their water availability (Table 1.1). For instance, Canada, a huge, sparsely populated country with significant **precipitation** over much of its surface, has 109 510 cubic metres per year per person. At the other extreme, Egypt has 40 cubic metres per year per person. Some countries have water supplies which permanently exceed demand, some have permanent deficits, and others, including the UK, shift between surplus and deficit water balances.

1.3 Water as a transfer system

In this book, we shall examine the important role of water as the agent of erosion, transportation and deposition of **sediment**. We are constantly reminded of the awesome power of rivers to create and to destroy. River channels are the main transfer pathways for water and sediment. It is vital therefore, that we understand how channels work and what their capabilities are: how much water they can hold; how much energy is available; and how much sediment can be moved. These understandings are becoming ever more important as human activities and settlements expand across river basins. Thus, a fundamental goal of water management techniques is to control the movement of water and sediment. This is achieved by modifying the stores and pathways of the drainage basin, e.g. building a dam to create a reservoir; channelising a river to improve flow, and so on.

1.4 Water quality

It is also important for us to study water quality. This is causing increasing concern throughout the world as human activities intensify. Issues in this book focus around the causes, character, levels, locations, impacts and remedies of water pollution. Remember, because the hydrological cycle works as a transfer and storage system, the effects of pollution may be felt at considerable distances from the source of the pollution.

Summary

- The hydrological cycle is the circulation of water in any of its forms – liquid, solid, gas – through the major stores of the global system: atmosphere, lithosphere, hydrosphere and biosphere.
- A drainage basin is a transfer system with a form of stores and pathways, and a function consisting of inputs, throughputs, processes and outputs.
- A drainage basin functions as an open system.
- Water, sediment and energy move through and are stored within the drainage basin system.
- Feedback is the term used for the processes which create adjustments to a system.
- Human activities are having increasing impacts upon the form and function of hydrological systems.

2 Drainage basin processes

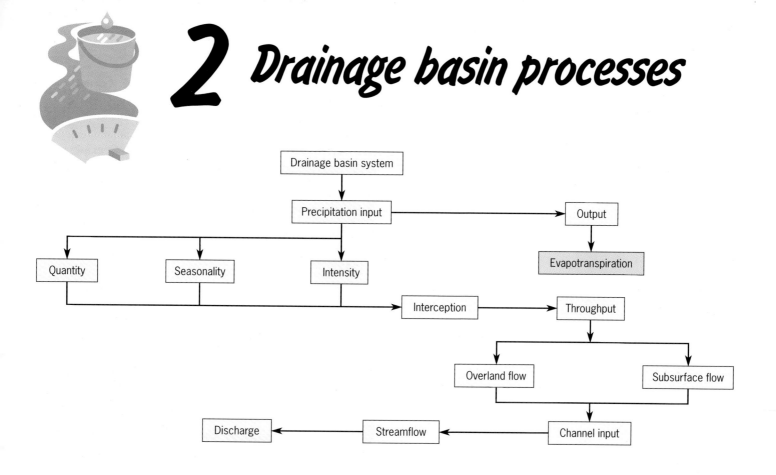

2.1 The drainage basin system

What is a drainage basin?

The **drainage basin** is the **catchment area** for water which drains into and flows down a single river channel, entering eventually into a sea or lake. It is the basic unit for studying hydrological processes. The drainage basin is a system as defined in Figure 2.1: inputs, stores and outputs, working within a definable boundary. This allows us to explore the inputs and outputs of the **hydrological cycle** in a manageable way. The water enters the system as **precipitation** and leaves as **streamflow** (measured in cubic metres per second, m^3/s, often called cumecs) or as **evaporation** or **transpiration.**

These hydrological processes do not operate in isolation. They are linked with geomorphological processes such as weathering and mass movement. Thus, the inputs, throughputs and outputs from the drainage basin system include **sediment** as well as streamflow. The whole system can be explained in terms of the relationships between water, sediment and available energy.

The system structure

Figure 2.1 shows the drainage basin system as a black box. Here, we can see the inputs and outputs are identified, but the contents of the box are not revealed. In this chapter we shall study the main processes at work within this drainage basin box.

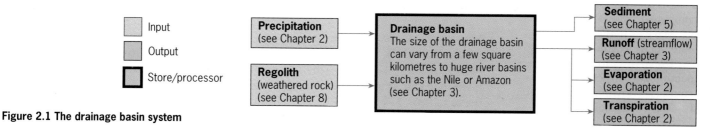

Figure 2.1 The drainage basin system

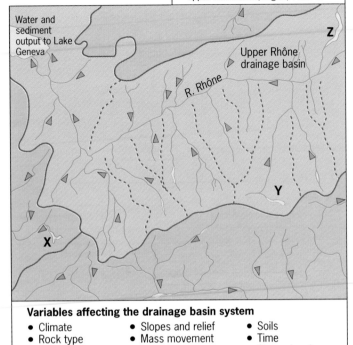

—— Main basin watershed	1. All rivers input water and sediment to the main Rhône channel.
---- Minor watersheds	2. Not all tributaries or minor watersheds are shown.
▲ Rivers showing direction of flow	3. A number of tributaries are glacier-fed. The glaciers show bluish to white in the upper catchments, e.g. X, Y and Z.

Water and sediment output to Lake Geneva

R. Rhône

Upper Rhône drainage basin

Z

Y

X

Variables affecting the drainage basin system

- Climate
- Rock type
- Geological structure
- Slopes and relief
- Mass movement processes
- Vegetation
- Soils
- Time
- Channel and valley form

Figure 2.2 The upper R. Rhône drainage basin, Valais, Switzerland, in partly completed diagrammatic form

Figure 2.3 Landsat image of the upper R. Rhône drainage basin

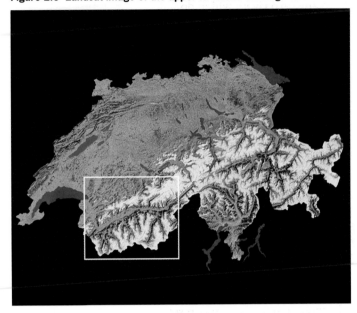

The component parts of the drainage basin are illustrated in diagrammatic form in Figure 2.2. The boundary of a drainage basin is the **watershed**. Within this rim of high relief, water and sediment move to and through the main river channel. The watershed forms the boundary between drainage basins. For example, in the western USA, the Rocky Mountains are a major watershed between the Colorado drainage basin to the west and the Mississippi drainage basin to the east. Within each drainage basin there are minor watersheds separating the catchments of the basin's tributary streams, i.e. sub-systems.

Each drainage basin is unique, with its distinctive size, shape and internal layout. The principal variables influencing the form and functioning of a drainage basin are listed on Figure 2.2. These variables affect how the hydrological and geomorphological processes will work within the basin, e.g. how much sediment will arrive in a river, where and when.

Streamflow

The usual way we observe the result of the inputs and processes – what is going on in a drainage basin – is as streamflow or **discharge**. We might expect streamflow to be determined mainly by the size of the drainage basin: the bigger the basin, the larger the streamflow. Figure 2.5 shows that this is too simple an assumption. For the 14 major drainage basins in England and Wales (Fig. 2.4), there is only a weak correlation between basin area and mean annual discharge. This means that there must be other factors which influence the amount of streamflow leaving the system. To find out what these factors are, and so to explain how rivers behave, we need to identify these factors and understand how they work.

1 Place tracing paper over Figure 2.2.
a Draw the main Rhône basin watershed.
b Mark as many minor watersheds as you can identify.
c Use arrows to show the location and direction of tributaries flowing into the Rhône.
d Mark the glaciers.

?

2 Study Figure 2.5.
a Name two rivers which show a close fit to the regression line on the scattergraph.
b Name two rivers which do not show a close fit to the regression line on the scattergraph.

3 On Figure 2.5 four clusters of drainage basins have been identified. Fit the following descriptions to each of the four groups.
a A small drainage basin area and a higher than average discharge.
b Medium-sized drainage basins with a larger than average discharge.
c Small drainage basin areas with a less than average discharge.
d A large drainage basin with a below average discharge.

4 The Spearman rank coefficient of correlation (r_s) for the two sets of data has been calculated as 0.72. Use Appendix 1 to interpret the significance of the correlation.

5 Evaluate the validity of the two techniques (scattergraph and Spearman rank) as ways of showing the relationship between drainage basin area and discharge.

6 Using Figure 2.4, suggest reasons for the level of correlation between drainage basin area and discharge for the 14 drainage basins in England and Wales.

Figure 2.4 The 14 major drainage basins in England and Wales

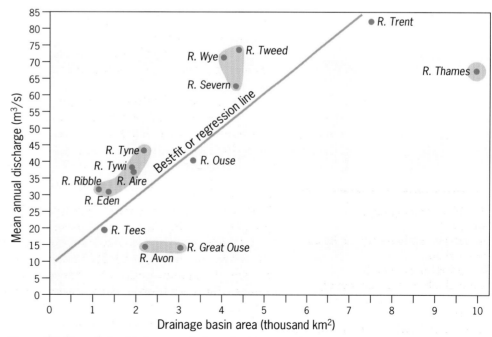

Figure 2.5 The relationship between drainage basin area and mean annual discharge for the 14 major drainage basins in England and Wales

Hydrological processes

In Figure 2.6 we can see the processes and stores within the drainage basin black box. The drainage basin consists of a series of stores linked by flows and processes which allow water to move through the system. As we have moved down in scale, each of the stores within the drainage basin is shown as a black box. Throughout the book we will open up each of these boxes by investigating the nature of the processes operating within the drainage basin system. Figure 2.7 introduces you to the key terms you will meet in this investigation. You should refer to this diagram and Figure 2.6 throughout.

Figure 2.6 Hydrological processes and stores in the drainage basin system (*After*: Ward and Robinson, 1990)

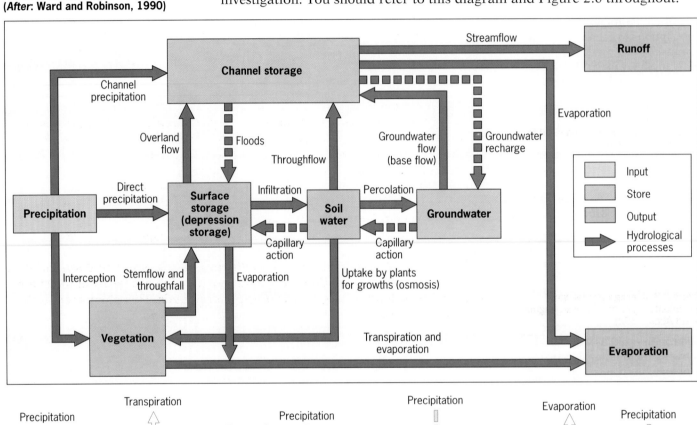

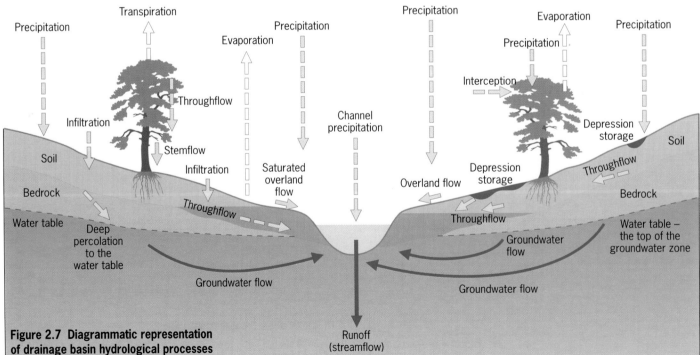

Figure 2.7 Diagrammatic representation of drainage basin hydrological processes

2.2 Drainage basin processes: above the surface

Precipitation

The precipitation input is an important factor affecting how rivers behave. Depending upon the size of the drainage basin, precipitation totals will influence the input (the potential amount of water which can enter a system) and the output (the eventual streamflow). The basic understanding is that precipitation varies over space and time at all scales. So, in a study of any river or drainage basin, we need to ask some key questions (Fig. 2.8). It is important also that we separate water delivery to a river into two stages: first, the precipitation as it falls, and second, what happens to it when it arrives at the surface. As only around one per cent of precipitation arrives as channel precipitation, i.e. falls directly on to the river surface, the journey of this second stage is crucial.

Where and how much? (Location and magnitude)

Figure 2.9 summarises precipitation at the global scale. The highest inputs to drainage basins are recorded in equatorial regions. This is because the constantly warm atmosphere and the convergence of the Trade Winds at the Inter-Tropical Convergence Zone (ITCZ) combine to generate high-energy storms which produce heavy rains. The lowest precipitation totals are recorded in two contrasting zones: high-latitude polar regions where cold air has a limited ability to hold and, therefore, to release water, and sub-tropical regions where descending air from the sub-tropical high pressure cells creates hot deserts.

The pattern of precipitation is also influenced by the size and distribution of land masses and oceans. Continental interiors, which are far from moist air mass sources, tend to receive low precipitation totals. This phenomenon is known as continentality. Relief and prevailing winds add further

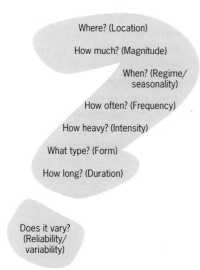

Where? (Location)

How much? (Magnitude)

When? (Regime/ seasonality)

How often? (Frequency)

How heavy? (Intensity)

What type? (Form)

How long? (Duration)

Does it vary? (Reliability/ variability)

Figure 2.8 The precipitation input to the drainage basin system

Figure 2.9 Average annual world precipitation (*Source:* Collins-Longman World Atlas, 1992)

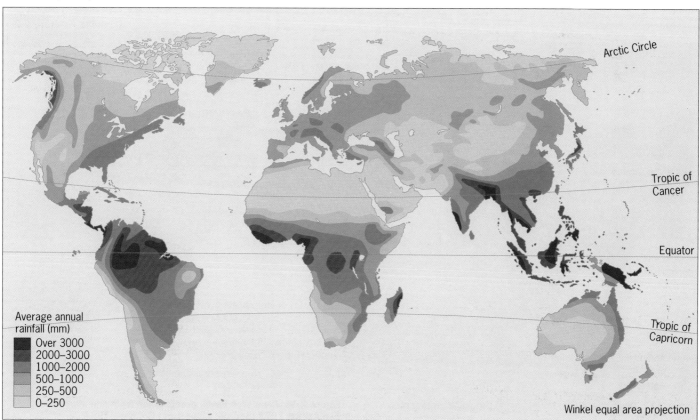

Arctic Circle

Tropic of Cancer

Equator

Tropic of Capricorn

Average annual rainfall (mm)

Over 3000
2000–3000
1000–2000
500–1000
250–500
0–250

Winkel equal area projection

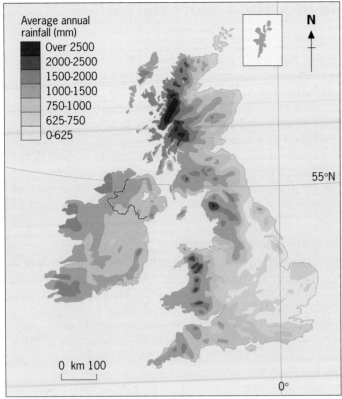

Figure 2.10 Average annual British Isles precipitation (*Source:* Collins-Longman World Atlas, 1992)

complications to the patterns. For instance, along much of the west coast of North America, prevailing onshore winds from the Pacific Ocean bring heavy precipitation totals to the coastal mountains. In the lee of the mountains, however, there is a marked rainshadow effect and reduced precipitation totals. We can see a similar pattern at a smaller scale across the British Isles (Fig. 2.10). The effects of relief and prevailing winds are clear, with areas of high precipitation (over 2500 mm) in the north and west, and lower totals (less than 600 mm) in the east and south.

We should, however, understand that average precipitation totals, such as those shown on Figures 2.9 and 2.10, are only of limited use. For instance, the British Isles are said to have 'reliable' rainfall, yet long-term records indicate significant fluctuations (Fig. 2.11). More recently, there has been the so-called 'Great Drought' of 1988–92 (see Chapter 8). In all localities, precipitation totals vary from year to year. Hydrologists cannot predict floods or advise people on land use, unless they have detailed data for each drainage basin showing how precipitation varies over time and space. Figures 2.12 and 2.13 illustrate these variations over a small area and in a short time. Other examples throughout this book demonstrate this essential feature of precipitation inputs.

Figure 2.11 Average annual rainfall for England and Wales, 1970–80

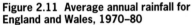

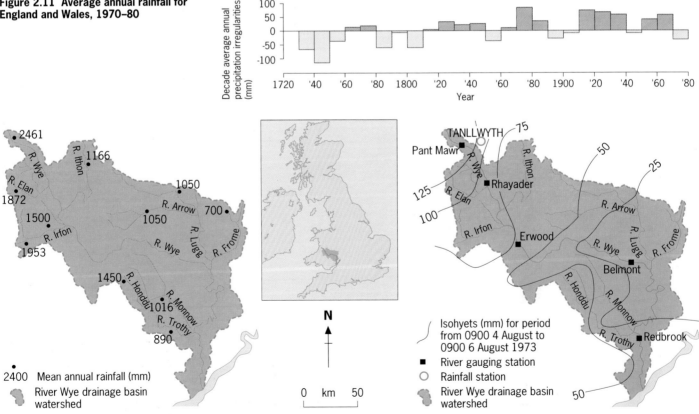

Figure 2.12 River Wye basin: mean annual precipitation (*Source:* Hilton, 1985)

Figure 2.13 River Wye basin: precipitation from one storm event, 5–6 August 1973 (*Source: Clowes and Comfort, 1987)*

Figure 2.14 The River Amazon, near Manaus. A 'tide mark' or 'trash line' can be seen running along this tropical rainforest. The upper limit of the brownish colouring marks the high water level of July. This photograph was taken in September, when the water had fallen by 6 m. By December the water levels will have dropped a further 8 or 9 m

When and how often? (Regime/seasonality and frequency)

Most regions have some seasonality in their precipitation which is reflected in their river **regimes** (Chapter 4). Even equatorial drainage basins such as the Amazon show marked seasonal discharge fluctuations (Fig. 2.14). Extreme seasonality occurs in monsoon climates, with a single wet season and a sequence of often rainless months (Fig. 2.15). Yet timing and frequency of rainfall vary considerably in such climates too, as Figure 2.16 shows

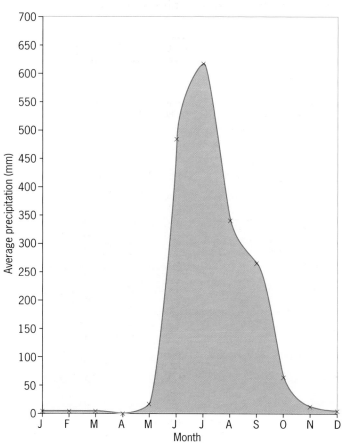

Figure 2.15 Annual rainfall for an Indian monsoon station

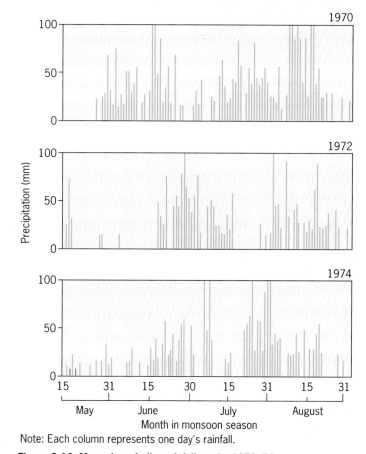

Note: Each column represents one day's rainfall.

Figure 2.16 Mangalore, India: rainfall totals, 1970–74

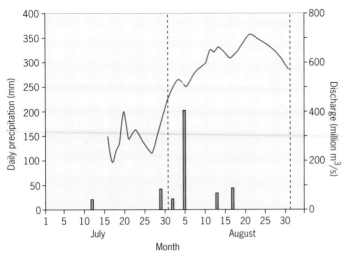

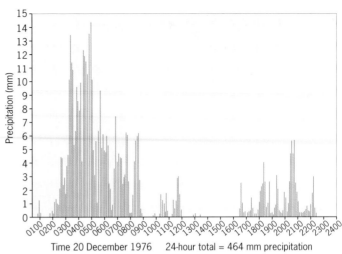

Figure 2.17 Khartoum, Sudan: daily rainfall, July–August, 1988 and discharge of the R. Nile (*Source: Weather*, Feb. 1989)

Figure 2.18 Babinda, Australia: daily rainfall, 20 December 1976. Each column represents a 6-minute period.

In arid environments there may be no seasonal regularity, but simply occasional and irregular storms, which may generate short-lived streamflows (Fig. 2.17). At the briefest time scales, rain may arrive in a series of pulses within a single storm (Fig. 2.18).

?

7 Describe and explain how Child's Glacier in Figure 2.20 acts as a store and input source for the Copper River. Consider how this influence varies seasonally and how this affects the river regime.

How heavy? (Intensity)

Rainfall intensity is measured in millimetres per hour (mm/h). It has a significant effect on the route water takes through the drainage basin system, and hence upon river flow. The intensity of steady drizzle is about 0.5 mm/hr, and for moderate rainfall 3 mm/h. Compare this with the intensities generated by tropical storms, which can yield more than 1mm of rain a minute (Fig. 2.18)! Convectional rainfall occurs typically as short, intense downpours. So, regions having frequent convection storms will experience high rainfall intensities. In the British Isles much of the precipitation occurs as a result of frontal processes. Even in such large-scale weather systems, rainfall intensity can vary considerably as the frontal system moves across a region (Fig. 2.19).

Figure 2.19 Composite rainfall map from a network of five radars, showing the distribution of rain associated with a frontal system crossing Wales and England. (*Source*: Ward and Robinson, 1990)

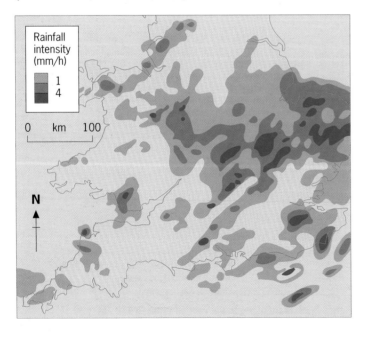

Figure 2.20 The Copper River, Alaska: ice as a water store

What type? (Form)

Water can enter the drainage basin as rain, snow, sleet or hail. If snow lies on the ground for days, weeks or months, there will be a delayed delivery of the water input to the stream system. In this way, snow acts as a temporary store of water in the drainage basin. The timing and speed of the snowmelt will determine the nature of the water input and thus affect the seasonal flood risk or the timing of water availability for irrigation. Snow and ice are important water sources (Fig. 2.20), including several of the world's major rivers, e.g. the Rhône in France (Fig. 2.3) and the Colorado in the USA. The 1983 floods along the Colorado were caused in part by a sudden late snowmelt in the mountain headwaters.

Interception

The second stage of the precipitation input to a drainage basin system begins once the water has arrived at the land surface.

The amount of incoming precipitation which reaches the ground surface directly depends not only upon its type, volume, intensity and timing, but also upon the surface cover. This may be artificial cover, such as roads and buildings (see Chapter 3), but is mainly natural or cultivated vegetation. The interruption in the arrival of precipitation at the surface is known as interception. This is important in determining when and how water moves through the drainage basin system. Some intercepted water will evaporate off vegetation and return to the atmosphere store. This is **interception loss**. Water also moves through vegetation cover to the ground surface (Fig. 2.21), where it may infiltrate into the soil or run over the ground surface as overland flow (see section 2.3).

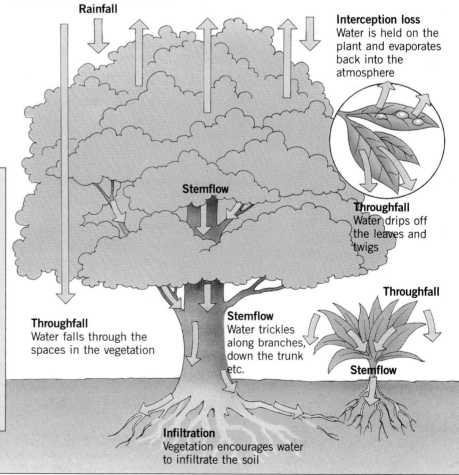

• Some of the water is held on the plant leaves and is then evaporated back into the atmosphere. This is called the interception loss. Precipitation is lost very quickly from the drainage basin system by this method and is therefore an important consideration for hydrologists.
• Some water falls through spaces in the vegetation directly to the ground, or drips off leaves and twigs to the ground surface. This process is called throughfall.
• Water which trickles along twigs, branches and down the main stem or trunk to the ground surface is called stemflow.
• All the water that is intercepted by the vegetation is stored temporarily. The amount which eventually moves on through the drainage basin, and when it does so, depends upon the storage capacity of the vegetation and the balance between interception loss, throughfall and stemflow.

Rainfall

Interception loss
Water is held on the plant and evaporates back into the atmosphere

Stemflow

Throughfall
Water drips off the leaves and twigs

Throughfall
Water falls through the spaces in the vegetation

Stemflow
Water trickles along branches, down the trunk etc.

Throughfall

Stemflow

Infiltration
Vegetation encourages water to infiltrate the soil

Figure 2.21 Vegetation interception

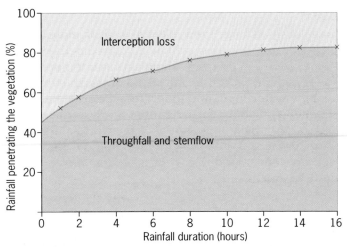

Figure 2.22 **The relationship between the amount of rainfall reaching the forest floor (mixed deciduous forest in Poland), interception loss and rainfall duration (*Source*: Ward and Robinson, 1990)**

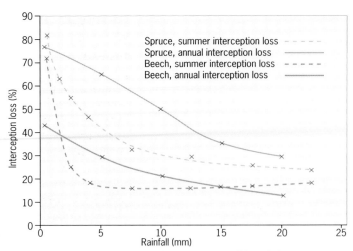

Figure 2.23 **Interception losses from spruce and beech forests (*Source*: Ward and Robinson, 1990)**

8 Use the information of Figure 2.22 to support the following statements:

a A drainage basin which receives frequent rainfall will lose more water by interception than one where rainfall events occur occasionally.

b Interception loss from intense rainfall will be smaller than from rain falling as slow drizzle.

9 Study Figure 2.23.

a Compare the annual interception loss from spruce and beech forests with less than 5 mm of rainfall.

b How do the two forest types compare in terms of interception loss when rainfall amounts reach 20 mm?

c Account for the differences you have described in parts **a** and **b**.

10 Explain why interception loss is high with both types of forest as rainfall begins.

11 Give reasons why interception loss declines rapidly in both types of forest with rainfall amounts less than 5 mm in the summer.

12 Essay: Compare and contrast the ways in which coniferous and deciduous trees control the precipitation interception storage and throughput processes. Use Figure 2.21 as the basis for your answer.

The amount of water intercepted is influenced by the characteristics of, first, the precipitation, and second, the vegetation. Significant features of the precipitation are its duration, frequency and type. For instance, interception loss is usually greatest at the beginning of a rainstorm, since the leaves and stems are dry. Each vegetation type has a storage capacity. So, as the leaves etc. become wetter, the water will begin to drip to the ground or run off as stemflow. The longer the duration of the rainfall, the less important interception loss becomes as the vegetation stores fill (Fig. 2.22). As a result, the frequency of the rainfall will be important, because it is in the early stages of each rainfall event that interception loss is greatest. Research suggests that interception loss from snow is very small, because most eventually falls off the vegetation to the ground surface.

Vegetation cover

The type of vegetation cover will determine the interception characteristics. For example, research on grasslands across California suggests that the annual interception loss is between 8 per cent and 13 per cent. Forests give much higher total annual interception losses: 25–35 per cent for coniferous forests and 15–25 per cent for deciduous woodlands. This difference between coniferous and deciduous forests is due to the seasonal leaf cover of deciduous trees. In winter, interception losses from deciduous trees may be as low as 4–7 per cent.

Figure 2.23 shows the contrasts between interception losses from spruce (coniferous) and beech (deciduous) forests. Notice that there are seasonal as well as annual differences, even though both types are in full leaf in the summer. The higher figures for spruce even in summer are due to the water droplets clinging to the individual needles, and the open texture of the needle system which allows air circulation and evaporation. This maintains the interception. In contrast, the larger beech leaves allow water droplets to merge and then to drip to the ground. Also, the denser leaf cover means that there is less air circulating and so evaporation is reduced.

Forest and woodland areas usually have a layered structure, e.g. the canopy, shrub and ground vegetation layers. Thus, some of the throughfall may descend by several stages to the ground surface. This is called secondary interception. This may be low during light rainfall, because most of the rain will be intercepted by the main canopy. However, during longer, heavier storms, secondary interception becomes increasingly important as the vegetation stores progressively fill up.

Evaporation and transpiration

Some of the precipitation input does not find its way to become streamflow. Instead, it is lost from the system by the process of evaporation. This is the process where water liquid is changed into a gas (water vapour). This evaporated part of the precipitation input is returned directly to the atmosphere (Fig. 1.4). In terms of the total amount of water returned, evaporation from oceans and seas is by far the most important. Within drainage basins, evaporation occurs from intercepted water on vegetation surfaces, from bare soil, from artificial surfaces, and from water surfaces such as rivers and lakes.

Equally important in many environments is transpiration. This is the process where water is drawn through living plants and evaporated as it emerges from the stomata. Thus, although this water has reached and penetrated the ground surface, it has been taken up by plants and so has not moved on through the drainage basin. For transpiration to occur there must be a supply of moisture from the soil. Many plants adapt their structures or annual rhythms of leaf fall to reduce transpiration rates when soil water may not be available, e.g. the stomata of some desert plants are sunken; the leaves of some plants drop off in the dry season.

In all but unvegetated deserts and snow or ice fields, the surface will consist of a mixture of bare ground and vegetation. Thus, evaporation and transpiration are usually at work together (Fig. 2.24). For this reason, we combine evaporation and transpiration losses to the atmosphere as **evapotranspiration.** Several factors influence how much water leaves a drainage basin by evapotranspiration.

Temperature

The main energy source for evaporation is solar radiation. As this varies across the earth, so will the potential for such loss. Higher temperatures allow more evaporation than cooler conditions. Consequently, evaporation rates will vary in different parts of the world (Fig. 2.25), at different times of the year, and at different times of the day.

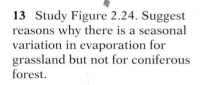

13 Study Figure 2.24. Suggest reasons why there is a seasonal variation in evaporation for grassland but not for coniferous forest.

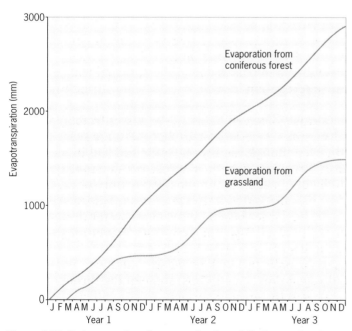

Figure 2.24 Estimates of total evaporation from fully forested and grassed areas in upland mid-Wales over a three-year period (*Source:* Oliver, 1988)

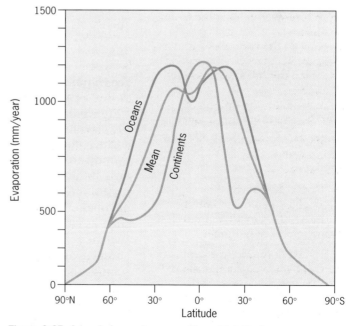

Figure 2.25 Annual change in evaporation with latitude (*Source:* Barry and Chorley, 1985)

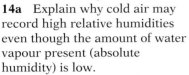

14a Explain why cold air may record high relative humidities even though the amount of water vapour present (absolute humidity) is low.
b Suggest what effect this can have upon the working of the hydrological cycle in cold environments.

Relative humidity

Relative humidity is the amount of water vapour in the atmosphere expressed as a percentage of the total amount the air could hold at that temperature. As air temperature increases, so air can hold more moisture per unit volume, i.e. warm air can hold more moisture than cold air. At any given temperature, air becomes **saturated** when its relative humidity reaches 100 per cent. It can hold no more moisture at that temperature. So, when relative humidities are high, e.g. above 70 per cent, the air feels 'damp', and little evaporation will occur. With low relative humidities, the air at that temperature has the capacity to absorb more moisture.

Wind

Air immediately in contact with the water body, land or vegetated surface is first to become saturated. Air movement mixes this saturated layer with the drier layers of air above, allowing further evaporation and saturation. Thus, at any given temperature, evaporation is greater in windy, turbulent conditions than in calm air. We could call this the 'hair-dryer effect'.

Albedo

The albedo is the proportion of incoming solar radiation which is reflected by the earth's surface. The albedo varies for different types of vegetation cover or soil type. The amount of solar radiation not reflected, but absorbed by the vegetation and other surfaces, will influence the amount of energy available for evaporation. Grassland absorbs 70–80 per cent of solar energy and forests 90 per cent. However, snow, with a high albedo, absorbs only 20 per cent. Darker soils have a lower albedo than lighter-coloured soils and retain more solar energy for evaporation and heating of the atmosphere.

Soil texture and depth

The size and number of the spaces within the soil, i.e. its **porosity**, affect how soil water is held, and how much there will be. Evaporation tends to be high from coarse-textured soils, with their large spaces between the particles. **Capillary action** through the open pore spaces brings the moisture to the surface. Finer soils, such as silts and clays, have numerous, but tiny, spaces and allow low rates of evaporation. Capillary action is more restricted in such soils.

Potential evapotranspiration

Hydrologists are less interested in the water loss from individual plants than the total evapotranspiration losses from areas with the same vegetation and surface characteristics. As a result they use the concept of **potential evapotranspiration (PET)**. This is the water loss which would occur from an area if there was a constant supply of water to the surface and the transpiring vegetation (Fig. 2.26). Thus PET is the maximum possible water loss for a particular environment. This loss is dependent upon atmospheric factors such as solar energy, precipitation, cloud cover and wind. In many regions, such as semi-arid environments, soil moisture supply is not constant, and actual evapotranspiration (AET) is less than PET. Even in moist environments such as the British Isles, the PET-AET relationship is complex (Figs 2.27 and 2.28).

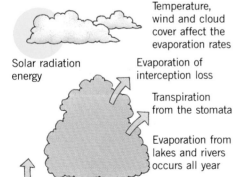

Temperature, wind and cloud cover affect the evaporation rates

Solar radiation energy

Evaporation of interception loss

Transpiration from the stomata

Evaporation from lakes and rivers occurs all year

Evaporation

Soil moisture provides a constant supply of water all year

Figure 2.26 The concept of potential evapotranspiration

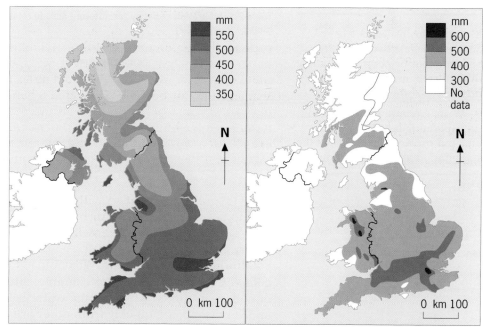

?

15 Study Figure 2.27.
a Compare PET in the UK:
• from north to south
• between coastal areas and inland areas
• between upland areas and lowland areas.
b Suggest reasons for any differences you have identified.

16 Study Figures 2.27 and 2.28. How do the AET rates in the UK compare with the potential values?

17 Explain how Figures 2.27 and 2.28 support the hypothesis that a higher proportion of incoming precipitation is likely to remain in the drainage basin system and reach the stream channels in the north and west of the UK.

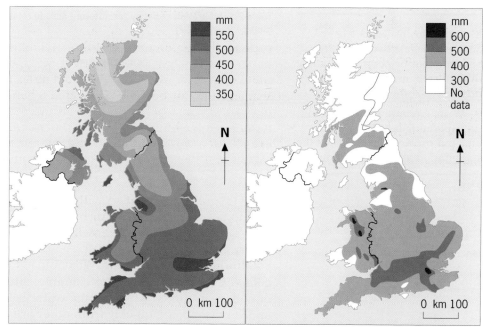

Figure 2.27 Spatial distribution over the UK of mean annual potential evapotranspiration (*Source*: Ward and Robinson, 1981)

Figure 2.28 Spatial distribution over the UK of mean annual actual evapotranspiration (*Source*: Ward and Robinson, 1981)

Figure 2.29 Factors affecting the amount of infiltration

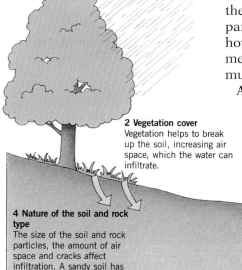

1 Intensity of precipitation
Rainfall of great intensity, i.e. downpour, is less likely to infiltrate than low intensity rainfall, e.g. drizzle.

2 Vegetation cover
Vegetation helps to break up the soil, increasing air space, which the water can infiltrate.

3 Angle of slope
Water will run off a steeper slope more easily than a gentle slope. The quicker the water runs off, the less likely it is to infiltrate.

Rainfall which does not infiltrate runs over the ground surface as overland flow. The soil might be washed away, causing erosion.

4 Nature of the soil and rock type
The size of the soil and rock particles, the amount of air space and cracks affect infiltration. A sandy soil has larger particles and more air spaces than a clay soil. This encourages infiltration.

water table

5 Depth of the water table
If the water table is near to the surface, the soil will become quickly saturated and less infiltration will occur.

6 Time
If rainfall occurs over a long period of time, infiltration will decrease as the soil store fills up, i.e. high antecedent moisture conditions.

2.3 Drainage basin processes: at and below the surface

Infiltration

Infiltration is the process whereby water enters the soil surface. Hydrologists usually study this water movement by measuring the **infiltration rate** and **infiltration capacity** of the water. We need to be clear about the meaning of these terms. The infiltration capacity is the maximum rate at which a particular soil under specific conditions *can* absorb precipitation. That is, how much water can pass through a given unit of soil in a certain time, measured in cubic millimetres per hour. The infiltration rate refers to how much water *is* passing through in a certain time.

At any given time, infiltration at a particular site (Fig 2.29) depends upon a

18 On a copy of Table 2.1, complete the last two columns to show whether or not precipitation will infiltrate into the land uses and soil types shown.

19 Write a paragraph describing and explaining how the type of soil, land use and the nature of the precipitation affect infiltration.

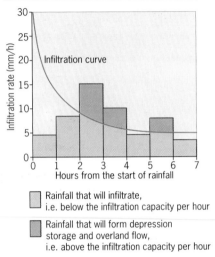

Figure 2.30 An infiltration curve imposed on a rainfall histogram to show the rainfall in excess of infiltration capacity (*After*: Weyman and Wilson, 1975)

20 Group exercise: Examining water storage and throughflow processes.
a Produce a plan of your school/college site, showing different surface types.
b For a single rainstorm event, or a series of events:
• Record the nature and length of the event. Include whether the surfaces were wet or dry before the rain began.
• As soon as possible after the rain stops, plot on your map the location of standing water, and the location and direction of overland flow.
• Repeat your mapping at regular intervals until surface storage and flow have disappeared.
c Briefly describe your results.

Figure 2.31 The processes of infiltration, throughflow and deep percolation

Table 2.1 Infiltration capacity for different soils in relation to typical UK rainfall statistics (*Source*: Burt, 1987)

Soil type and use	Infiltration capacity (mm/h)	Rainfall type (mm/h)			
		Drizzle (0.5)	Moderate rain (2.5)	Heavy rain (10)	Violent rainstorm (50)
Old pasture	60	Yes	Yes		
Moderately grazed pasture	20	Yes	Yes		
Heavily grazed pasture	5	Yes	Yes		
Bare soil after compaction by rainbeat: Clays	2	Yes	No		
Silts	5	Yes	Yes		
Sands	7.5	Yes	Yes		
Freshly ploughed soil	100	Yes	Yes		
Woodland soil	150	Yes	Yes		
Dry clay soil under grass	20	Yes	Yes		
Moist clay soil under grass	10	Yes	Yes		
Wet clay soil under grass	0.5	Yes	Yes		

complex set of variables. For example, after a rainstorm, look at the school or college grounds: why is it that water is lying on the surface in some places, and yet disappears quickly from other areas? Rainfall intensities and surface/soil characteristics are crucial variables (Table 2.1).

Infiltration is a key process in the drainage basin, because precipitation which arrives at the surface but does not infiltrate is likely to run off quickly into the streams and rivers as **overland flow**. The infiltration capacity decreases rapidly over time during a storm (Fig. 2.30). This is because the air spaces (pores) in the soil become progressively filled with water. (Soil moisture movement and storage are discussed in more detail in Chapter 8.) As the infiltration capacity of the soil falls, further precipitation will be unable to infiltrate (Fig. 2.30).

How quickly the soil store fills up depends not only on rainfall intensity and the infiltration capacity, but also on the weather conditions over the previous days and weeks. It is particularly important to know the antecedent rainfall, i.e. rainfall in the days preceding the rainfall event we are studying. If there has been significant rainfall, then the soil store may already be partially full, and so overland flow will occur quickly at the arrival of further precipitation.

Throughflow

Water which does infiltrate the soil will move vertically downwards at first. Then movement swings progressively downslope due to the effects of gravity, and the decrease in infiltration capacity of the soil with increasing depth. As Figure 2.31 shows, soils become more compacted with depth: they have fewer spaces and cracks in the lower horizons of the profile. Also, horizons in the soil profile vary in their infiltration capacity. This downslope movement of soil water is called **throughflow**.

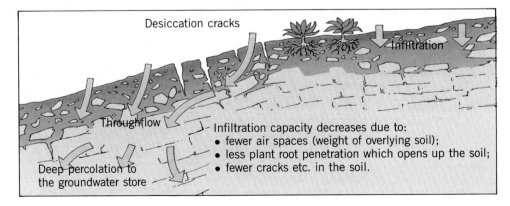

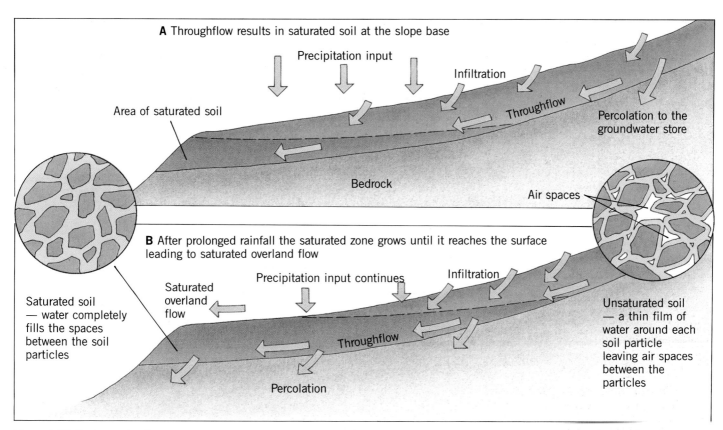

Figure 2.32 Processes leading to saturated overland flow

Unless the soil contains many spaces, root systems and animal burrows, throughflow is a slow process. Research suggests that movement ranges between 0.01 mm and 1 mm per minute. Eventually, however, the water arrives at the slope base or slope foot.

Percolation

Some water will continue downwards to the **water table** by the process of deep **percolation**. At the water table it becomes part of the **groundwater store**. (This is considered fully in Chapter 8.)

Overland flow

Water which cannot infiltrate collects on the ground surface in any hollows and depressions as **depression storage.** If these hollows become full, then the water may flow over the ground surface in trickles, rivulets and even thin sheets as overland flow. Vegetation-covered surfaces have a high infiltration capacity (Table 2.1) and, consequently, overland flow is relatively rare under natural conditions. It is most likely to occur if the ground surface is frozen in winter, or has dried (desiccated) leaving a surface crust, or if there is an unusually violent rainstorm. Human activities which result in soil compaction, e.g. the passage of farm machinery, or trampling by animals, can increase the occurrence of overland flow.

Soils at the slope foot readily become saturated due to the downslope movement by throughflow. This prevents further infiltration and results in the process of saturated overland flow following a rainfall event (Fig. 2.32). Saturated overland flow becomes increasingly important with a long rainstorm, or during a series of wet days. It is more common under natural conditions than overland flow, due to the precipitation input exceeding the infiltration capacity. The occurrence of saturated overland flow is a key process in the delivery of water quickly to river channels and has an important effect upon the nature of the storm hydrograph (Chapter 3).

2.4 Overview

This chapter has followed the journey of water into and through the drainage basin system as far as the slopes surrounding the stream channels. We have taken each process separately, but the important understanding is that all are closely interlinked. Some processes take the water out of the system, e.g. evapotranspiration. Others, such as infiltration, lead the water into the basin. Figure 2.33 summarises how precipitation and runoff in the drainage basin stores and flows vary during a rainstorm.

A second important understanding is how variable the inputs and processes are, both within individual basins and between different basins. Each basin is unique in the way it works, and may change over time. Yet all work by the same variables and principles. These understandings provide an essential foundation for our investigation of stream channels as transfer systems for water and sediment (Chapter 5). They are a basis too, for the study of drainage basin management (Chapters 7 and 9).

?

21 Study Figure 2.33.
a Read off the percentage of rainfall in each store or process at:
- the beginning of the storm,
- midway through the storm,
- at the end of the storm.
b Explain any differences in the percentage of rainfall entering the water stores or moving by different processes over the duration of the storm event.

22 Essay: Discuss the value of a systems approach to understanding the hydrological processes operating in a drainage basin.

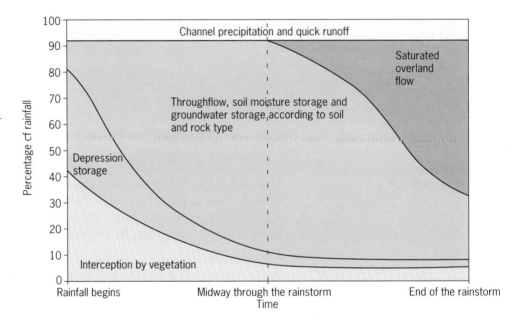

Figure 2.33 Components of the rainfall–runoff process as they vary in proportion during a rainstorm

Summary

- A drainage basin is the catchment area within which water collects and drains into a main river channel.
- The drainage basin works as an open system and is the basic unit for the study of hydrological processes.
- The precipitation input variable, and the processes at work in the basin, combine to determine streamflow.
- Aspects of precipitation which influence the drainage basin system are magnitude, regime, location, frequency, duration, intensity, reliability and form.
- When precipitation arrives, it may fall directly on to the river or lake surfaces, or on to soil or the ground, or it may be intercepted by the vegetation cover, and so reach the surface indirectly.
- Some precipitation is lost to the drainage basin by evaporation and transpiration; the rest is delivered at varying speeds, by several surface and subsurface routes, to stream channels.
- The balance between infiltration, subsurface movement and overland flow is influenced by the nature of the precipitation, the character of the soil and the antecedent conditions.

3 Streamflow and human influences

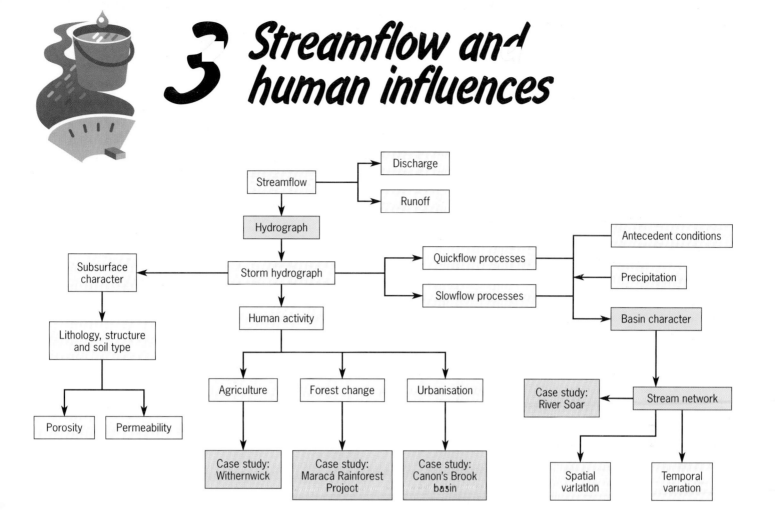

3.1 Introduction

From Chapter 2 we have learned how water enters and is stored in the **drainage basin** system. In this chapter we shall investigate the effects these stores and processes have upon **streamflow**. We shall use the **hydrograph** for this investigation, as it is the basic technique for recording and predicting fluctuations in the channel flow.

As there are few regions of the world where human activity has no influence on hydrological processes, later sections of the chapter introduce the impacts of these activities on streamflow and hydrographs. People influence the ways that drainage basin systems work both intentionally, e.g. by flood control schemes, irrigation projects, energy generation, and unintentionally, e.g. deforestation, urbanisation. The changes affect the processes in the basin and the streamflow, and are recorded in the changing hydrographs.

3.2 Streamflow in the river channel

Streamflow is generated by the outputs from the stores in the drainage basin system. As Figure 3.1 illustrates, it occurs when the stores fill up, or when they have sufficient water to release it steadily. We know from Chapter 2 that the stores release water at different rates and at different times. Also, the processes which deliver the water to the river channel operate at different speeds. At times of extreme conditions, water inputs may not enter a store, but move directly to the stream by **overland flow**. As a result, streamflow is constantly fluctuating.

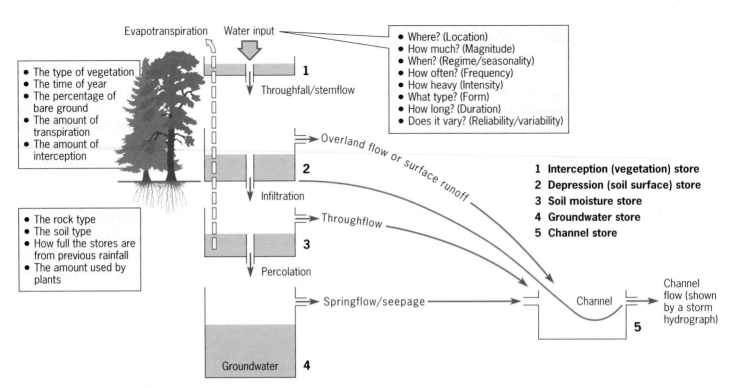

Evapotranspiration   Water input

- Where? (Location)
- How much? (Magnitude)
- When? (Regime/seasonality)
- How often? (Frequency)
- How heavy (Intensity)
- What type? (Form)
- How long? (Duration)
- Does it vary? (Reliability/variability)

- The type of vegetation
- The time of year
- The percentage of bare ground
- The amount of transpiration
- The amount of interception

1 Throughfall/stemflow

Overland flow or surface runoff

2

Infiltration

- The rock type
- The soil type
- How full the stores are from previous rainfall
- The amount used by plants

Throughflow

3

Percolation

Springflow/seepage

Channel

Groundwater **4**

1 **Interception (vegetation) store**
2 **Depression (soil surface) store**
3 **Soil moisture store**
4 **Groundwater store**
5 **Channel store**

Channel flow (shown by a storm hydrograph)

5

Figure 3.1 Drainage basin stores and flows which affect streamflow in the river channel (*Source*: Newson, 1979)

We measure this varying streamflow in two ways:

1 Discharge (Q) is the volume of water passing a specific gauging station per unit of time. Discharge is expressed as cubic metres of water per second (m^3/s), often abbreviated to cumecs.

2 Runoff is the volume of water passing a **gauging station**, represented as the thickness of water spread over the drainage basin area above the gauging station (Fig. 3.2). Runoff is expressed as millimetres per month or year. Measuring runoff allows us to compare the amount of water discharged by a river system with the **precipitation** inputs over the drainage basin.

Recording channel flow – the hydrograph

A hydrograph is a continuous record of fluctuating streamflow. Time is plotted along the *x* axis. Discharge, in m^3/s, is plotted on the *y* axis. Figure 3.3 is a typical example. It tells us, for instance, that during 1989, at the Craigiehall gauging station, the River Almond's mean daily discharge ranged from less than 1 m^3/s to over 90 m^3/s.

Figure 3.2 A gauging station

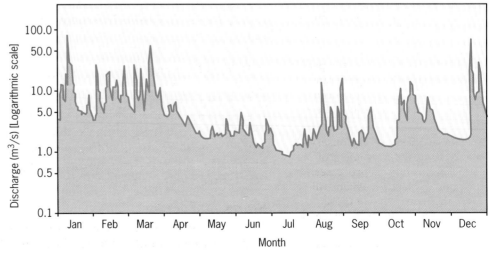

Figure 3.3 River Almond, Craigiehall (a catchment area of 369 km²): daily flow hydrograph, 1989 (*Source*: Institute of Hydrology, 1989)

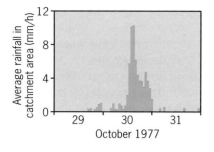

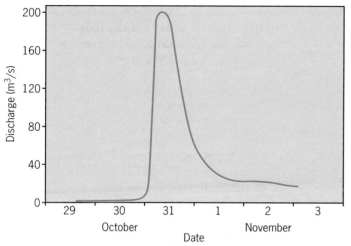

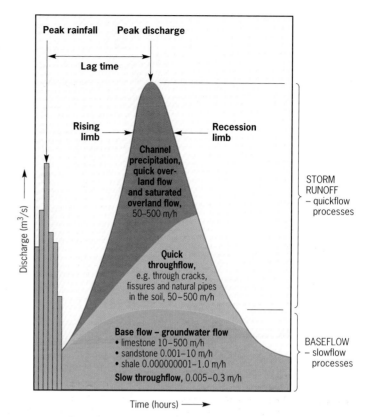

Figure 3.4 River Almond, Craigiehall: storm hydrograph, 29 October 1977 (*Source*: Institute of Hydrology, 1977)

Right: **Figure 3.5 The storm hydrograph: terminology and processes**

1a Make a copy of Figure 3.4 and annotate it with the following terms:
• peak rainfall, • peak discharge, • rising limb, • recession limb, • lag time, • storm runoff, • base flow.

b Give precise figures to illustrate the times and amount of discharge at each stage.

2 Explain how saturated overland flow can cause the peak of the storm hydrograph, even though it does not operate as a process until the middle of the storm.

3 Figure 3.5 shows the observed range of rates of movement of water by the various processes. Describe the factors which will affect the actual rate of these processes at a particular place or time.

The storm hydrograph

A **storm hydrograph** records the discharge pattern of a river at a specific gauging station, following a single rainstorm event (Fig. 3.4). In order to show the relationship between the precipitation input and the discharge of the water past the gauging station, most storm hydrographs include the rainfall graph. This relationship is important to the hydrologist because it determines the speed and scale of the rise in discharge, and therefore the likelihood of flooding.

Figure 3.5 takes a closer look at a storm hydrograph and how it helps our analysis of streamflow. During dry spells, a permanent stream maintains a low discharge known as its **base flow**, sustained by **slowflow processes**. Following a rainfall event, streamflow rises by storm runoff, supplied by **quickflow processes**. The hydrograph plots this increased input along the rising limb. Eventually, discharge peaks; an important piece of information is the lag time between the rainfall maximum and this peak. As the water inputs to the channel fade, the hydrograph records this along its recession or falling limb.

3.3 Understanding streamflow patterns and hydrographs

A hydrograph only *describes* what happened to streamflow. We need to be able to interpret the graph in order to *explain* what happened. In turn, this will help us to predict and forecast what might happen. Such forecasting is difficult because the inputs, stores and processes in a drainage basin change constantly over time and space.

Stores and flows

The antecedent moisture conditions will influence how a drainage basin responds to a rainfall event (see Section 2.3). Thus, the same storm may cause a different discharge response and hydrograph pattern at different seasons. In the British Isles in summer, drainage basin stores are unlikely to be full, and **evapotranspiration** will be relatively high. In winter, water stores tend to be nearer to capacity and evapotranspiration rates are lower. As a result, the same storm in January is likely to have a greater and quicker effect on streamflow than it would in July. The storm hydrograph for the January event would be higher and steeper than the July pattern. In the shorter timescale, the same storm will have a different impact on streamflow and the hydrograph if it follows several wet days than if it ends a dry spell.

In January 1994, much of Britain experienced serious flooding (see Fig 7.1). Hydrographs showed steep rising limbs, high peaks and short lag times. (We call such steep, high patterns 'flashy' hydrographs.) Hydrologists identified three conditions which caused the hydrograph patterns and the floods:

1 Rainfall was prolonged.
2 The water stores in the drainage basins were already full.
3 Evapotranspiration ouputs were low.

Rainfall intensity

If we look again at Figure 3.1 it is clear that steady rainfall, even over several days, will allow the various water stores to fill up gradually and efficiently. This controls the speed and volume of runoff to the stream channels. This will be reflected in a broad, flat hydrograph. If, however, the precipitation input is intense and exceeds the soil **infiltration** and vegetation **interception** capacities, quickflow processes, e.g. overland flow, dominate, even when the basin stores are not full. Discharges rise suddenly and flooding is likely – a situation identified by a 'flashy' hydrograph.

Simulation: a drainage basin hydrograph

In order to show clearly the way in which a hydrograph is generated, we need to simplify reality. We will therefore make three assumptions:
1 The drainage basin is a smooth surface without surface depressions and with no permanent stream.
2 The basin is completely impermeable, so all rainfall immediately runs off as overland flow.
3 The overland flow moves at a constant velocity of 0.1 m/s, i.e. there is no variation with discharge.

A hypothetical drainage basin is shown in Figure 3.6. Let us say that a rainstorm of 4.5 mm lasts four hours (Fig. 3.7). If overland flow moves at the rate of 0.1 m/s, the one-hour isochrone (line of equal time of travel to the gauging station) will be 360 m from the gauging point (0.1 m x 3600 s).

In this exercise we are assuming that water will flow on a flat surface and we are not taking into account drainage basin relief. We can draw isochrones for two and three hours from the gauging station. The area within each isochrone contains the water which will reach the gauging station in hourly intervals:
- time zone I, 0–1 hours after the start of the rainfall;
- time zone II, 1–2 hours after the start of the rainfall;
- time zone III, 2–3 hours after the start of the rainfall;
- time zone IV, 3–4 hours after the start of the rainfall;

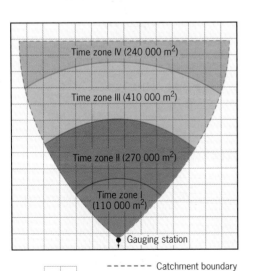

Time zone IV (240 000 m^2)

Time zone III (410 000 m^2)

Time zone II (270 000 m^2)

Time zone I (110 000 m^2)

Gauging station

0 m 200

- - - - - - - Catchment boundary
——————— Isochrone

Figure 3.6 A hypothetical drainage basin with simple isochrone pattern (ignoring contour effect)

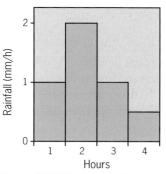

Figure 3.7 **A hypothetical four-hour rainstorm**

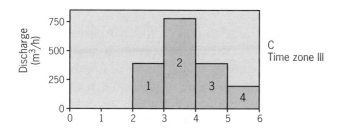

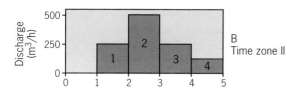

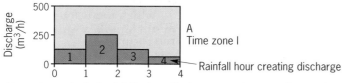

Hours from start of rainfall when discharge reaches gauging station

Figure 3.8 **The hydrographs created by each time zone according to the time the water arrives at the gauging point**

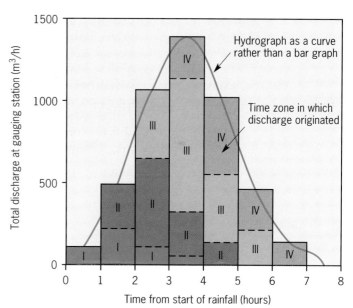

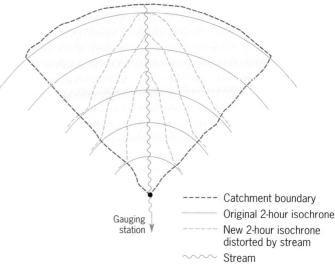

Figure 3.9 **The total basin hydrograph with the origin of each discharge unit shown**

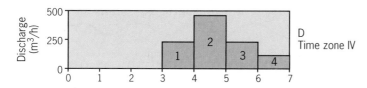

Figure 3.10 Streamflow is faster than overland flow. The original arc-shaped overland flow isochrones are distorted with the introduction of streamflow

We can calculate the area of each time zone and thus the amount of rainfall which runs off from each time zone. For example, for time zone II:

- hour 0–1: 0.001 m rain x 270 000 m^2 = 270 m^3
- hour 1–2: 0.002 m rain x 270 000 m^2 = 540 m^3
- hour 2–3: 0.001 m rain x 270 000 m^2 = 270 m^3
- hour 3–4: 0.0005 m rain x 270 000 m^2 = 135 m^3.

We can graph this information and repeat the calculation for each time zone (Fig. 3.8).

The drainage basin hydrograph

The runoff from each successive time zone starts to arrive one hour later than runoff from the preceding zone and finishes one hour later. Thus, water from time zone I starts to arrive at zero hours and finishes at four hours; water from time zone II starts to arrive at one hour and finishes at five hours; water from time zone III starts to arrive at two hours and finishes at six hours, etc.

Drainage basin hydrograph

The total volume of water arriving at the gauging station for each hour is added to give a final basin hydrograph (Fig. 3.9).

In this simulation the hydrograph is shown both as a bar graph and a line graph. However, hydrographs are usually only curved line graphs, because time intervals are shorter when the line graphs are produced.

The effect of streamflow

In the above simulation we assumed that overland flow ran evenly across the drainage basin at a constant speed. This simplification helps us to understand the lag effect. In reality, however, drainage basin characteristics vary, and much of the water is delivered to the gauging station by a stream. Streamflow transfers water more quickly than overland flow. The result is the distortion of the isochrones and time zones, as shown in Figure 3.10.

3.4 The effect of drainage basin size and shape on the hydrograph

Basin size

The runoff which forms the stream discharge shown on the hydrograph is generated upstream of the gauging station. The volume of runoff and the time lag increase with the size of the drainage basin, as the model of Figure 3.11 illustrates. This model may be applied to humid environments such as the British Isles. However, in arid and semi-arid regions, such as the Sahel of Africa, runoff and discharge volume may decrease downstream, i.e. as basin size above a gauging station increases. This is due to high evaporation rates, loss by seepage of water into the channel bed, and the absence of inputs from tributaries.

Basin shape

The shape of a drainage basin will affect the pattern of the time zones and therefore the shape of the storm hydrograph (Fig. 3.12). An elongated basin will take longer to achieve a throughput of water from a rainstorm than a short, broad basin. The most efficient shape is one in which the **watershed** is circular and all the water disappears down a hole in the middle – rather like a circular washbasin!

Figure 3.11 The effect of increasing basin size on the hydrograph (*Source:* Gregory and Walling, 1973)

4 Construct a three-hydrograph model (see Fig. 3.11) for a gauging station in a:
a small,
b medium,
c large drainage basin in a semi-arid environment. Use the same axes as in Figure 3.11. Describe and explain the patterns of the graphs you have drawn.

5 Describe and explain the relationship between the basin shape and hydrograph pattern for the three examples of Figure 3.12.

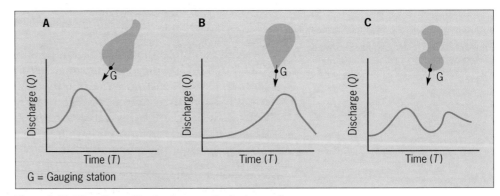

Figure 3.12 The effect of basin shape on the hydrograph
a In a triangular-shaped basin with the apex in the upper catchment, the largest area is in the early time zones. This causes an early peak of the hydrograph.
b In a triangular-shaped basin with the apex near to the gauging station, there will be a delayed peak because the largest time zone is furthest from the gauging station.
c A basin with a small area in the middle time zones, increasing near to and far from the gauging station will produce a double peak.
(*Source:* Gregory and Walling, 1973)

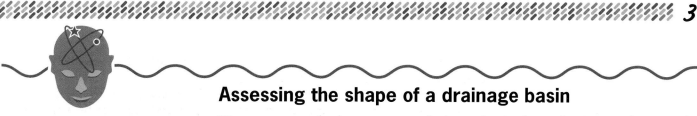

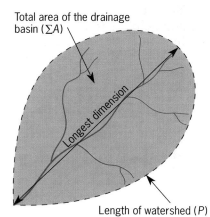

Figure 3.13 Basin circularity and basin elongation are ways of describing objectively the shape of a drainage basin. Comparisons can then be made between drainage basins.

Assessing the shape of a drainage basin

We use two methods to measure drainage basin shape: basin circularity and basin elongation. Remember that both assume that rainfall is evenly distributed across the drainage basin. In reality this is rarely the case.

Basin circularity

We use basin circularity to compare the area of the drainage basin to the area of a circle of the same circumference.

If $P = \pi D$, then $D = \dfrac{P}{\pi}$ and $A_O = \pi \left(\dfrac{D}{2}\right)^2$

Basin circularity $= \dfrac{\Sigma A}{A_O}$ where:

P = the length of the perimeter of the basin, i.e. the watershed
D = the diameter of a circle equivalent in circumference to P
A_O = area of the circle, of diameter D
ΣA = the total area of the drainage basin

The nearer the answer is to 1, the more circular the drainage basin shape.

Basin elongation

Basin elongation compares the longest dimension of the basin to the diameter of a circle of the same area as the basin.

$\Sigma A = \pi r^2$, therefore: $r = \sqrt{\dfrac{\Sigma A}{\pi}}$

Basin elongation $= \dfrac{Dl}{d}$ where:

ΣA = the total basin area
Dl = the longest dimension
d = the diameter, i.e. 2r.

Defining and measuring stream network characteristics

The pattern of streams within a drainage basin influences the transfer of water and consequently the shape of the hydrograph, i.e. the reponse to rainfall events. The two key variables are stream density and stream order.

Calculating stream density

We define stream density as the total length of the drainage channels divided by the drainage basin area.

$Dd = \dfrac{\Sigma L}{\Sigma A}$ where:

Dd = the drainage density in kilometres per square kilometres
ΣL = the sum of the total stream lengths in kilometres
ΣA = the **catchment area** in square kilometres.

For example, the River Wallington (Fig. 3.15) has a drainage density of 1.22 km of channel length per square kilometre.

Calculating stream order

Stream order refers to the way the various stream channels in a drainage basin fit together. The most widely used method for describing this stream arrangement has been devised by A N Strahler (1952). This is based on a hierarchical set of stream orders. Figure 3.14 shows that, if we count the number of streams of each order and plot them against stream order on logarithmic graph paper, we find a clear negative relationship. This constant ratio between the number of streams and stream order is called **Horton's law of stream numbers**.

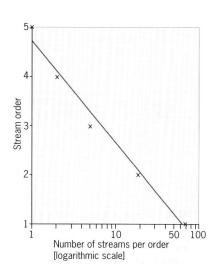

Figure 3.14 River Wallington: number of streams against stream order

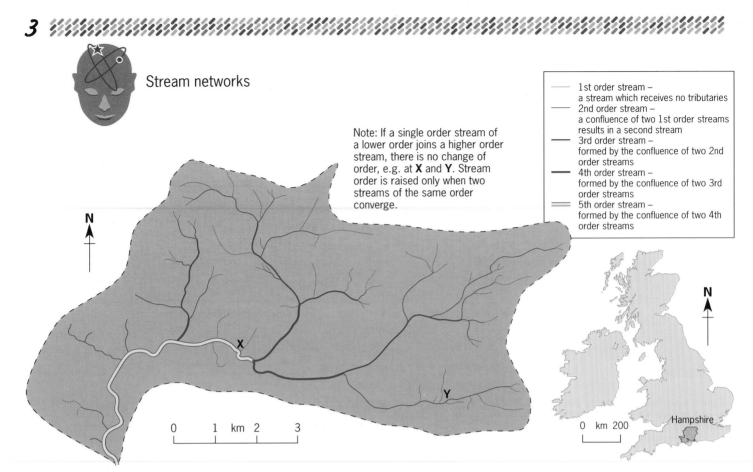

Stream networks

Note: If a single order stream of a lower order joins a higher order stream, there is no change of order, e.g. at **X** and **Y**. Stream order is raised only when two streams of the same order converge.

—— 1st order stream –
a stream which receives no tributaries
—— 2nd order stream –
a confluence of two 1st order streams results in a second stream
—— 3rd order stream –
formed by the confluence of two 2nd order streams
—— 4th order stream –
formed by the confluence of two 3rd order streams
═══ 5th order stream –
formed by the confluence of two 4th order streams

N

X

Y

0 1 km 2 3

N

0 km 200

Hampshire

Figure 3.15 The drainage network of the River Wallington, Hampshire, showing stream orders according to Strahler's system

The bifurcation ratio (R_b)

The rate of change of stream order is shown by the **bifurcation ratio (R_b)** This is calculated using the formula:

$$R_b = \frac{\text{number of streams in order}}{\text{number of streams in the next highest order}}$$

For example, for the River Wallington (Fig. 3.15) for first and second order streams:

$$R_b = \frac{69 \text{ (number of streams in order)}}{19 \text{ (number of streams in the next highest order)}} = 3.6.$$

If we repeat the calculation for second and third order streams, and third and fourth order streams, we can then find the average bifurcation ratio for the drainage basin. The results for the River Wallington are shown in Table 3.1. Most bifurcation ratios for natural streams lie between 3 and 5. Lower values indicate a low level of stream development, higher values indicate a high level of stream development.

Table 3.1 River Wallington: network characteristics

Stream order	Number of streams	Bifurcation Index	Total stream length (km)	Mean stream length (km)	Ratio of stream lengths
1	69		26.3	0.38	
		3.6			2.8
2	19		20.5	1.08	
		3.8			1.4
3	5		9.8	1.96	
		2.5			1.7
4	2		6.5	3.25	
		2.0			2.0
5	1		6.5	6.50	
		R_b=2.97	L=69.6		R_L=1.97

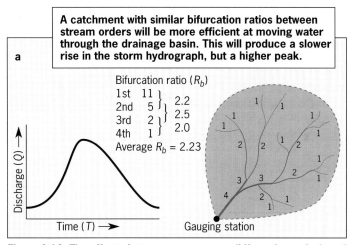

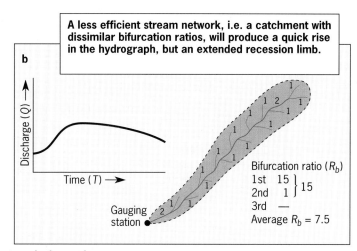

Figure 3.16 The effect of stream arrangement (bifurcation ratios) on the storm hydrograph

3.5 Factors influencing stream networks and the hydrograph

Drainage network measurements allow us to compare drainage basins and to predict how they would respond to precipitation inputs. It is important, therefore, that we understand the factors which influence these networks. For instance, research by Gregory (1976) in the UK produced two main findings:

1 As precipitation increases, so does the drainage density.
2 Impermeable drainage basins have higher drainage densities.

High drainage densities transfer precipitation inputs relatively quickly to the main river channels. So, each of these situations is likely to produce steep

a A drought situation, discharge is $0.00056\,\text{m}^3/\text{s}$

b A normal situation, discharge is $0.0084\,\text{m}^3/\text{s}$

c A flood situation, discharge is $0.056\,\text{m}^3/\text{s}$

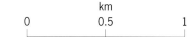

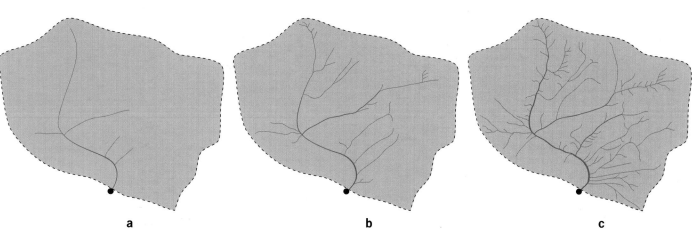

Figure 3.17 Seasonal variation of drainage density and stream network, Swildon stream, Somerset, England (*Source*: White et al 1986)

?

Draw copies of Figures 3.17 a, b and c.

6 Label the three stream networks according to Strahler's system of stream ordering.

7 Calculate the bifurcation ratios for each stream network.

8 For each situation, draw the shape of the storm hydrograph you would expect to see. Add notes to explain the shape of your graphs.

hydrographs and increase the likelihood of flooding. Notice too that the evolution of a high-density drainage network is one way a drainage basin responds to the need to deal with the precipitation input. It is a form of **negative feedback.**

Seasonal variation in drainage density

Precipitation inputs and conditions in the drainage basin water stores vary seasonally, e.g. in the UK rising **groundwater** levels and **saturated** soils during wetter winter months produce increased runoff. The result is noticeable variations in the extent and density of the stream network (Fig. 3.17). Over longer time periods, drainage densities increase as a network evolves across a landscape. The sequence could be similar to that shown on Figure 3.17.

River Soar, Leicestershire, England

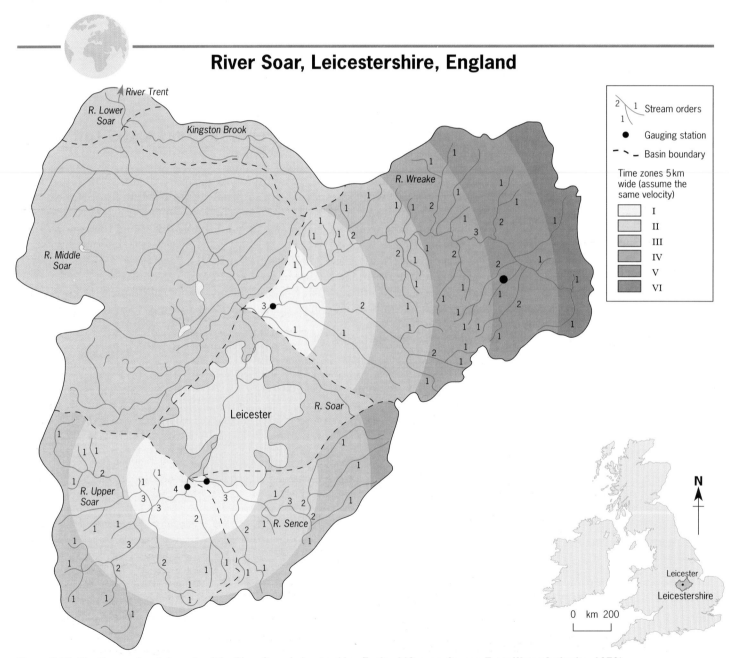

Figure 3.18 The three sub-catchments of the River Soar, Leicestershire, England (*Source*: Severn–Trent Water Authority, 1978)

Table 3.2 Characteristics of the River Soar sub-catchments

Sub-catchment	Area (km²)	Mean annual flow (m³/s)	Basin perimeter (km)	Basin circularity	Basin elongation	Drainage density*
Upper Soar	202	1.44	60.75	0.69	0.87	0.48
Sence	133	1.02	61.56	0.44	1.46	0.44
Wreake	414	2.80	87.8	0.67	1.33	0.52

*These drainage density figures are relatively low since they only include main channels

The Rivers Upper Soar, Wreake and Sence (Fig. 3.18–21) have similar rock types – impermeable Keuper Marl, Rhaetic and Lias clays. Their relief height is also similar, although the River Wreake has a larger area of higher relief extending further downstream in the drainage basin. This results in a large number of low-order streams.

Table 3.3 Stream orders and bifurcation ratios for the River Soar sub-catchments

Stream order	Soar	R_b	Sence	R_b	Wreake	R_b
1	18		8		35	
		3		2.66		3.5
2	6		3		10	
		3		3.0		10.0
3	2		1		1	
		2				
4	1		-		-	
		R_b=2.67		R_b=2.83		R_b=6.75

Figure 3.19 R. Sence at Kilby Bridge, looking upstream Jan. 1994.

Figure 3.20 R. Wreake at Syston, looking upstream Jan. 1994.

Figure 3.21 R. Soar at Narborough, looking upstream Jan. 1994.

?

9 Use Figure 3.18 and Tables 3.2-3.3. Link statements a-h with each drainage basin. Using a-h, explain how drainage basin characteristics affect the storm hydrograph. As more than one characteristic will apply to each of the three drainage basins, the actual hydrograph may be quite complex (Figs 3.22-3.24).
a The largest drainage basin (the greatest number of time zones) which will produce a higher peak discharge but a longer lag time on the hydrograph.
b An elongated basin relative to its size which results in a longer lag time on the hydrograph.
c A relatively circular basin which will be efficient at moving water through the system, giving a relatively short lag time and a higher peak discharge on the hydrograph.
d A well-developed stream network with similar bifurcation ratios producing a slower rise but a higher peak discharge on the hydrograph.
e A less-developed stream network which has dissimilar bifurcation ratios resulting in a quick rise but a more drawn-out hydrograph.
f A higher-order stream giving a lower peak and a longer time lag on the hydrograph.
g A high drainage density which drains the basin efficiently giving a rapid response in the storm hydrograph.
h A small drainage basin giving a short lag time but a smaller peak discharge on the hydrograph.

10 Which basin has the most efficient shape? Explain.

11 How would you expect the time zones of each drainage basin to affect their storm hydrographs? Consider the stream density in each time zone in your answer.

River Soar

12 Essay: Study Figures 3.22 to 3.24 and compare the responses of the three sub-basins to the same storm events. Does the response of the three sub-basins follow the theoretical ideas concerning drainage basin size, shape, drainage density and stream arrangement? Support your answer with precise evidence from the storm hydrographs.

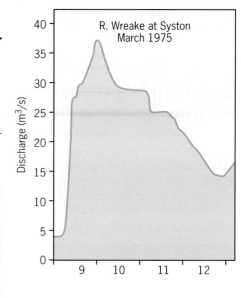

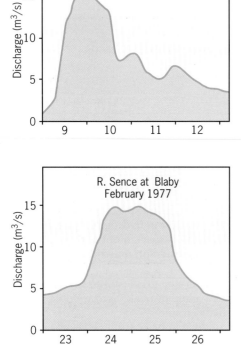

Figure 3.22 Flood hydrographs for the River Sence at Blaby (*Source:* Severn–Trent Water Authority, 1978)

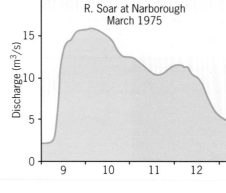

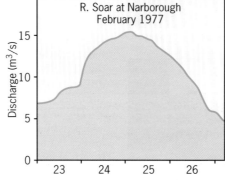

Figure 3.23 Flood hydrographs for the River Soar at Narborough (*Source:* Severn–Trent Water Authority, 1978)

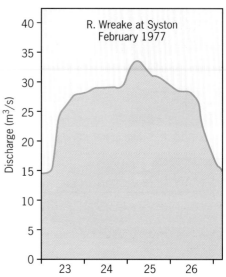

Figure 3.24 Flood hydrographs for the River Wreake at Syston (*Source:* Severn–Trent Water Authority, 1978)

Table 3.4 Porosity of various materials (*Source:* Ward and Robinson, 1990)

Material	Average porosity	Range (%)
Soils	55	50-65
Clay	50.5	42-59
Silt	43.5	37-50
Sand	35	30-40
Gravel	34	29-39
Sand & gravel	27	20-34
Sandstone	18	8-28
Limestone	20	5-35
Shale	8	2-14
Crystalline rock	5	1-10

3.6 The effect of structure and lithology on the hydrograph

As we have learned in Chapter 2, a proportion of the precipitation input passes through the soil store, to **percolate** more deeply into the **groundwater store**. It is the groundwater store which regulates the slow flow supply and base flow of streams. (Chapter 4 looks at river **regimes** and so examines base flow.) The behaviour of this store is influenced by the geological structure, i.e. folding, faulting, tilting of rock formations, and the lithology, i.e. rock type. Together they are an important control upon both the surface stream network and the subsurface transmission of water. In any hydrographs we study, we need to take them into account. (The groundwater store is studied in more detail in Chapter 8.)

13 Study Figures 3.25 and 3.26 carefully, then:

a Describe the streamflow of each for 1986.

b Compare and contrast the two hydrographs.

c Suggest how lithology might explain any differences you identify.

Rocks vary in their **porosity** (Table 3.4) and **permeability**, and so in their ability to hold and transmit water. For instance, crystalline, igneous and metamorphic rocks often have low porosity and permeability. In moist environments, drainage basins underlain by such rocks are likely to have dense drainage networks. They will be dominated by the quickflow processes of soil **throughflow** and overland flow. However, even rocks of low porosity may transmit water efficiently if they are well-jointed and criss-crossed by fissure systems. For example, Carboniferous Limestone is crystalline and has a low porosity, but generally has joint, bedding plane and fissure systems which give it permeability.

The hydrographs of Figures 3.25 and 3.26 are for two catchments within the Thames drainage basin. Both are for the same year, and both catchments experienced similar weather conditions. Note that the Kennet basin is bigger than the Loddon basin. The key difference is in their geological foundation: the Kennet basin is largely permeable, while the Loddon is underlain mostly by impermeable rocks.

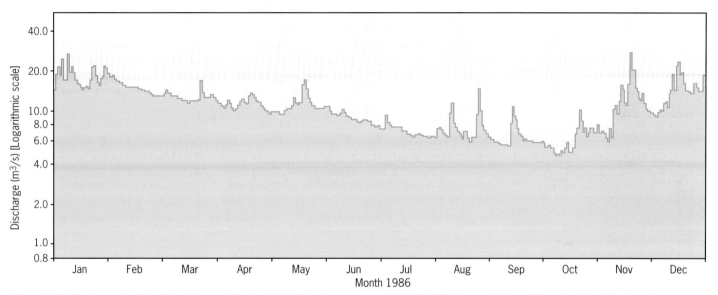

Figure 3.25 Hydrograph of the River Kennet, Theale, 1986 (Catchment area of 103.4 km²) (*Source*: National Water Archive, Institute of Hydrology, 1993)

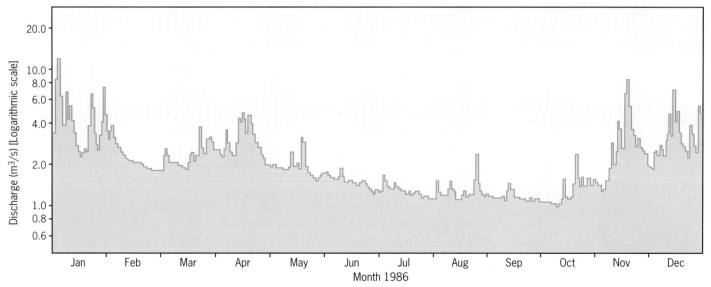

Figure 3.26 Hydrograph of the River Loddon, Sheepbridge, 1986 (Catchment area of 164.5 km²) (*Source*: National Water Archive, Institute of Hydrology, 1993)

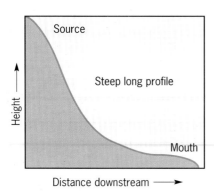

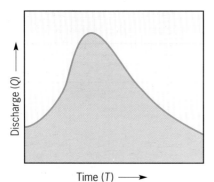

Figure 3.27 Steep long profile

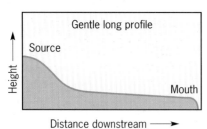

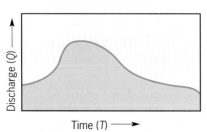

Figure 3.28 Gentle long profile

Figures 3.27 and 3.28 The effect of basin relief on the hydrograph

?

14 Suggest reasons for the impacts of changing the ploughing patterns in the former USSR.

3.7 The effect of basin relief upon the hydrograph

The importance of slopes

A drainage basin with steep slopes is likely to show more quick flow, a shorter lag time and higher peak discharge on the hydrograph than a basin which has gentle slopes and low relief. This is because steeper slopes encourage more overland flow, faster runoff and faster throughflow processes which produce rapid water collection at the slope base and saturated conditions. Basins with strong relief are also likely to give relatively steep stream **long profiles** (Figs 3.27 and 3.28). We must beware, however, as steeper channel gradients do not always mean higher flow velocities.

The importance of soil structure

When considering relief and slopes we must not forget the role of the soil store. Generally areas of high relief tend to have shallow soils. Except where there is a peat 'blanket', these soils have limited storage and transmission capacities, which encourage overland flow and high drainage densities. Extensive areas of the uplands of northern and western Britain illustrate these characteristics. However, the typical scarp-and-vale topography of lowland England contradicts this general rule: drainage densities are low on the higher relief, thin soils and permeable rocks of the Chalk Downs and the Cotswolds. In contrast the nearby impermeable clay vales have higher drainage densities.

3.8 The effects of agriculture on hydrological processes

Farming activity may speed up or slow down delivery of surface and subsurface water to the stream. For instance, many soil conservation measures are designed to reduce runoff and soil erosion which accompany overland flow. Popular strategies are hill-slope terracing (Fig. 3.29), or planting of permanent grassland on vulnerable soils. These techniques will reduce quick flow. In contrast, the purpose of land drainage is to accelerate the transfer of water to the stream channel.

In general, the more intensive the farming, the greater the modification of the natural processes. When high technology is added to intensive farming, the hydrological regime is likely to be changed fundamentally, e.g. large-scale water basin transfers for irrigation in arid regions.

Intensive farming

Intensive farming practices change the way water is stored and its movement through the soil horizons. Firstly, changes in vegetation cover will affect interception, surface runoff, infiltration and percolation. Secondly, ploughing, the application of fertiliser, and the impact of equipment and animals all alter the soil texture and so the storage and infiltration capacities. The timing of activities can be important. For example, in the former USSR, ploughing fields in the autumn rather than the spring reduced runoff in the forest zone by 1.5–2 times. In the forest-steppe zone the reduction was 2–4 times, and in the steppe zone 4–8 times. In each zone there was also an increase in recharge of the groundwater store.

Land drainage

The primary aim of most land drainage schemes is to lower the **water table** and so prevent waterlogging. This is done by a combination of cutting deeper ditches and laying pipes beneath the field surfaces. The improved drainage permits the intensification of farming practices, e.g. a change from grazing to arable cropping.

Figure 3.29 Rice terraces, Bali

15a Make a sketch of the rice terraces in Figure 3.29
b How are hydrological processes modified by the terraces? Add these as annotations to your sketch.

16 You live beside a river down-stream from a large farm. The owner of this farm wants to put in a field drainage scheme. Most of the farm soils are heavy clays. Write a letter to the farmer, stating what effect the scheme will have upon your property, and whether you support or oppose the proposal.
b Would your opinion be the same if the soils on the farm were light sand? If not, say why.

The Institute of Hydrology in the UK has carried out research into the impacts of field drainage and stream channel improvement, and makes these key conclusions:
• The drainage of heavy clay soils, which when undrained are prone to prolonged surface saturation, generally results in a lowering of large and medium peaks on the storm hydrograph of neighbouring streams. This is because their natural response is 'flashy', resulting from limited soil water storage capacity. When these soils are drained, however, surface saturation and therefore quickflow surface runoff is largely eliminated.
• On more permeable soils, which are less prone to surface saturation, the usual effect of drainage is to improve the speed of subsurface discharges. This tends to increase hydrograph peak flows in nearby streams.
• Stream base flows are higher from drained rather than undrained lands, mainly as a result of an increase in channel depth.
• At the river catchment scale, main channel improvements lead to larger peak flows downstream, due to higher channel velocities and a reduction in overbank flooding and storage.
• The combined effect of field drainage and main channel improvement is to increase streamflow peaks and dry weather base flows.
• At the drainage basin scale, artificial drainage produces a significant shortening of hydrograph lag times.

Withernwick, Holderness, England

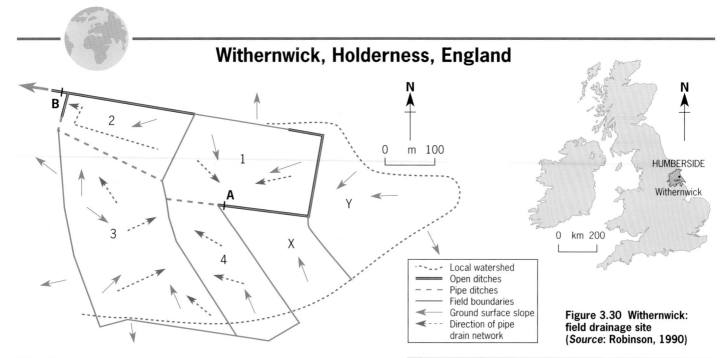

Figure 3.30 Withernwick: field drainage site (*Source*: Robinson, 1990)

The field drainage scheme

Withernwick lies on the flat, intensively farmed Holderness plains (Fig. 3.30). The local soils consist of clay loams increasing in density and massive structure with depth. Between 1974 and 1975, hydrologists studied four fields on Westland Farm before and after a field drainage scheme was completed on 81 per cent of the area.

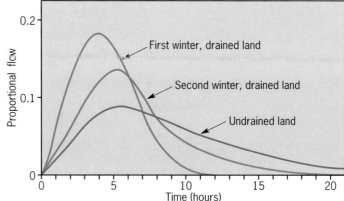

Figure 3.32 Comparison of one-hour unit hydrographs, before and after drainage. Delivery of rainwater to the drainage ditches was accelerated by the field drainage network (*Source*: Robinson, 1990)

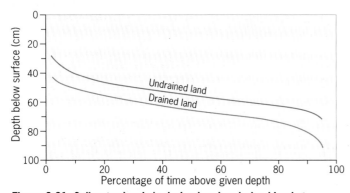

Figure 3.31 Soil water levels in drained and undrained land at Withernwick. The mean water table levels fell by approximately 10-15 cm after drainage (*Source*: Robinson, 1990)

17 Study Figure 3.30 and outline the purpose of field drainage scheme and how it works.

18 Using Figures 3.30 to 3.33, describe and explain the effects of field drainage upon streamflow.

19 Study Figure 3.30. Suggest what the effects might be on the water flow through fields 1 to 4, if similar drainage improvements were applied to fields X and Y.

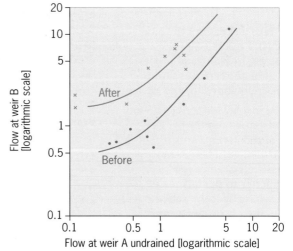

Figure 3.33 Base flows, i.e. stream discharge during dry weather, at Withernwick as the percentage of the study area artificially drained was increased from 25 to 56 per cent (*Source*: Robinson, 1990)

20 Study Figures 3.34 and 3.35. Describe and explain the changes in runoff, infiltration and evapotranspiration on: •flat ground, •sloping ground.

3.9 The impacts of changing forest cover

Afforestation

Afforestation of watersheds is a popular technique used to slow down runoff and control erosion. The aim is to even out stream discharge and 'flatten' the hydrographs, making them less 'flashy'. The increased **transpiration** losses also divert some of the precipitation inputs. Trees are thirsty organisms, and their removal frequently results in rising water tables and wetter soils, e.g. the extensive peat cover of the Scottish Highlands is the result of Medieval forest clearance causing waterlogging. A more recent example comes from southern Australia where the natural eucalyptus woodland has been cleared for cattle and sheep grazing. Water tables have risen and soil salinity has become a serious problem. As a result reforestation schemes are under way, whose purpose is to 'suck up' water and so lower the water tables once more.

Deforestation

Deforestation has become a high profile global issue. One aspect of the impacts is the acceleration of runoff and erosion, leading to an increased likelihood of flooding. A well-known example is the claim that deforestation in the Himalayas, the headwater catchments for the River Ganges, is increasing flood frequency and intensity in Bangladesh. In Europe, forest clearance for ski developments in the Alps is blamed for increased flood damage in farmland and settlements downstream. Figures 3.34 and 3.35 summarise the impacts of deforestation on the routes water takes through the **hydrological cycle** and hence the input to streamflow.

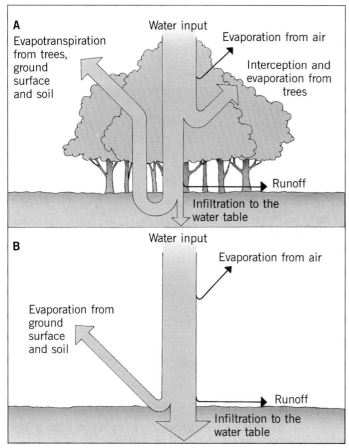

Figure 3.34 The hydrological cycle (a) before and (b) after deforestation on flat ground (*Source:* Tivy and O'Hare, 1981)

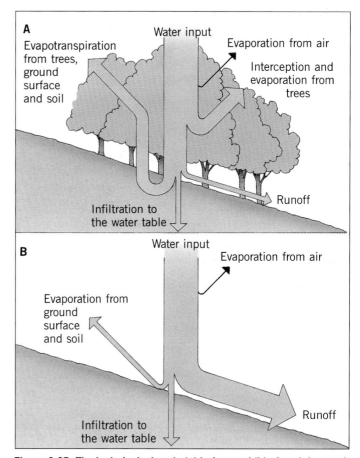

Figure 3.35 The hydrological cycle (a) before and (b) after deforestation on sloping ground (*Source:* Tivy and O'Hare, 1981)

These changes depend on:
- the size of the deforested area;
- the slope of the land;
- the climatic and meteorological conditions, especially the amount and intensity of the rainfall;
- soil texture and organic content;
- the nature of the remaining or succeeding vegetation.

Perhaps the most controversial deforestation issues focus on the tropical rainforests. The hydrological cycle interacts with this complex ecosystem in a very special way, and forest clearance can have severe impacts (Fig. 3.36). For example, in the central Amazon basin in Brazil there are growing concerns that deforestation is causing greater extremes of flow.

Figure 3.36 Hydrological processes in undisturbed tropical rainforest

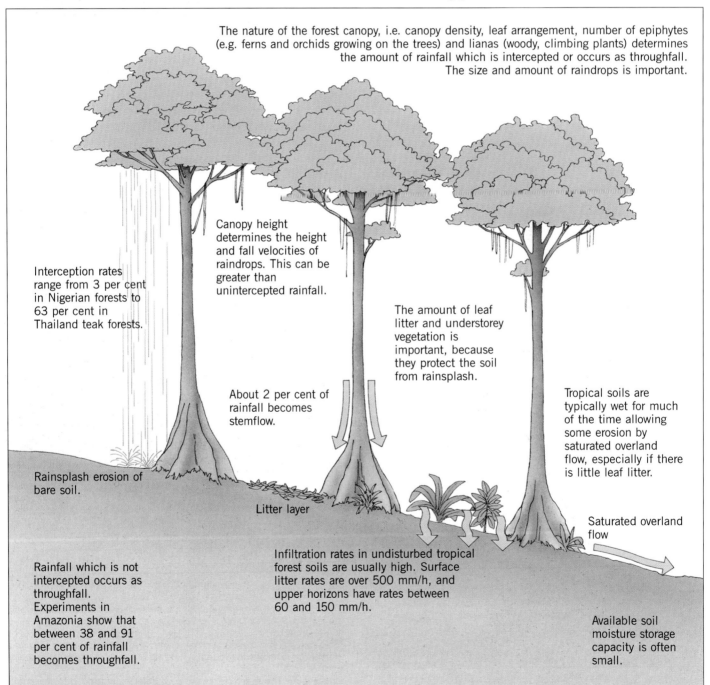

The nature of the forest canopy, i.e. canopy density, leaf arrangement, number of epiphytes (e.g. ferns and orchids growing on the trees) and lianas (woody, climbing plants) determines the amount of rainfall which is intercepted or occurs as throughfall. The size and amount of raindrops is important.

Interception rates range from 3 per cent in Nigerian forests to 63 per cent in Thailand teak forests.

Canopy height determines the height and fall velocities of raindrops. This can be greater than unintercepted rainfall.

The amount of leaf litter and understorey vegetation is important, because they protect the soil from rainsplash.

About 2 per cent of rainfall becomes stemflow.

Tropical soils are typically wet for much of the time allowing some erosion by saturated overland flow, especially if there is little leaf litter.

Rainsplash erosion of bare soil.

Litter layer

Saturated overland flow

Rainfall which is not intercepted occurs as throughfall. Experiments in Amazonia show that between 38 and 91 per cent of rainfall becomes throughfall.

Infiltration rates in undisturbed tropical forest soils are usually high. Surface litter rates are over 500 mm/h, and upper horizons have rates between 60 and 150 mm/h.

Available soil moisture storage capacity is often small.

The Maracá Rainforest Project, Brazil

The Ilha de Maracá in northern Brazil was studied as part of a project undertaken by the Royal Geographical Society (RGS) in 1987 at the invitation of the Brazilian Environment Secretariat. It provided a rare opportunity to study an area of little-disturbed, moist tropical forest. The RGS established experimental plots to investigate the effects of partial and complete forest clearance on hydrological processes (Fig. 3.39). The soils of the experimental area are coarse-textured and quartzitic, with a thin layer of surface organic matter. Laterite occurs at depths of about 1000–1200 mm. This is exposed at the surface where erosion has occurred. The forest canopy height is between 20 and 25 m, with a large number of understorey palms, especially near stream channels.

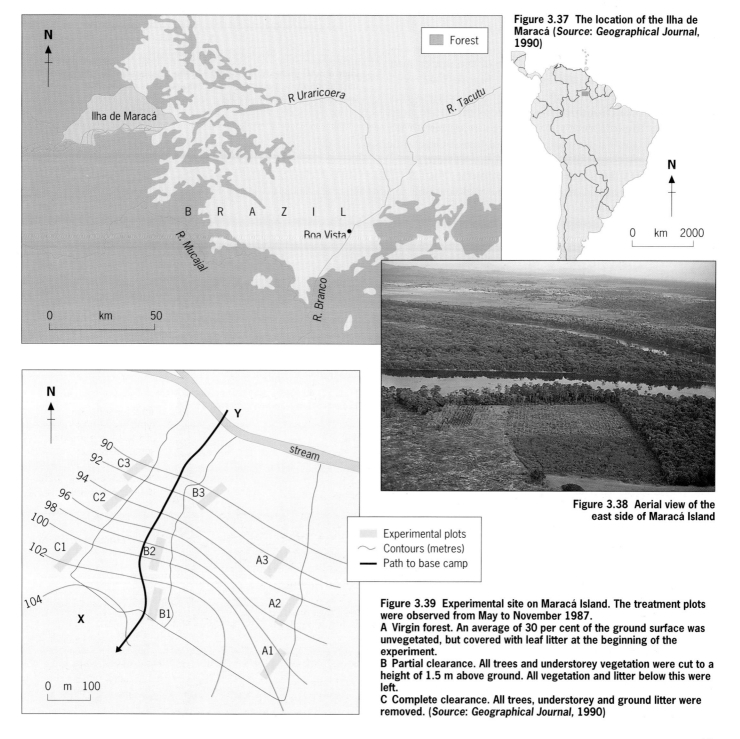

Figure 3.37 The location of the Ilha de Maracá (*Source: Geographical Journal*, 1990)

Figure 3.38 Aerial view of the east side of Maracá Island

Experimental plots
Contours (metres)
Path to base camp

Figure 3.39 Experimental site on Maracá Island. The treatment plots were observed from May to November 1987.
A Virgin forest. An average of 30 per cent of the ground surface was unvegetated, but covered with leaf litter at the beginning of the experiment.
B Partial clearance. All trees and understorey vegetation were cut to a height of 1.5 m above ground. All vegetation and litter below this were left.
C Complete clearance. All trees, understorey and ground litter were removed. (*Source: Geographical Journal*, 1990)

Maracá Rainforest Project

Throughflow

In the wet season, throughflow on the totally cleared plots was higher than on the partially cleared and uncleared plots. We can partly explain this by the total clearance. However, if this was the only reason, we would expect the totally cleared plots to respond more sensitively to storm events, i.e. show increased throughflow after each rainfall event as water infiltrates the cleared plot, and not respond as in Figure 3.40.

The explanation lies in the linkage of the upper and lower slopes by strong throughflow. Figure 3.42 explains what is happening. Throughflow feeds water to the slope foot (**floodplain**) and keeps moisture high. This offsets the different rates of forest transpiration and excess runoff losses as a result of forest clearance. The cleared plots are like 'windows' in a system dominated by subsurface water movement. The lateritic layer hinders drainage in the wet season, encouraging saturated overland flow.

21 Study Figure 3.39. Draw a cross-section from X to Y.

22 Using Figure 3.40, describe the rate and pattern of throughflow on the three types of plot in response to the dry season rainfall on 15 October.

23a Explain why the three types of plot behave in a similar pattern in the dry season.
b Suggest why the forest plot shows faster soil water movement than the totally cleared plot.

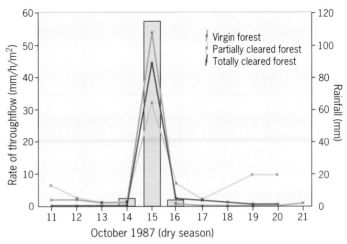

Figure 3.40 Rate of throughflow in the dry season. Soil moisture conditions were monitored using neutron probes. (*Source: Geographical Journal*, 1990)

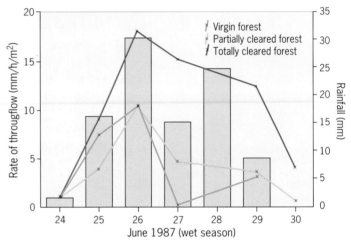

Figure 3.41 Rate of throughflow in the wet season (*Source: Geographical Journal*, 1990)

Figure 3.42 Store and flow model of Maracá hillslope hydrology (*Source: Geographical Journal*, 1990)

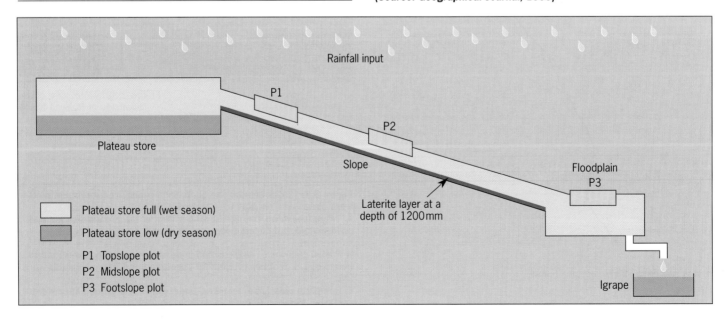

Rainfall input

Plateau store

Slope

P1

P2

Laterite layer at a depth of 1200 mm

Floodplain
P3

Igrape

Plateau store full (wet season)

Plateau store low (dry season)

P1 Topslope plot
P2 Midslope plot
P3 Footslope plot

Subsurface processes

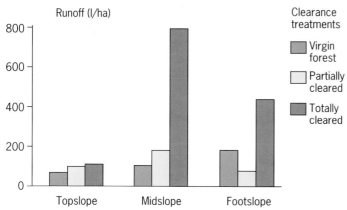

Runoff (l/ha)

Clearance treatments
- Virgin forest
- Partially cleared
- Totally cleared

Topslope Midslope Footslope

Figure 3.43 Runoff levels for the three plots (*Source: Geographical Journal*, 1990)

24a Study Figure 3.40. Compare the responses of the three types of plot to the rainfall inputs in the wet season.
b Why do you think overall soil moisture movement is slower in the wet season than in the dry season?

25 Study Figure 3.41 and 3.42. How does the lateritic layer affect surface and subsurface soil water movement at the study sites?

26 Use Figure 3.43 to compare runoff for the three plots.

27 Draw two annotated diagrams, similar to Figure 3.36, to show the hydrological processes on partially cleared and completely cleared plots.

28 Essay: Evaluate the findings of the work at Ilha de Maracá and their importance for users of tropical forest areas.

3.10 The effects of urbanisation on hydrological processes

Impermeable surfaces

The most obvious change that urbanisation brings to a drainage basin is that it replaces vegetated soils with less permeable surfaces, e.g. tarmac roads (Fig. 3.44). There is less surface storage and less water enters the soil and groundwater stores. The reduced surface water storage and vegetation cover mean lower evapotranspiration outputs. Consequently, the percentage of rainfall that runs off increases.

Figure 3.44 The effects of urbanisation on hydrological processes (*Source:* Hollis, 1988)

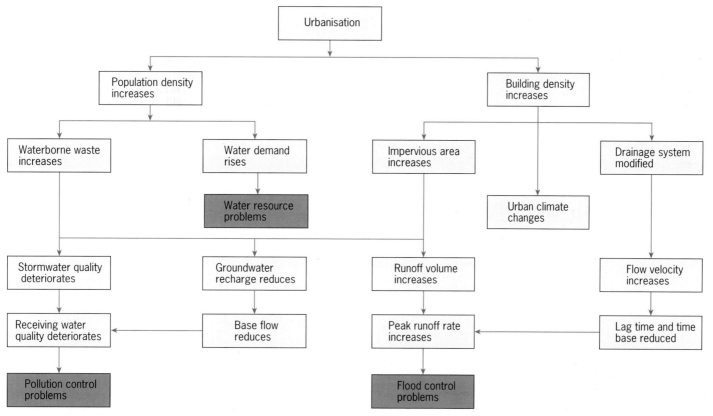

Figure 3.45 In the UK, impermeable surfaces cover 20 per cent of urban areas built after 1945. This rises to 90 per cent in city centres and falls to under 5 per cent in areas of suburban detached housing. Water is moved quickly and efficiently by gutters, drains and sewers. They are designed to be smooth and efficient at transferring water, usually into the nearest river channel

Urban areas are designed to shed water quickly (Fig. 3.45). For example, roads have cambers and gutters to remove surface water and roofs are shaped for rapid shedding of water. However, all surfaces absorb some water and are therefore affected by antecedent moisture conditions. Surfaces have irregularities which store water. Studies in Redbourn, Hertfordshire, show that runoff from roads averages 11.4 per cent and roofs 56.9 per cent. As with all surfaces, runoff will also depend on the amount and intensity of rainfall.

Effects on the storm hydrograph
The urbanised part of a drainage basin responds quickly to a rainfall event. We can identify this in the storm hydrograph which is typically steeper with a shorter lag time (Figs 3.46 and 3.47). The amount of water reaching a river by slow flow processes of throughflow and groundwater flow is reduced. This means that base flow is lower. Water managers have to respond to these changes in the storm hydrograph in order to prevent flooding in the urban area or downstream.

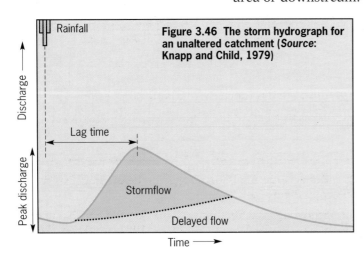

Figure 3.46 The storm hydrograph for an unaltered catchment (*Source:* Knapp and Child, 1979)

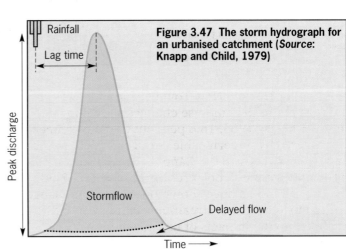

Figure 3.47 The storm hydrograph for an urbanised catchment (*Source:* Knapp and Child, 1979)

The Canon's Brook basin, Harlow, England

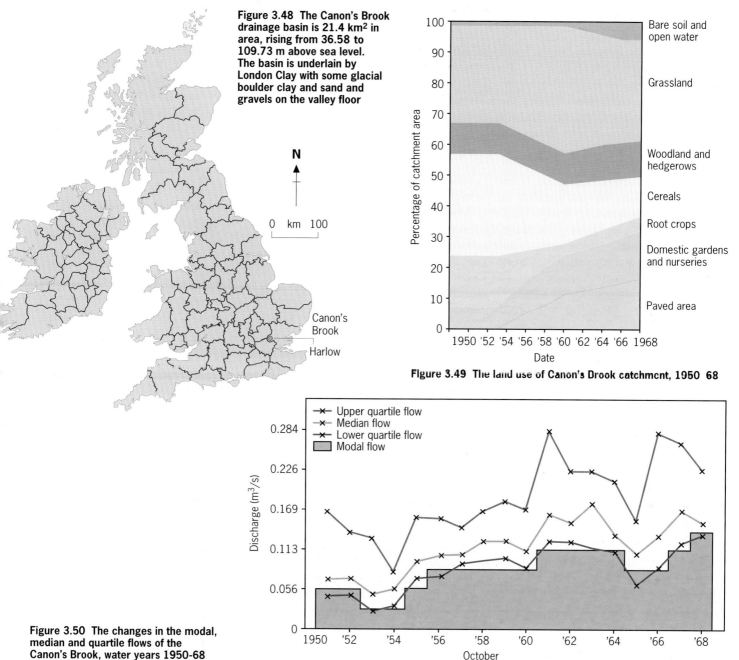

Figure 3.48 The Canon's Brook drainage basin is 21.4 km² in area, rising from 36.58 to 109.73 m above sea level. The basin is underlain by London Clay with some glacial boulder clay and sand and gravels on the valley floor

Figure 3.49 The land use of Canon's Brook catchment, 1950–68

Figure 3.50 The changes in the modal, median and quartile flows of the Canon's Brook, water years 1950-68

Building for Harlow New Town began in late 1951 and resulted in the land use changes shown in Figure 3.49. By 1968, 16.6 per cent of the catchment was covered by impermeable surfaces which drained via sewers directly to the Canon's Brook. The changes in the flows of the Brook are shown in Figure 3.50. The rainfall inputs have shown no significant changes and so any changes in streamflow can largely be attributed to the impacts of urbanisation. A 15 per cent paving of the catchment increased runoff by 59.4 mm, i.e. an increase of about 30 per cent above the rural catchment runoff.

29 Describe the land use changes in the drainage basin shown in Figure 3.49.

30 Study Figure 3.50. Compare the quartile, median and modal flows of the Canon's Brook for 1952, 1960 and 1968.

The Canon's Brook basin

Seasonal variations

An interesting finding was in the seasonal variations in the increased runoff (Fig. 3.51). The urbanised catchment produces noticeably higher flows than the simulated rural catchment during the summer months or during relatively dry years. There is also an increased frequency of high flows due to thunderstorms over the developed catchment compared to rural areas.

Urbanisation appears to have little effect on winter flows. The reasons for this are that the urban catchment responds to every rainfall event, because water is quickly shed into the stream. In the rural catchment, summer flows tend to be low as a result of soil moisture storage and higher evapotranspiration losses. Only moderate to heavy rainfall would produce a response in the stream of the simulated rural catchment. Thus, low flows in the summer of

0.028–0.057 m³/s per second for the pre-urban catchment have been replaced by higher flows of 0.100–0.283 m³/s per second in the urbanised catchment. In the winter, the rural catchment's clay soils would be saturated, causing storm rainfall to run off rapidly. This would behave in a similar way to a paved area after building work.

31 Study Figure 3.51.
a In which years is the simulated (rural) flow at its greatest difference from the gauged (urban) flow?
b For the years 1966–68 inclusive, find the amount and time of year with the greatest difference between the simulated rural flow and the gauged urban flow.
c Suggest reasons for the simulated rural flow being greater than the urban flow in late 1965.

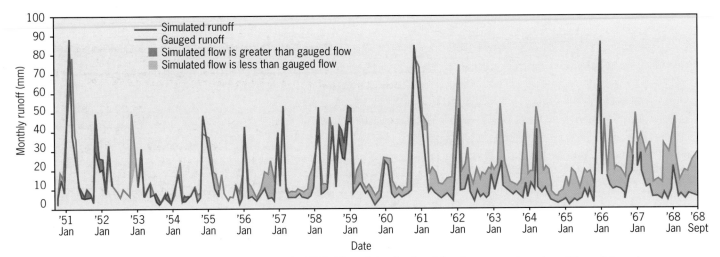

Figure 3.51 **Gauged monthly flows from the Canon's Brook, 1950–68, and the simulated flow from a rural version of the catchment**

Managing urban hydrological systems

Urban development increases flood frequency by reducing hydrograph lag times and increasing peak discharges. However, since urban water management involves storm drains and sewage systems, their combined effect on flooding is more complex than simply increasing quickflow processes from impermeable surfaces.

River system management includes water storage, **abstractions** and transfer of water for urban supply. Thus, urban areas frequently have inputs of water from outside the drainage basin for public water supply. After use in homes and businesses, it is passed on for treatment in sewage works before being discharged into the urban river. How this management operates has a significant effect upon the discharge and hydrograph downstream. Figure 3.52 sets out four types of management system.

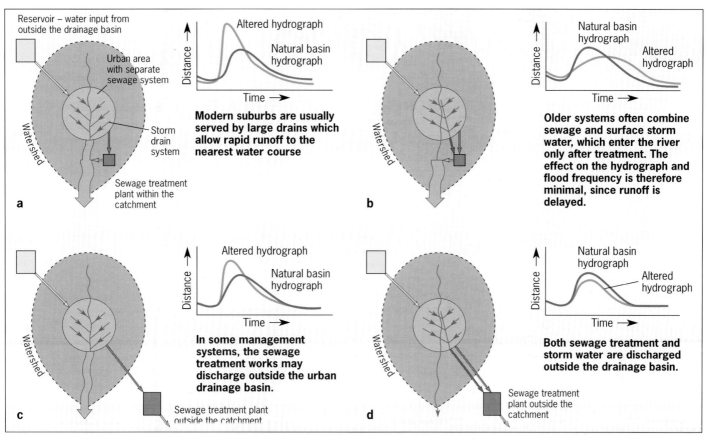

Figure 3.52 Variability of urban hydrological systems in the UK and the implications for changes in flood hydrographs (*Source*: Roberts, 1989)

?

Study Figure 3.52.

32 Construct a table to show the four types of urban hydrological system in the UK under the following headings:

a 'Type of system (A–D)'

b 'Comments on sewage and storm water management'

c 'Impact on discharge downstream'

d 'Impact on flood hydrograph'

33 For each of the four types of urban water management system, explain the impact on the amount of discharge downstream and on the flood hydrograph.

34 What will be the implication of urban hydrological management on:

a the river that the water is abstracted from?

b the river that the water is discharged into?

35 What factors should be considered when deciding on the water management system in an area of new urban development?

Summary

- The amount of water in a river is expressed as discharge or runoff and consists of two components: base flow and quick (storm) flow.
- Streamflow takes place in response to changes in the status of stores of the drainage basin. Changes in streamflow are shown by hydrographs.
- Rainfall intensity, persistence and periodicity influence the form of the hydrograph.
- Base flow results from slowflow processes, and storm flow from quickflow processes.
- A key quickflow process is saturated overland flow which results from the combined effects of prolonged rainfall inputs and high antecedent soil moisture conditions, high water tables, i.e. water stores are full, and low evapotranspiration outputs.
- Drainage basin characteristics – size, shape, relief, geology, soil, geological structure, stream density and arrangement – have important effects on the nature of the storm hydrographs.
- The porosity and permeability of the soil and rock types in a drainage basin have important impacts on the balance between quickflow and slowflow processes.
- Human activities have major impacts on runoff processes and the nature of the storm hydrograph. The largest effects are produced by agricultural enterprises and changes in land use, e.g. deforestation and urbanisation.

4 Water balance and river regimes

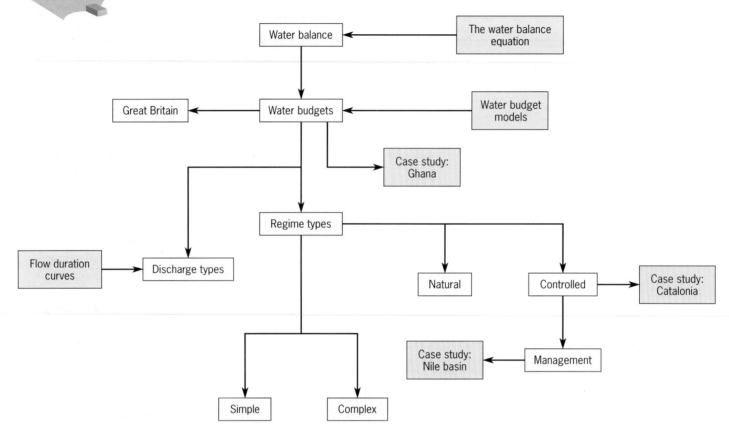

4.1 Introduction

Our study of **hydrographs** in Chapter 3 emphasised that **streamflow** varies constantly – from day to day, from month to month, and from one year to another. None the less, if we examine records over longer periods of time, we find that the main river in any **drainage basin** has, under natural conditions at least, a seasonal rhythm of **discharge**. We call this rhythm the river **regime**. The regime varies in amplitude, but it is always present. It is controlled by the varying availability of water in the drainage basin. This water supply or input is ample in some months, scarce in others. We express this fluctuation in terms of the **water balance** or **budget**.

The purpose of this chapter is to examine the relationship between the water balance in a drainage basin and the streamflow regime. This is a particularly important topic, as the rhythms of all life forms, including humans, are influenced by the annual rhythm of water availability.

Figures 4.1 and 4.2 are a vivid illustration of how water availability varies from season to season within the same environment. Our understanding of the processes affecting the water balance and how to manage water supply effectively is becoming increasingly urgent as global water demands expand. Water resource management modifies the water balance and the river regime. We therefore need to distinguish between natural and controlled balances and regimes.

_____ **?** _____

1 Compare Figures 4.1 and 4.2 and describe the implications of seasonal river flow for water availability.

Figure 4.1 The Black Volta River, Ghana, at base flow during the dry season

Figure 4.2 The Black Volta River, Ghana, nearing high flow during the wet season

4.2 The water balance

Streamflow can only occur when the water stores in the drainage basin are capable of releasing water, and when there is direct surface runoff. Thus, in order to understand the pattern of streamflow, or the regime of a river over the year, we need to understand the shifting balance between the three key variables: precipitation; **evapotranspiration**; soil and **groundwater storage**.

The water balance equation

The dynamic relationship between precipitation, evapotranspiration and soil and groundwater storage can be expressed in terms of the water balance equation:

Precipitation (P) = streamflow (Q) + evapotranspiration (E) $\pm$ change in storage (S).

Transposing this in terms of streamflow, it becomes:

$Q = P - E \pm S$.

The water balance at the global and continental scale

Geographers classify the world aridity regions (Fig. 4.3) using the balance between precipitation and evapotranspiration, for natural conditions, i.e. without accounting for human interference.

Water balance at the drainage basin scale

Within an individual drainage basin we can expect to find a seasonal rhythm in the water balance (Figs 4.1 and 4.2). This should be reflected in the streamflow regime. Remember, the greater the proportion of the precipitation input which is transferred to streams as runoff, the more positive is likely to be the water balance.

The River Thames at Kingston and the River Taw at Umberleigh, Devon, illustrate this seasonal rhythm (Tables 4.2 and 4.3). Notice that the fluctuation in water balance is more marked than the seasonal rainfall variation. Thus, in regions with strongly seasonal rainfall we can expect even wider fluctuations in water balance (see Ghana case study).

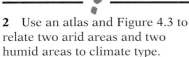

2 Use an atlas and Figure 4.3 to relate two arid areas and two humid areas to climate type.

3 Use a map of world population distribution to identify one area in each continent which is likely to have severe water management problems, i.e. both an arid climate and a dense population.

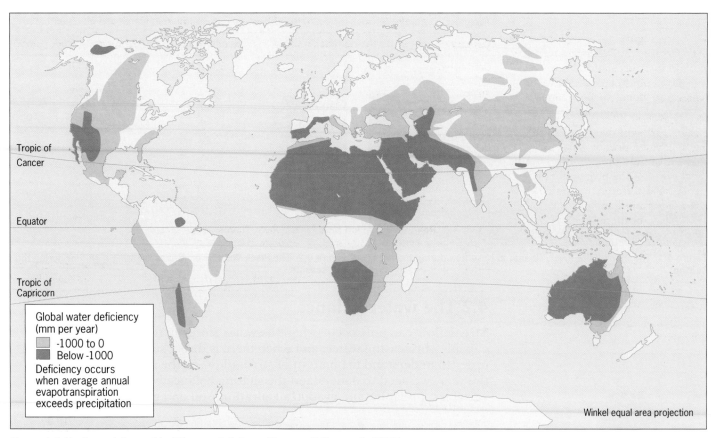

Figure 4.3 Regions of the world with water deficiency (*Source*: *Falkenmark, 1977*)

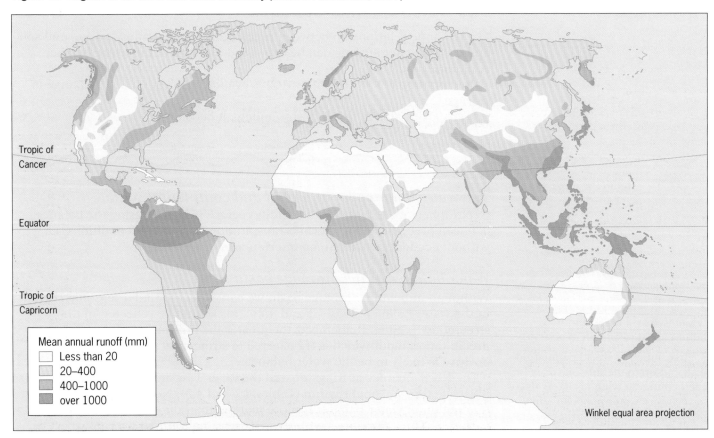

Figure 4.4 Simplified world map of mean annual runoff (*Source*: Lvovitch, 1973)

4 Trace Figure 4.4 and place it over Figure 4.3. Describe and explain any correlation between the global physical availability of water and global surface runoff.

5a On an outline map of Western Europe, present the data in Table 4.1 as located proportional pie graphs. Use the precipitation input for the size of the proportional circles. Use different colours to shade the runoff and evapotranspiration outputs.
b Describe and explain as fully as you can the variations in the water balance equations over Western Europe.
c Classify the countries of Western Europe into those having a surplus of water, and those with a deficit.

6 Using Tables 4.2 and 4.3, draw line graphs on the same axes to show the percentage of precipitation occurring as runoff for both drainage basins. Show the two lines in different colours and add a title and a key.

7 For the two drainage basins:
a In which month(s) are water losses from the drainage basin highest? Suggest why.

b Suggest how groundwater storage and seepage will affect the runoff figures.

8 Use your understandings of the way a river drainage basin system works to explain the patterns and relationships revealed by Tables 2.2 and 2.3 and your graphs. Look especially at identifiable seasonal rhythms and the differences between the two basins.

Table 4.1 The water balance for countries of Western Europe (*Source*: Marsh and MacRuairi, 1993)

Country	Precipitation (mm)	Runoff (mm)	Evapotranspiration (mm)
Switzerland	1500	1000	500
Norway	1450	1250	200
Austria	1200	670	530
Great Britain	1090	550	540
Italy	1000	600	400
Portugal	900	220	680
Belgium	850	360	490
France	750	300	450
Germany	750	260	490
Netherlands	750	250	500

Table 4.2 Rainfall and runoff data for the River Thames at Kingston (*Data source*: National Water Archive, Institute of Hydrology)

Month 1883–1991	Mean precipitation (mm)	Mean runoff (mm)	Mean precipitation as runoff (%)
January	65	37	57
February	49	33	67.3
March	53	31	58.5
April	48	22	45.8
May	54	17	31.5
June	53	13	24.5
July	58	9	15.5
August	63	9	14.3
September	57	9	15.8
October	72	13	18.0
November	72	21	29.2
December	72	30	41.7
Total	716	245	34.2

Location: SE England
Catchment area: 9948 km²
Maximum altitude: 330 m
Rocks and land use: diverse

Table 4.3 Rainfall and runoff data for the River Taw at Umberleigh (*Data source*: National Water Archive, Institute of Hydrology)

Month 1953–87	Mean precipitation (mm)	Mean runoff (mm)	Mean precipitation as runoff (%)
January	129	116	89.9
February	84	82	97.6
March	91	67	73.6
April	71	46	64.8
May	73	31	42.5
June	68	17	25.0
July	71	15	21.1
August	87	19	21.8
September	92	24	26.0
October	116	62	53.4
November	130	92	70.8
December	139	119	85.6
Total	1151	690	56.0

Location: SW England
Catchment area: 826.2 km²
Maximum Altitude: 604 m
Rock and land use: Dartmoor granite and Devonian shales and sandstones/ agriculture
Note: The percentage of precipitation which forms runoff has been calculated using the water balance equation, i.e. $Q = P - E$. It is not possible to calculate short- or long-term groundwater storage with this type of data.

?

9 Interrogate Table 4.4 to support or reject the hypothesis: 'As both the grassland (upper Wye) and forested (upper Severn) catchments receive similar precipitation totals, the runoff arriving in stream channels will be similar in both catchments.'

Effects of vegetation on the water balance

We know from Chapter 3 that runoff and, therefore, water balance will be influenced by a number of variables. One important variable is vegetation cover, which affects **interception**, **infiltration**, soil **throughflow** and evapotranspiration.

For more than 20 years researchers have been comparing two catchments, the upper Wye and Severn on the edges of Plynlimon in upland Wales (Fig. 4.5). One of their objectives has been to discover the effects of afforestation on river regimes and the water balance. Some researchers argue that afforestation improves water storage and produces a steady release of water as soil and groundwater flow to the stream. This reduces seasonality of regime, 'flattens' storm hydrographs, increases lag times and so reduces the likelihood of downstream floods. Other researchers claim that coniferous plantations take up more water than grassland and plagioclimax moorland ecosystems. This moisture is then lost to the drainage basin through transpiration. Thus, although the forest modifies the stream regime and dampens the likelihood of floods, it does not benefit the water balance of the drainage basin.

The upper Wye catchment has a grassland and moorland cover, and the upper Severn catchment has a 62 per cent cover of coniferous forest. Both catchments have a similar mean annual rainfall of around 2400 mm and range in altitude from 370 m to 700 m. The researchers measured 'catchment loss' for the two study areas, i.e. that part of the precipitation input which does not reach the stream. The amount of water moving into the groundwater store was similar for both catchments. So, if vegetation type is an influential factor, then catchment loss should be different in each catchment, i.e. that evapotranspiration is different and is the key variable (Table 4.4).

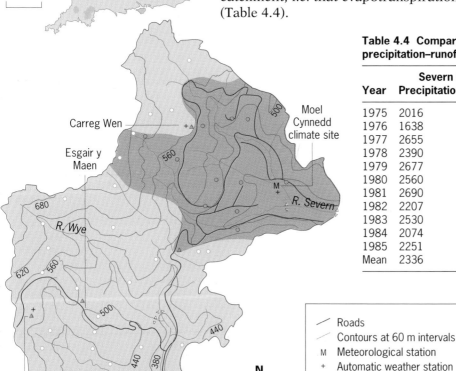

Table 4.4 Comparison of upper Severn forested area and Wye: the precipitation–runoff difference (*Source*: Institute of Hydrology)(mm)

| | Severn forested area | | | Wye | Forest–Wye |
Year	Precipitation (P)	Streamflow (Q)	P–Q	P–Q	Δ (P–Q)
1975	2016	1230	786	413	373
1976	1638	1061	577	378	199
1977	2655	1852	803	413	390
1978	2390	1787	603	341	262
1979	2677	2002	675	367	308
1980	2560	1887	673	300	373
1981	2690	2030	660	350	310
1982	2207	1737	470	325	145
1983	2530	1912	618	399	219
1984	2074	1442	632	320	312
1985	2251	1711	550	258	292
Mean	2336	1695	641	351	290

Land over 300m

N

Plynlimon

0 km 100

Moel Cynnedd climate site

Carreg Wen

Esgair y Maen

500

560

680

R. Wye

620

560

R. Severn

500

440

440

380

Eisteddfa Gurig

Cefn Brwyn

R. Wye

N

0 km 5

／ Roads
／ Contours at 60 m intervals
M Meteorological station
+ Automatic weather station
▲ Recording raingauge
◉ Ground–level raingauge
○ Canopy–level raingauge
▵ Stream gauging station
▨ Forest

Figure 4.5 The Plynlimon research catchments showing the Rivers Severn and Wye and their tributaries and the main measuring networks (*Source*: Institute of Hydrology)

The research has found that the forested catchment loses more water by evapotranspiration. Grassland returns about 16 per cent of the precipitation input to the atmosphere by **evaporation**, almost all as **transpiration** from the vegetation. In the forested catchment, evapotranspiration accounts for 30 per cent. The vital finding is that 25 per cent of all precipitation is lost from the forested area by evaporation of water which has been intercepted by the trees. Only 5 per cent is transpired from the stomata.

Water budget models

A useful way of investigating the water balance of a location over the year is by plotting temperature, precipitation and evapotranspiration rates on to a single graph to show the balance between them. These water budget graphs (Fig. 4.6) look quite complicated at first glance, but remember that they are only line graphs shown together.

Water budget graphs usually show **potential evapotranspiration (PET)**, i.e. the amount of water which would evaporate if an adequate supply was continuously available to the covering vegetation. **Actual evapotranspiration (AET)** will be less than this.

Figure 4.6 Southampton, England: the water balance of a temperate maritime climate

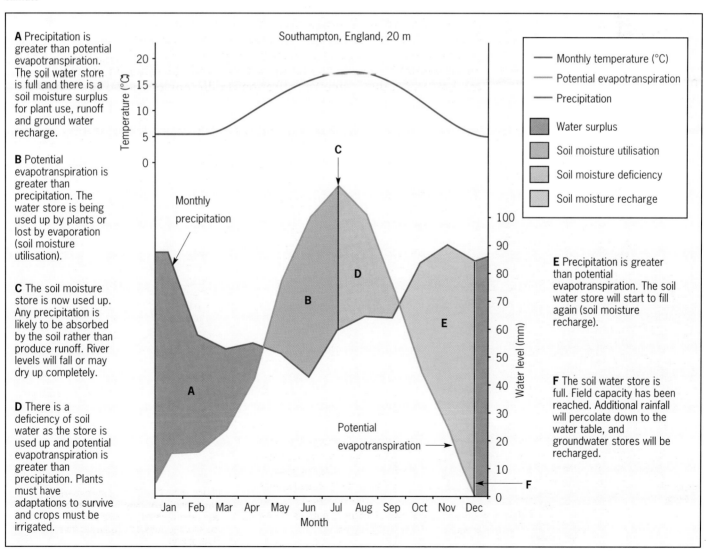

A Precipitation is greater than potential evapotranspiration. The soil water store is full and there is a soil moisture surplus for plant use, runoff and ground water recharge.

B Potential evapotranspiration is greater than precipitation. The water store is being used up by plants or lost by evaporation (soil moisture utilisation).

C The soil moisture store is now used up. Any precipitation is likely to be absorbed by the soil rather than produce runoff. River levels will fall or may dry up completely.

D There is a deficiency of soil water as the store is used up and potential evapotranspiration is greater than precipitation. Plants must have adaptations to survive and crops must be irrigated.

E Precipitation is greater than potential evapotranspiration. The soil water store will start to fill again (soil moisture recharge).

F The soil water store is full. Field capacity has been reached. Additional rainfall will percolate down to the water table, and groundwater stores will be recharged.

?

Study Figures 4.6, 4.7 and 4.8.

10 Describe the yearly pattern of the balance between temperature, precipitation and PET for the three climatic areas.

11 Suggest why the soil moisture surplus is greater for England than Bolivia, even though the precipitation input is smaller.

12 Which area(s) would require irrigation water for crops which continue to grow from year to year (perennial agriculture)?

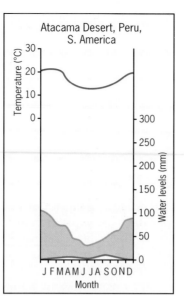

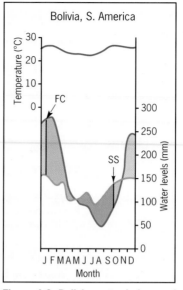

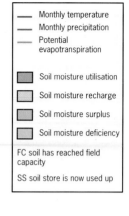

Figure 4.7 Atacama, Peru: water balance of a desert climate

Figure 4.8 Bolivia: water balance of a tropical forest climate

The water balance in Ghana, West Africa

Natural vegetation is adapted to the climate of an area. One purpose of this adaptation is for plants to survive periods of soil moisture deficit. However, many food and commercial crops may not have suitable adaptative mechanisms, although plant breeding tries to minimise the problems. The water balance model, as well as being a useful model for understanding runoff patterns in an area, allows agriculturalists to identify times when irrigation of food and commercial crops is likely to be necessary.

Ghana's climate is influenced by the seasonal movement of the Inter-Tropical Convergence Zone (ITCZ) where the trade winds meet. It is responsible for the seasonality of the rainfall over the country. Ghana has high temperatures throughout the year (Fig. 4.11), producing high PET rates. As a result, large areas experience a water balance deficit for part of the year.

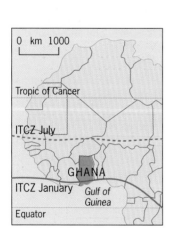

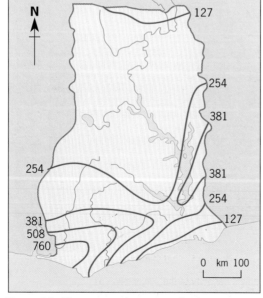

Figure 4.9 Ghana: annual water surplus in mm

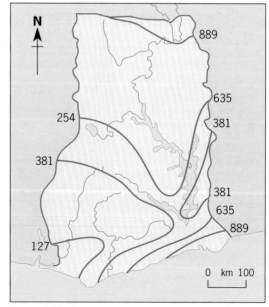

Figure 4.10 Ghana: annual water deficiency in mm

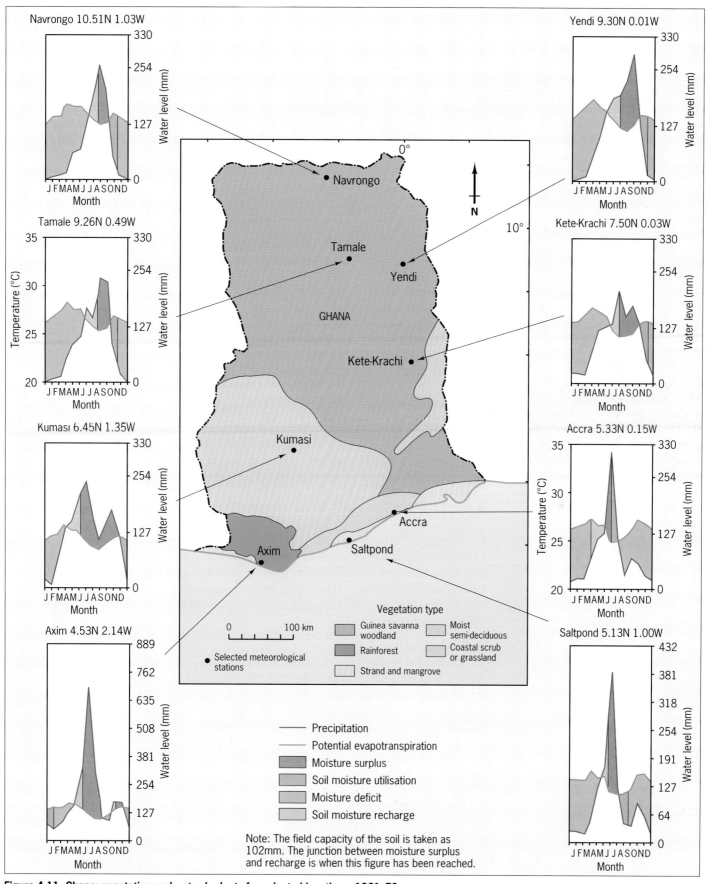

Figure 4.11 Ghana: vegetation and water budgets for selected locations, 1961–70

Water balance in Ghana

Soil moisture conditions

PET rates are low in the wet season, but more than double in the dry season. As the PET rises following the wet season, soil moisture is used up rapidly, leading to a desiccated state, particularly in the north and south-east. Any rainfall is quickly evaporated during these drier months. The AET rates will depend upon the amount of water available for evaporation and the transpiration rates of the vegetation type in the area.

In the north and east of Ghana, the savanna grassland dies down as the **soil moisture deficit** increases.

The **field capacity** of the soils in Ghana is taken as 102 mm. Once this amount of water has been absorbed, as **soil moisture recharge**, the soils will have a **soil moisture surplus**. Surface runoff and infiltration to the subsoil and groundwater stores will occur. After the rainy season, soil moisture take-up by plants or evaporation of at least 102 mm will result in a soil moisture deficit. The areas of maximum aridity or water deficiency occur in the north and along the east coast.

?

13 A wet month in Ghana is defined as when rainfall is 102 mm or more, and is over and above the PET for that same month. Using Figure 4.11, compare the duration of the wet season at: •Axim, •Accra, •Tamale, •Navrongo.

14 For Axim, Accra, Kumasi and Navrongo, give a precise comparison of the water balance. Explain any differences that you find.

15 Compare the actual amount and the seasonal pattern of PET over Ghana.

16 Relate the vegetation types at Axim, Kumasi and Navrongo to the water budgets of the area.

17 Draw the expected river regime graph for a river starting at Yendi. Put time on the *x* axis and discharge on the *y* axis. No figures are needed – it is the pattern of flow over the year that you need to show.

18a On an outline map of Ghana, divide the country into three areas:
• areas needing little or no irrigation;
• areas needing irrigation for three months of the year or less;
• areas needing irrigation for over three months.
b Which areas would you recommend solving the water shortage times by:
• storing water from the wet season;
• transferring water from 'wet' areas if they are to grow crops successfully all year?

4.3 River regimes

Ephemeral, intermittent and perennial regimes

The river regime is controlled by fluctuations in the water balance equation and the changing contributions from **quickflow** and **slowflow processes**. Each drainage basin produces its unique streamflow regime, but the rhythms can be grouped into three types according to their flow duration: ephemeral; intermittent; perennial.

Ephemeral streams

Ephemeral streams are found in arid and semi-arid environments with permanent moisture budget deficits. Streamflow occurs irregularly for short episodes, and the stream channel, often poorly defined, is dry for long periods (Fig. 4.12). Precipitation inputs arrive in localised, occasional, sudden downpours. Vegetation cover is sparse and, as a result, rainfall interception is minimal. Thus, when rainfall intensity exceeds the infiltration capacity of the surface materials, quickflow processes, e.g. **overland flow**, deliver water directly to the channel.

The result is a 'flash flood' which flows in a rapid surge downstream (Fig. 4.13). Streamflow may only last a few hours after the rain ceases. Because the water input is short-lived, the discharge declines rapidly downstream as water infiltrates the channel bed to recharge the soil and groundwater stores. For example, in the 150 km^2 of the Walnut Gulch catchment in Arizona, USA, only 15 per cent of the runoff entering the channel actually leaves the drainage basin.

Figure 4.12 Armagosa Valley, California

Figure 4.13 Armagosa River, flash flooding

A Uniform regime

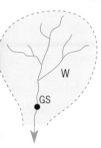

Environmental conditions, including climate, are consistent across the drainage basin (W). The regime, as recorded by the hydrograph at the gauging station (GS), reflects this simple pattern. A uniform regime is typical of small drainage basins.

B Dual regime

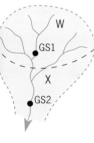

The headwater catchment (W) has different conditions, including precipitation inputs, from the lower basin (X). The regime is determined by the environment at W, and the dominant pattern is given by the hydrograph of gauging station GS1. As the river crosses X, the regime is modified. The hydrograph at GS2 will be a modified version of that at GS1.

C Complex regime

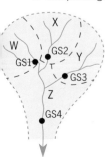

The headwater catchments extend across several environments with different precipitation inputs (W, X and Y). Each of the gauging stations in the upper basin (GS1, 2 and 3) produces a distinct hydrograph. The regime recorded by the hydrograph of GS4 will reflect elements of each of the upper catchment discharge regimes. The complex regime is typical of large drainage basins.

Figure 4.14 A model of classification

Intermittent streams

Intermittent streams are seasonal streams. They are characteristic of climates with well-defined wet and dry periods and strong seasonal contrasts in the water balance, e.g. monsoon, tropical savanna (Fig. 4.11) and Mediterranean climates. During the wet season there is a water budget surplus, and quickflow and slowflow processes combine to give high flows. When the rains end, quickflow processes cease. As the water balance graphs indicate, slowflow processes from the soil and groundwater stores sustain flows during the early part of the dry season. Eventually, however, this supply ends and the streams dry up. Except during rare 'freak' storms, any rain falling during the dry season is likely to remain in the drainage basin as recharge to the soil and groundwater stores.

In years, or series of years, with above average rainfall, streams flow longer into the dry season and may maintain some discharge all year. In contrast, during dry years flows may be brief. This variability has serious implications for animals and for human communities. For example, most stream networks of Africa's Sahel are intermittent. During the great drought of 1968–73, streamflow shrank in extent and duration. Also, recharge of the soil and groundwater stores was reduced.

Perennial streams

Perennial streams are permanent streams. They flow throughout the year, even where there is a period of lower precipitation and moisture deficit. Thus, although quickflow processes may cease, slow flow from the groundwater store is sufficient to sustain **base flow**. For example, major rivers in Britain maintain baseflow discharge even during summer droughts.

In many drainage basins there may be streams of more than one category. In the chalk catchments of southern England, headwater stretches may be intermittent as the **water table** rises and falls. Downstream, the streams become permanent due to the water table level and the groundwater zone which feeds the channel. (See Chapter 9 for the effects of the UK 1988–92 drought on stream networks.)

Simple and complex river regimes

The natural regime of a river is controlled by the environmental conditions of the drainage basin, especially the precipitation inputs. As each drainage basin is unique, so the regime, as recorded by the hydrograph, is unique. Within this diversity two classes of regime have been identified: simple and complex. A generalised model of this classification is set out in Figure 4.14.

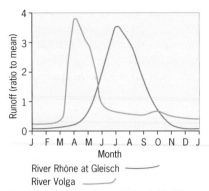

Figure 4.15 Simple regime of the River Volga (plains snowmelt) and River Rhône (glacier melt) (*Source*: Ward and Robinson, 1990)

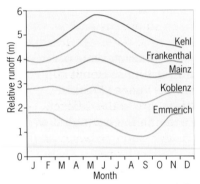

Figure 4.16 The complex regime of the River Rhine, Europe (*Source*: Ward and Robinson, 1990)

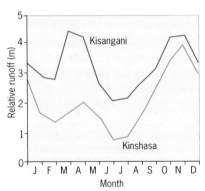

Figure 4.17 The complex regime of the River Zaire, Africa (*Source*: Ward and Robinson, 1990)

?

19 Using Figures 4.18 to 4.23, list the river regimes which show:
• the most, • the least variation from the mean flow. Suggest reasons for your answer in each case.

Figures 4.18 to 4.23 European river regimes (*Source*: Institute of Hydrology)

Simple regimes

Simple river regimes are divided into distinct periods of high and low flow. Water inputs are delivered from a headwater catchment of a single environmental type. The simplest pattern, called the **uniform regime**, occurs typically in small river basins, such as those draining from Exmoor to the north Devon coast. Even some larger rivers, such as the Volga in the Russian Federation (Fig. 4.15), whose regime is strongly influenced by severe winters followed by snowmelt across the majority of the basin, show these simple rhythms.

Other rivers may be glacier and snowmelt-fed in their headwater catchments, e.g. the River Rhône in France (Fig. 4.15). However, their lower basins may lie in quite different environments, and the regimes are progressively modified towards the river mouths. These are defined as **dual regimes**.

Complex regimes

Large river basins are likely to include headwater catchments with different runoff patterns and stream regimes. Each imposes a distinct discharge rhythm upon the main river. The result is a complex regime which shows the influences of several headwater catchments. Furthermore, there is progressive change as a river crosses its lower basin. The Nile and Mississippi both have complex regimes.

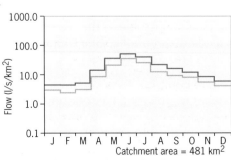

Figure 4.18 R. Vascão, Portugal

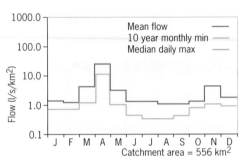

Figure 4.19 R. Vorona, Russia

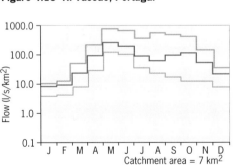

Figure 4.20 R. Roggiasca, Switzerland

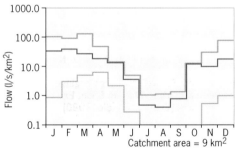

Figure 4.21 R. Valescure, France

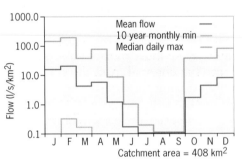

Figure 4.22 R. Kara-Samur, Russia

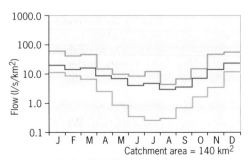

Figure 4.23 R. Wold, Netherlands

20 Match the six regime hydrographs in Figures 4.18 to 4.23 to the following descriptions, giving reasons for your answer in each case:

a West coast, temperate oceanic climate.

b Glacier melt, mountain climate.

c Mediterranean climate, river with intermittent flow.

d East European continental climate with snowmelt and summer maxima rainfall.

e Mediterranean climate with semi-permanent flow.

f Continental interior with spring snowmelt.

21 For each of the regimes in Figures 4.18 to 4.23, state whether it is simple, dual or complex.

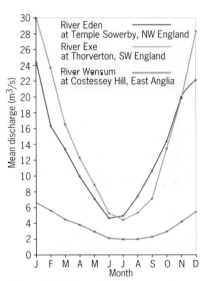

Figure 4.24 Annual discharge regimes for three English rivers: the Eden, Exe and Wensum (*Source*: Goudie, 1990)

22 Figure 4.24 shows the discharge regimes for three rivers in different parts of England.

a Suggest reasons why the Eden and the Exe show a more varied discharge over the year than the Wensum.

b Explain how these river regimes support the work of Ward and Robinson in Figures 4.25 and 4.26.

In Europe, the Rhine (Fig. 4.16) is fed by glaciers and snowmelt in its upper catchment, to give early summer peak flows. Downstream it receives tributaries which are increasingly influenced by temperate oceanic climates. These produce low flows during the summer, e.g. the River Mosel, France. Thus, by Emmerlich at the Dutch border, the meltwater input from upstream gives the Rhine a secondary summer peak.

In equatorial Africa, the River Zaire (Congo) has a complex regime produced by the distinct climates of the northern and southern hemisphere. The river at Kisangani shows the double peak regime which reflects the equatorial rainfall pattern (Fig. 4.17). However, large parts of its headwater catchments lie in the southern hemisphere, with December rainfall maxima. This complicates the regime downstream at Kinshasa. Although Kinshasa is in the northern hemisphere, the river regime shows the influence of the southern hemisphere tributaries.

4.4 River regimes and human activity

British rivers are small by world and even European standards and, as with all rivers, they show variability of flow. Most have simple regimes. However, some rivers in the north and west of the UK show more complex regimes due to spring snowmelt or reduced summer evapotranspiration. Periods of maximum runoff show a tendency to come later in the year towards the south and east of the UK (Figs 4.25 and 4.26). This is due to the differences in evaporation patterns, but also the nature of the rocks. In the north and west the rocks are mainly older, impermeable metamorphic and igneous rocks which will encourage more quickflow processes. The south and east are dominated by younger, permeable sedimentary rocks which release water slowly into the channel from the groundwater store.

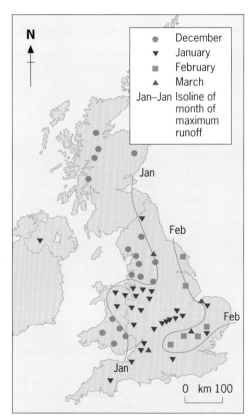

Figure 4.25 The UK: month of maximum runoff (*Source*: Ward and Robinson, 1990)

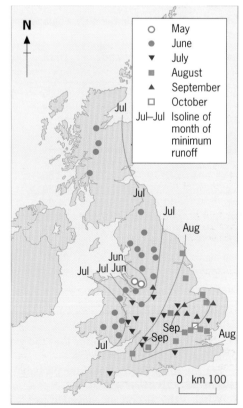

Figure 4.26 The UK: month of minimum runoff (*Source*: Ward and Robinson, 1990)

Flow duration curves

A useful way of showing the variation in flow of a river is the **flow duration curve** (Figs 4.27 and 4.28). This shows the percentage of time that a given discharge is exceeded, or the probability of the river having a certain discharge. Flow duration curves which are steeply sloping throughout show highly variable flows due to the importance of quickflow processes, e.g. the Rivers Tees and Tamar. Rivers which have gently sloping curves, e.g. the Rivers Ver and Wharfe, are largely fed by base flow and respond more slowly to rainfall inputs.

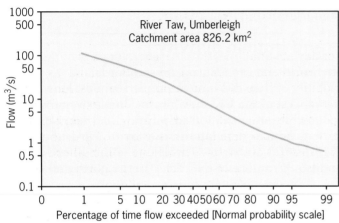

Figure 4.27 River Taw, Umberleigh

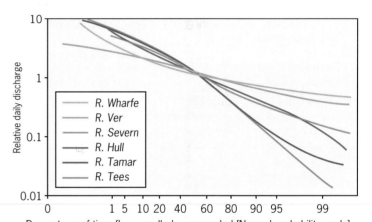

Figure 4.28 Flow duration curves for six British rivers (*Source*: Ward and Robinson, 1990)

Table 4.5 River Taw, Umberleigh, England: mean monthly discharge data (m³/s) for 1980–7 (*Data source*: National Water Archive, Institute of Hydrology)

Month	1980	1981	1982	1983	1984	1985	1986	1987	Mean	Min.	Max.	Standard deviation
Jan	28.18	29.83	40.86	48.92	62.10	26.03	42.73	20.00	?	20.00	62.10	13.03
Feb	43.82	16.86	18.54	19.18	36.47	19.95	7.16	19.45	22.68	7.16	43.82	10.95
Mar	27.45	52.14	42.17	14.44	7.45	15.65	15.19	27.28	25.22	7.45	52.14	14.34
Apr	14.49	7.78	6.04	17.89	5.48	25.02	24.08	28.85	16.20	5.46	28.85	?
May	2.42	19.55	2.46	37.00	2.26	3.56	13.28	3.58	10.51	2.26	37.00	11.65
Jun	9.84	9.11	2.72	4.47	1.33	5.99	9.54	5.09	6.01	1.33	9.84	3.02
Jul	8.79	2.75	8.56	1.65	0.79	3.97	3.31	3.59	?	0.79	8.79	2.77
Aug	5.63	2.21	2.59	0.84	0.80	19.13	18.01	1.74	6.37	0.80	19.13	7.19
Sep	11.43	9.80	4.28	3.25	3.59	9.62	7.91	1.81	6.47	1.81	11.43	3.43
Oct	40.53	47.73	24.26	14.98	20.64	9.49	19.15	32.38	26.14	9.49	47.73	?
Nov	28.95	24.21	52.83	11.13	49.39	6.64	54.32	34.17	32.71	6.64	54.32	17.25
Dec	33.35	46.35	55.45	46.91	37.38	36.83	47.04	15.96	?	15.96	55.45	11.26
Year mean	21.17	22.52	21.81	18.48	18.92	15.15	21.91	16.12	19.51	15.15	22.52	2.62

23 Study Figure 4.27. Notice that the graph has a logarithmic scale on both axes.
a For the River Taw, what is the probability of a discharge of:
• 1.0 m³/s? • 10 m³/s? • 80 m³/s?
b What is the discharge exceeded for:
• 90 per cent of the time? • 20 per cent of the time?

24 Standard deviation is a measure of the dispersal of the discharges for each month around the mean for that month. The larger the standard deviation, the more variable the discharge data for that month. The smaller the standard deviation, the less variation there is around the mean.
a Complete Table 4.5.

?

b Using your data:
• Draw a hydrograph of river flow to show the characteristic regime. Plot line graphs in different colours on the same axes for mean, minimum and maximum figures for each month.
• Present the standard deviation figures as a bar graph on the same piece of graph paper and with the months on the same scale as your hydrographs.

c Interpret the data as fully as possible. Include flow pattern over the year, months of high and low discharges and months when discharge variation is smallest and greatest from the mean.
d What factors could explain the patterns you have described in c?

Water resource problems in Catalonia, Spain

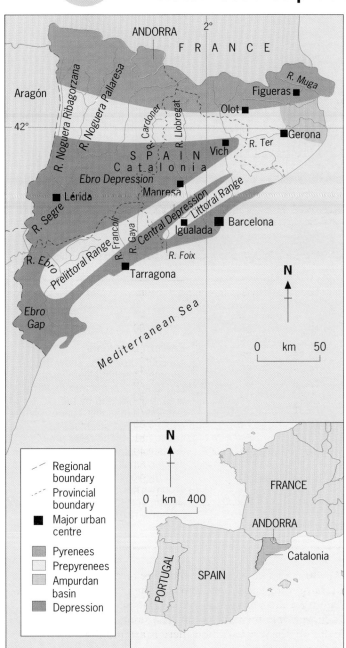

Figure 4.29 Catalonia: location and geography

Catalonia in north-east Spain (Fig. 4.29) is a popular holiday destination. It is also a thriving agricultural and industrial region, centring on Barcelona (population two million; 42 per cent of Catalonia's total). Urban and industrial water demands are not specifically seasonal, but agriculture and tourism have strong summer demand peaks. May to September is the period of water budget deficits, minimal runoff and base flow discharges. So, if we are lucky enough to be enjoying a Mediterranean holiday in Catalonia and to relax in a leisurely shower or bath after a long day in the sun, we are consuming a scarce resource.

The Mediterranean climate in this region gives hot, dry summers, with spring and autumn rainfall maxima (Fig. 4.30). The general rhythm of river regimes follows this pattern, with summer minima and floods most likely in early spring. However, the individual drainage basin regimes in Catalonia vary widely (Fig. 4.31). This is a reflection of the climatic differences, influenced by the physical geography of

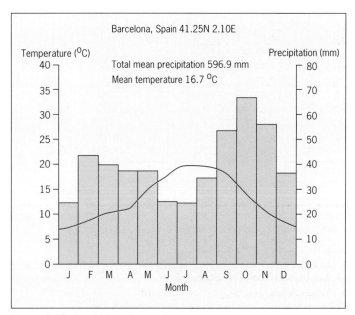

Figure 4.30 Catalonia: climate data

 Problems in Catalonia

the region. For instance, if we compare the physical and climatic maps (Figs 4.29 and 4.31) we can see that the higher precipitation totals of over 1000 mm in the north are explained by the presence of the Pyrenees mountains. The Lérida basin in the west lies in the rainshadow of the coast ranges and so has rainfall totals of less than 400 mm.

Equally important in determining the river regimes is the low proportion of the precipitation inputs which becomes runoff. For example, even in the cooler, wetter north, only 38 per cent of the rainfall reaches the river channels. The figures then decline southwards, as evapotranspiration rates increase. Varying amounts of rainfall enter the groundwater store.

Figure 4.31 Catalonia: the geography and flow regimes of selected rivers, and rainfall in mm (*Source: Geography, 1988*)

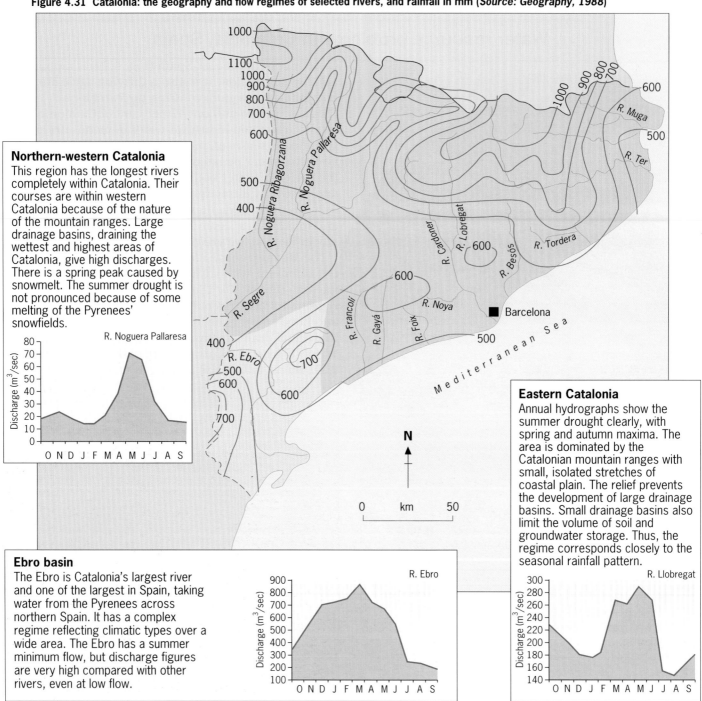

Northern-western Catalonia
This region has the longest rivers completely within Catalonia. Their courses are within western Catalonia because of the nature of the mountain ranges. Large drainage basins, draining the wettest and highest areas of Catalonia, give high discharges. There is a spring peak caused by snowmelt. The summer drought is not pronounced because of some melting of the Pyrenees' snowfields.

Eastern Catalonia
Annual hydrographs show the summer drought clearly, with spring and autumn maxima. The area is dominated by the Catalonian mountain ranges with small, isolated stretches of coastal plain. The relief prevents the development of large drainage basins. Small drainage basins also limit the volume of soil and groundwater storage. Thus, the regime corresponds closely to the seasonal rainfall pattern.

Ebro basin
The Ebro is Catalonia's largest river and one of the largest in Spain, taking water from the Pyrenees across northern Spain. It has a complex regime reflecting climatic types over a wide area. The Ebro has a summer minimum flow, but discharge figures are very high compared with other rivers, even at low flow.

Table 4.6 Drainage areas and discharge characteristics of the principal Catalan rivers (Source: Geography, 1988)

Region	Drainage basin	Drainage area (km²)	Total annual flow (hm³)	Average discharge (m³/s)
Eastern Catalonia	Muga	854	117	2.5
	Fluviá	1125	225	6.8
	Ter	3010	840	17.4
	Torderá	894	127	0.7
	Besós	1039	78	0.8
	Llobregat	4948	630	12.3
	Foix	312	9	0.3
	Gayá	424	28	0.4
	Francolí	838	48	1.5
North and western Catalonia	Noguera Ribagorzana	1100 (2046)	720	24.3
	Noguera Pallaresa	2820	1489	31.6
	Segre	11934 (22579)	3148	90.0
Ebro basin	Ebro	14950 (85550)	18842	615.0

Note: The figures within brackets indicate the total drainage area of basins lying only partially within the region. The discharge statistics are based on the lowest gauging station in the basin and exclude therefore any subsequent increases in flow.

Figure 4.32 Catalonia: the geographical distribution of water demand and potential supply (Source: Geography, 1988)

25a Use the data in Table 4.6 to carry out a Spearman rank correlation of drainage basin area and total annual flow for Catalonia's rivers.
b For the three regions of Catalonia, calculate the mean drainage basin area, total annual flow and average discharge figures for the rivers.
c On a copy of Figure 4.29 draw located proportional bar graphs or symbols to show the mean drainage basin area, total annual flow and average discharge for the rivers.

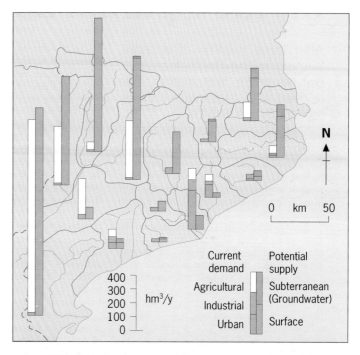

Water supplies

Water availability in Catalonia, therefore, varies spatially. The crucial issue for water resource managers is that the geographical distribution of demand is not well matched with this potential supply (Fig. 4.32). Water for industrial, domestic and agricultural use comes from two main sources: rivers and their reservoirs, and the groundwater stores. Reservoirs are used to store spring and autumn high river flows. A conflict exists in this storage policy. Many reservoirs are primarily for hydro-electric power (HEP) generation which supplies 21 per cent of Catalonia's electricity needs (Fig. 4.33). HEP requires a constant high head of water to drive the turbines. Thus, the reservoirs cannot be drawn down too low during the shortage periods of summer drought.

To attempt to overcome the shortfall, several small-scale inter-basin transfer schemes have been built. However, these are inadequate and groundwater stores are increasingly used. Fortunately, the major river valleys in the east contain up to 200 m of Pleistocene sands and gravels. These

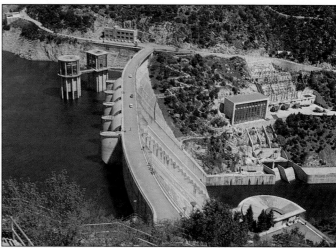

Figure 4.33 HEP generation in Catalonia

Problems in Catalonia

unconsolidated **sediments** are highly permeable, creating useful **aquifers** (see Chapter 8 for coverage of aquifers). Winter recharge of the aquifers becomes available for summer **abstraction**. In addition, the local geology of limestones and sandstones provides useful aquifers which people draw upon for agriculture in particular.

What of the future?

The Government has been working for the past eight years on a draft national water plan. Its aim is to ensure that by the next century all the regions of Spain are adequately supplied with water. There is no doubt that water managers see water transfer, rather than increased water storage, as the way forward (Figs 4.34 and 4.35). This reflects the geographical mismatch between potential supply and actual demand.

Water war threatens to divide Spaniards

After three months of drought, farmers in the South face ruin. But Madrid's water plan has revived old regional conflicts, reports Frank Smith.

JUAN GONZALVEZ will not forget this summer in a hurry. At the beginning of it, he was one of the most popular men in the small town of Campote'jar in the region of Murcia, on Spain's eastern Mediterranean coast.

Now, after his first stint as head of the community's fruit growers, he has had the most un-enviable of tasks, having to supervise the distribution of water in a region where not a single drop has fallen for the past three months.

'One man came begging for water to save his peaches and apricots. I had to refuse. What I didn't realise was that he had *already* stolen the water to irrigate his trees …'

Others were less subtle. The wardens who supervise the irrigation of orchards — in effect, the water police — say they have frequently been threatened along the lines of: 'Either you open the tap or I will — and remember, the shotgun is in my car.'

As president of the fruit growers, Gonzalvez has the power to fine offenders. But sanctions of £2,500 do not deter those who stand to gain five times that amount by saving their crops with stolen water. And private householders with summer houses in the area have come across a new phenomenon this year – the disappearance of the water from their swimming pools. In regions such as Murcia and Valencia, in the South, water has become like liquid gold.

So severe has been the drought this summer (it is calculated that the growers of Murcia alone have lost as many as 15 million fruit trees) that the Spanish government intervened at the end of July, ordering the diversion of 55 million cubic metres of water from the River Tagus in the community of Castilla–La Mancha to the basin of the River Segura, which waters both Mediterranean regions. But in doing so Madrid started a national water war, every bit as intense and furious as the local disputes to save precious fruit crops.

As a country which divides, geographically, into a wet North and a dry South, Spain is no stranger to regional disputes over water. One of the perennial ambitions of every Spanish government since the republic of the early Thirties has been to redress the water imbalance between the haves and the have-nots.

The Socialist government has been working for the past eight years on the draft of a national water plan, whose main aim is to ensure that by the next century all the regions of Spain are adequately supplied with water, 80 per cent of which is used on irrigation.

The fundamental problem is political. Some of the diversions involve transferring water between regions of different political persuasion. The first serious dress rehearsal of the battles that loom ahead took place last year between the Aragonese regionalist party and the Catalan nationalists, when it was revealed that the water plan envisaged diverting water from the Ebro northwards to Catalonia.

'Over my dead body,' the Aragonese president was hear to mutter. The president of Castilla–La Mancha, Jose Bono, said he would not let a 'single drop of water' be transferred from the region southwards, claiming that his own people were running short. When he was overruled by Madrid, he threatened to challenge the government's decision in the courts. At a subsequent meeting of the Socialist party executive, Bono was accused of lacking solidarity. 'Water', he was told, 'belongs to nobody and is everybody's. Only the government can decide how best to share it out.'

The water was duly transferred, by Cabinet decision, to the thirsty regions of Valencia and Murcia. The government may thus claim to have won the first battle, but the war promises to be a long, drawn-out affair.

During the past 17 years, the country has gone a long way down the road of decentralisation — further than any of its European partners, with the exception of Germany. Each of its 17 autonomous regions enjoys a degree of self-rule, and when central government tries to rule on matters considered to be of national interest, such as the distribution of water, it keeps coming up against a growing willingness on the part of the regions to flex their muscles in the new political area.

Figure 4.34 National water transfer (*Source: The Observer*, 4 September 1994)

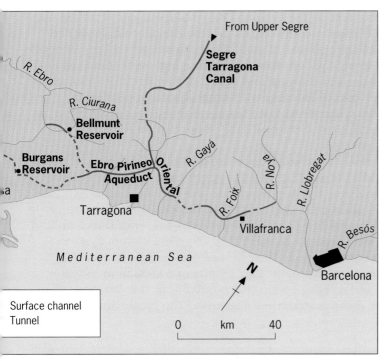

Figure 4.35 Proposed water transfer schemes in southern Catalonia (*Source: Geography, 1988*)

26 Using Figure 4.34 and an atlas, explain the proposed water transfers within Spain. Think in terms of supply, i.e. climatic data, major rivers, and demand, e.g. population density and agricultural areas.

27 Explain how political decentralisation in Spain has made a national water policy problematic. Refer to actual examples in your answer and to the situation in Catalonia.

28 Use Figures 4.30 to 4.35 to comment upon the hydrological basis for the two proposed water transfer schemes in Catalonia.

29 Suggest why the schemes shown in Figure 4.35 are likely to be technologically difficult and expensive. (Refer back to Figures 4.29 to 4.31.)

30 Spanish water managers consider large-scale water transfer schemes as the answer to water supply shortages. Suggest other possible methods. Think about other sources of supply in the water cycle, and water storage and use.

31 Essay: Use the results of your statistical analysis and the information in the case study to write an account of the hydrology and river regimes in Catalonia.

32 Study Table 4.7.
a Which two water regions in England and Wales have the highest and lowest amount of water abstraction?
b Suggest reasons for the amount and type of abstraction.

Water use

Water is abstracted from rivers for domestic consumption, industrial and irrigation purposes (Table 4.7). The reasons for water abstraction will vary according to country and region depending upon climatic conditions, irrigation demands and the level of economic activity, especially urban and industrial development.

Abstraction for urban use will alter the regime of a river, because, although much of the water is returned via sewerage systems, the amount and timing of the return may be different to the natural regime. The sources of water

Table 4.7 Abstraction from surface water and groundwater by purpose and region, 1990 (*Source*: Newson, 1992)

Region	Piped mains water (megalitres/ day)	Agriculture (megalitres/ day)	Industry Electricity generating companies (megalitres/ day)	Industry Other (megalitres/ day)	Abstraction of surface water (megalitres/ day)	Abstraction of groundwater (megalitres/ day)	Total (megalitres/ day)
Anglian	1928	231	2	295	1365	1091	2456
Northumbria	1060	1	–	38	1037	61	1098
North West	1883	8	161	734	2457	330	2787
Severn–Trent	2421	77	2991	451	4914	1026	5940
Southern	1621	38	–	1184	1500	1343	2843
South West	630	35	210	28	955	48	1003
Thames	3827	26	111	167	2594	1537	4131
Welsh	2671	18	8475	310	11 393	81	11 474
Wessex	798	32	–	137	546	421	967
Yorkshire	1498	39	662	351	2184	367	2551
England and Wales	18 336	507	12 612	3795	28 945	6305	35 250

33 Use Table 4.7 to describe the main purposes of water abstractions and identify any regional variations. How can these be explained?

may be remote from and outside the drainage basin of the areas of actual use (see Chapter 8). Yet sewerage systems discharge into the nearest river. The net result is a transfer of water between drainage basins. Up to 34 per cent of the flow volume of the River Trent in England during average conditions is provided from sewerage rather than natural sources. Some of this input may have originated in other basins. Because of evapotranspiration losses, a smaller proportion of the water abstracted for agricultural use is returned to the river. (Water abstractions and returns have important implications for water quality – see Chapter 10.)

Abstractions of river water have significant impacts on levels in lakes along their courses. The world's largest lake, the Caspian Sea in Asia, has fallen by 3 m since 1929. Human usage has contributed to this fall. In central Asia, the Aral Sea has shown a dramatic fall and a fourfold increase in **salinity** since water was abstracted from its two main feeder rivers – the Amu Darya and Syr Darya – for irrigation purposes. Water is lost from the system by evapotranspiration during irrigation. The reduced return flow from the irrigated soils has a higher salt content. This results in a reduction in water quality for human use and a reduction in fish numbers. In the Aral Sea, all native fish species have disappeared, thus destroying the local fishing industry (Fig. 4.36).

Figure 4.36 The Aral Sea, central Asia: boats left stranded by the shrinking of the water area

34 On an outline map of the world, present the data from Table 4.8 as proportional symbols.

35 Describe the growth of world dam construction shown in Figure 4.37.

36 Study Figure 4.38.
a For discharges of 0.116 Ml/d and 1.16 Ml/d, compare the pre- and post-dam occurrences.
b What are the pre-dam and post-dam discharges which were equalled or exceeded for:
• 1 per cent of the time?
• 50 per cent of the time?
• 95 per cent of the time?
c Describe how the dam has changed the flow pattern for low, medium and high flows.

Dam construction

River flow is directly regulated by the building of **dams** and reservoirs (Fig. 4.40). Dams may have a specific purpose, e.g. water storage, HEP, flood control or navigation; or they may be multi-purpose involving some or all of these (Fig. 4.37). In the UK most dam building has been for water storage purposes. Storage of water in the reservoir behind the dam allows water managers to regulate the release of water through the dam, and thus regulate the discharge and regime of the river.

The change to the regime and discharge of a river can be shown by the flow duration curve (see Section 4.4). The Windamere Dam, New South Wales, Australia, was built in 1984 to provide irrigation water for the Cudgegong valley and public water supply for the towns of Mudgee and Gulgong. From the flow duration curve, we can see that flood magnitudes downstream have been reduced by 57–72 per cent (Fig. 4.38).

37a Suggest what physical and human factors will affect the number of dams built in a region. (Think in terms of the dam site, economic development and the reasons for dam construction.)
b Using Table 4.8 and your map, suggest what regional differences can be identified in the number of large dams.

Table 4.8 Large world dams, 1986 (*Source*: World Resource Institute, 1992)

Location	Total over 15 m in height		Total over 30 m in height		Under construction	
	Number	%	Number	%	Number	%
Africa	885	2.4	256	3.3	58	5.7
N. and C. America	6663	18.2	1530	19.9	39	3.8
S. America	885	2.4	333	4.3	69	6.7
Asia	23 555	64.4	3568	46.4	615	59.9
Europe	3945	10.8	1680	21.9	202	19.7
Former USSR	132	0.4	101	1.4	18	1.8
Oceania	497	1.4	217	2.8	25	2.4
World	36 562	100	7685	100	1026	100

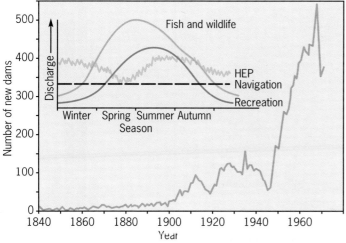

Figure 4.37 The growth in world dam construction since 1840 and the regime requirements for different uses (*Source*: Newson, 1992)

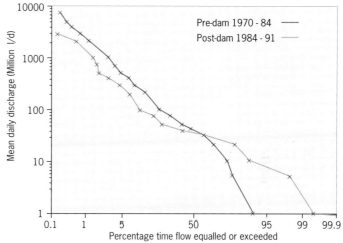

Figure 4.38 Cudgegong River, New South Wales, Australia: flow duration curves downstream of the Windamere Dam (*Source*: Benn and Erskine, 1994)

38 How does the ideal regime for various uses vary? Suggest reasons for the variations and identify the areas of possible conflict.

There is, however, increasing concern about the detrimental impacts of dams, particularly on the environment. In the former USSR, dams have reduced the natural discharge from the Dnestr, Dnepr, and Don rivers by 50–60 per cent. This has increased the accumulation of salts and pollutants in the Black Sea coastal waters. Dams have also blocked the migratory routes of some fish. The Russian commercial sturgeon fisheries of the Black, Azov and Caspian Seas were once amongst the most productive in the world. Dam construction has virtually eliminated them. (The impacts of dams on sediment flows in rivers and on processes and landforms are discussed in Chapters 5 and 7.)

The Nile basin, Africa: water balance and resource issues

The UN Secretary General, Dr Boutros Boutros-Ghali, who is an Egyptian, has prophesied that, 'the next war in our region will be over the waters of the Nile'.

The River Nile and its tributaries drain an area of 2.9 million square kilometres and cover nine countries. The source of Nile water is predominantly from the headwater countries, where rainfall is abundant but seasonal, resulting in different runoff patterns of the Nile tributaries. The Nile water is not static in amount or location, and there is evidence that it may be declining due to climatic change.

The Nile is managed by a series of dams and barrages, especially in the Sudan and Egypt. The main purpose of the dams is for low-season water storage for irrigated agriculture, although the Owen Falls Dam on the White Nile at Lake Victoria is primarily for HEP. In the Sudan, the Sennar Dam was built on the Blue Nile in 1925, to irrigate the Gezira area. The Roseires Reservoir expanded this scheme.

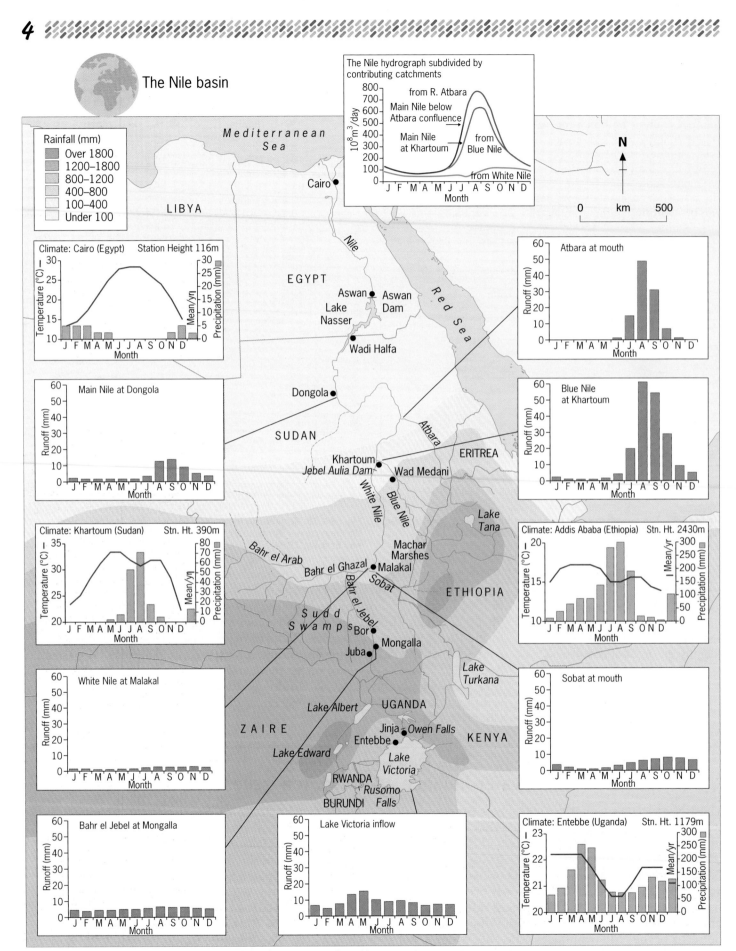

Figure 4.39 The Nile basin: climatic data and mean monthly runoff figures (*Source*: Sutcliffe and Lazenby, 1990)

The impacts of the Aswan High Dam

The Aswan High Dam was completed in 1963. Prior to the management of the River Nile at Aswan, the regime of the river strongly influenced Egyptian rural life. At the end of July, the rising floodwaters would inundate the fertile **floodplain** agricultural land, replenishing the soil and groundwater stores, and adding a layer of fertile silt. When the floodwaters receded, farmers would plant their crops.

This cycle had sustained Egyptian agriculture for thousands of years, but the country was subjected to droughts or devastating floods when the river's flow varied. In modern Egypt, with a rapidly expanding population, this variable flow and loss of food production during the inundations and low flows posed a major problem. The regulation of the river below Aswan has allowed all-year-round (perennial) irrigation and crop production, e.g. double cropping.

The Aswan Dam has clearly benefited Egypt's 48 million people, but has caused much controversy (Fig. 4.40). The USA refused finance for its building and Egypt nationalised the Suez Canal to raise the capital itself. Eventually financial support was provided by the former USSR. The project was multi-purpose. Although irrigation was crucial, the amplitude of the high and low flow fluctuations has been reduced (Fig. 4.41) and the dam is used to generate HEP.

?

39a Describe the runoff regimes of the main Nile and its tributaries shown in Figure 4.39.
b Explain these patterns using climate data to support your answer. Think in terms of the water balance equation.

40 The impacts of the Aswan Dam in Figure 4.40 have not been prioritised. Construct a table to arrange these under social, economic and environmental costs and benefits. Give each impact a score between –5 and +5, i.e. high negative impact to high positive impact. Justify your scoring in each case.

- Egyptian agriculture has been revolutionised with year-round (perennial) irrigation, a 2.8 million hectare increase in the irrigated area, and an increase in cropping intensity and yields. This has allowed food production to help keep pace with the rapid population increase.
- Storage of water in Lake Nasser protected Egypt from drought in the upper basin during the mid-1980s.
- The groundwater store is under-utilised.

- Lake Nasser inundated the town of Wadi Halfa and flooded fertile agricultural land in Sudanese Nubia. Egypt had to pay compensation to Sudan.
- There is high annual water loss at 10% of the storage capacity of the lake. This is by evaporation and seepage.
- Sedimentation in the lake has reduced the sediment load of the river. The result has been degradation of the river valley below the dam and erosion of the fertile Nile delta (see Chapter 5).

- Year-round (perennial) irrigation has caused waterlogging and rising water tables.
- Irrigation practices have caused an increase in the levels of salt in the soil and water. A pipe drainage scheme, with World Bank finance, is helping to solve some of the problems.
- The still waters of the irrigation canals have led to an increase in diseases such as malaria and schistosomiasis ('sleeping sickness').

- Lake Nasser fisheries have been successfully developed. Fish is an important source of protein. In Egypt fish is now half the price of meat and poultry.
- The Nile delta fisheries have been greatly reduced. The Nile sediment nutrients do not replenish the delta area and, as a result, the sardine fisheries have declined from 18,000 tonnes to virtually nothing. Thirty thousand fishers have lost their jobs.
- The fertilising and leaching benefits of the annual flood have been lost. The use of artificial fertilisers has increased, which adds to water pollution.
- Fertiliser, chemicals and effluent from towns and industries are not washed away by annual floods. The rodent population has increased. Water quality has deteriorated, but does not represent a health hazard yet.
- Archaeological sites had to be moved when Lake Nasser flooded.
- HEP generation from the dam provides Egypt with 45% of current requirements. However, the full capacity has not been achieved, because the dam has never been full.
- Flood control saved lives in 1964, 1967, 1975 and 1987, and the costs of flood damage were avoided.
- Nile navigation has improved. This has increased from seasonal to year-round. An important benefit of this is the tourism aspect of the Nile for larger cruise boats.

Figure 4.40 Impacts of the Aswan High Dam. The vertical aerial photograph shows part of Lake Nasser.

The Nile basin

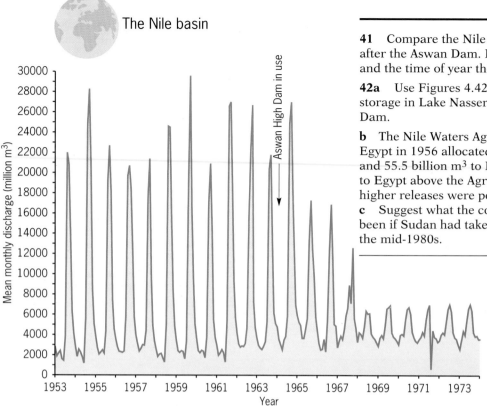

Figure 4.41 The impacts of the Aswan High Dam on the flow regime of the Nile

41 Compare the Nile flow regime (Fig. 4.41) before and after the Aswan Dam. Include details of peak and low flows and the time of year these occur.

42a Use Figures 4.42 and 4.43 to describe the amount of storage in Lake Nasser and the output from the Aswan High Dam.

b The Nile Waters Agreement between the Sudan and Egypt in 1956 allocated 18.5 billion m³ water to the Sudan and 55.5 billion m³ to Egypt. In which years were releases to Egypt above the Agreement level? Explain why these higher releases were possible.

c Suggest what the consequences for Egypt might have been if Sudan had taken its full share of Nile water during the mid-1980s.

Hydropolitical issues

There is a wide diversity of ethnic, religious and political characteristics among the nine countries of the Nile basin and almost all are faced with problems of poverty and high population growth. **Hydropolitical** issues are not crucial yet, but are likely to become more so in the future. The current importance of the Nile waters to the countries of the drainage basin is wide-ranging. The upper basin states of Tanzania, Rwanda, Burundi, Kenya, Uganda and Zaire are using only 0.5 billion cubic metres of Nile water among them. Ethiopia provides 86 per cent of the Nile waters, but only uses 0.6 billion cubic metres at the present time, despite devastating droughts and famines. The key user is the desert state of Egypt, with a demand of 55.5 billion cubic metres (Table 4.9) and the Nile provides 86 per cent of the freshwater supply. The second most important user is the Sudan, with a current consumption of 18.3 billion cubic metres and rising slowly. The external sources of their water raise important management issues.

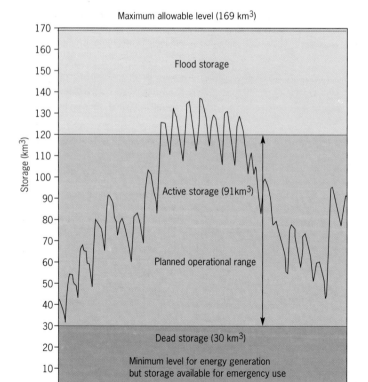

Figure 4.42 Lake Nasser: storage zones and storage levels, 1968–89 (*Source*: Howell and Allan, 1990)

Right: Figure 4.43 Releases from the Aswan High Dam, 1970–86 (*Source*: Howell and Allan, 1990)

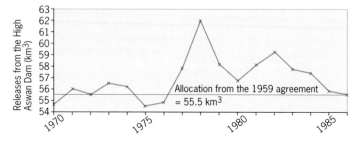

Table 4.9 Estimated water use in Egypt
(*Source*: Howell and Allan, 1990)

		Volume (billion cubic metres)
Inflow	Aswan release	55.5
Outflow	Edfina to sea	3.5
	Canal tails to seas	0.1
	Drainage to sea and Fayoum	13.9
	Evaporation from water surfaces	2.0
	Sub total	19.5
Water use	Municipal and industrial	2.4
	Irrigation)	33.6
	Subtotal	36.0

Egypt and the Sudan currently use 60 per cent of Nile water for irrigation; 10–15 per cent is lost by evaporation and seepage from storage reservoirs; 20 per cent flows north to the Mediterranean to flush out the heavily salinated water at the end of the system. Only 7–8 per cent is currently for urban and industrial uses (Table 4.9). However, this demand will increase as the economies of Egypt and the Sudan develop. Also, the potential for HEP has only just begun to be harnessed. As electricity is an exportable commodity, the likelihood for expansion of HEP schemes is high.

Future water management

Egypt currently uses all the Nile waters it was allocated in the 1959 Agreement (Fig. 4.43). For the future it will have to look to increase irrigation efficiency. In recent years the releases from Lake Nasser have been in excess of the inputs. It is only the high flood flows of 1987 which saved Egypt from potentially serious water shortages.

International discussion has so far been mainly between Egypt and the Sudan. Future management issues are likely to focus upon the increasing use of water by the upper basin states, especially Ethiopia. Ethiopia has plans to dam the waters of the Blue Nile source at Lake Tana. However, political problems, such as civil war, and economic difficulties in both Ethiopia and the Sudan, have inhibited large-scale projects.

In the White Nile catchment, development is likely to focus on water conservation schemes. At present the flow of the Nile is much reduced by the Sudd Swamps in southern Sudan. If these huge swamps are drained and the water transferred northwards via a canal, there would be important water savings available for the Sudan and Egypt.

In order to safeguard its future interests over Nile waters, especially inputs from the upper basin, Egypt has recently set up a consultative group, called the Undugu Group, of the Nile countries to propose a long-range scheme for Nile development.

43 Present the data in Table 4.9 as a proportional flow line diagram.

44a State the evidence for a threatening water shortage between 1982 and 1987.
b Suggest what might have happened without the high inputs to Lake Nasser between 1987 and 1988.

45 Essay: Using all the evidence available, evaluate the Aswan High Dam Project in terms of Egyptian well-being, economic development and the environment.

Summary

- Each drainage basin has a unique water balance or budget and will experience varying periods of water surplus and deficit.
- The water balance or budget is determined by the relationship between precipitation inputs and the combination of evapotranspiration loss, storage and runoff.
- The main river in a drainage basin has a distinctive regime or annual rhythm of discharge.
- A natural river regime is controlled by the relationship between the pattern of precipitation inputs, the environmental conditions and the processes at work within the drainage basin.
- Streams are grouped into three types according to duration of flow: ephemeral; intermittent; perennial.
- Stream regimes may be simple (uniform and dual) or complex according to the character of the pattern revealed in the hydrograph.
- Human activities are having increasing impacts, both intentional and accidental, upon the water balance and streamflow in drainage basins.

5 Drainage basins and sediment yields

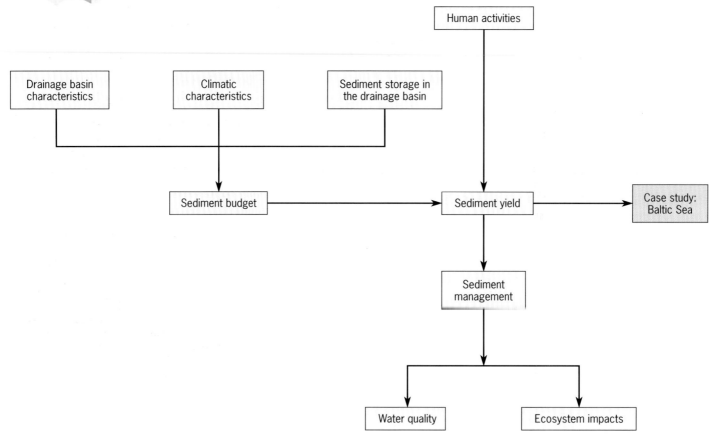

```
Human activities
```

| Drainage basin characteristics | Climatic characteristics | Sediment storage in the drainage basin |

```
Sediment budget  →  Sediment yield  →  Case study: Baltic Sea
                         ↓
                   Sediment management
                    ↓           ↓
              Water quality   Ecosystem impacts
```

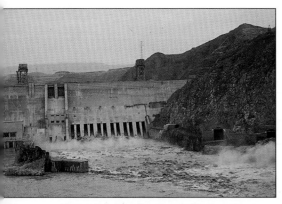

Figure 5.1 The Sanmenxia Dam on the Yellow River (Huang He), China. The bottom sluice gates of the dam are open to flush out the sediment from the reservoir bed behind the dam.

5.1 Introduction

The **sediment load** of the Yellow River in China (Fig. 5.1) is one of the highest in the world at 1640 million tonnes per year. This is because the river flows through easily eroded loess soils which have been cleared of their forest cover for farming. The sediment in this **drainage basin** causes problems for the water engineers managing the **dam**. The sediment collects in the reservoir behind the dam and reduces its storage capacity.

Sediment and water are the main outputs from the drainage basin system (Fig. 2.1). Therefore, information about the erosion, transfer and deposition of sediment is important for our understanding of how the drainage basin operates, and for management of the system.

Sediment is produced by natural processes in the drainage basin system. However, today, there are few rivers which do not show the effects of human activity in either increasing or decreasing the supply and transfer of sediment. Most rivers discharge their sediment load into the world's seas and oceans, although some basins, especially those in semi-arid areas, output into lakes and inland depressions, e.g. Lake Chad, West Africa and the Qattara depression of North Africa, or the tectonically formed depressions of the Dead Sea in the Middle East or Lake Baikal in the Russian Federation.

5.2 Sediment movement through the drainage basin

Sediment in rivers comes from two main sources. The largest amount is from the weathering and mass movement operating on the hill slopes of the drainage basin. A smaller amount is added by the erosion within the river channel itself. The transfer of sediment is a feature in the lowering and shaping (denudation) of landscapes and their evolution. Both natural processes and human activity will affect the amount, timing and location of sediment entering the system, i.e. the inputs.

Sediment produced by weathering and erosion does not all enter the river channel immediately. Much is stored in the drainage basin system for varying lengths of time. Eventually it is output as **sediment yield** (Fig. 5.2). This is measured in tonnes per square kilometre per year. A second measure is the total amount of sediment produced by the river basin. This is measured in tonnes per year, and does not allow for the size of the drainage basin as with the sediment yield data. The sediment output will depend upon the amount of erosion in the drainage basin and the amount of storage within the drainage basin system itself.

Figure 5.2 Sediment stores in the drainage basin. As with water (see Chapter 4), drainage basins have a sediment budget. The output from the drainage basin, i.e. the sediment yield, will depend upon the amount and nature of the inputs, and the short- and long-term storage within the drainage basin

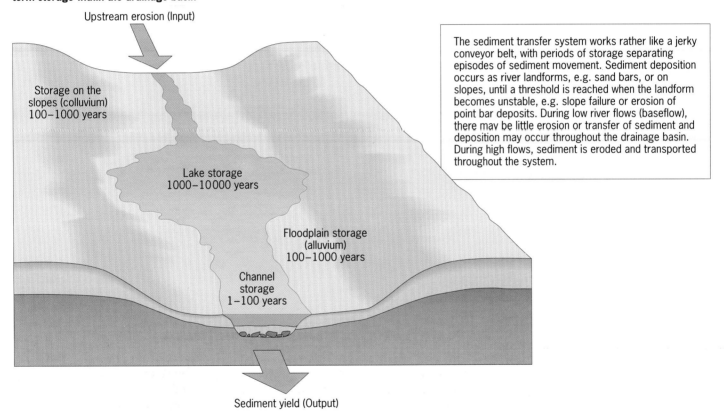

Upstream erosion (Input)

Storage on the slopes (colluvium) 100–1000 years

Lake storage 1000–10000 years

Floodplain storage (alluvium) 100–1000 years

Channel storage 1–100 years

Sediment yield (Output)

The sediment transfer system works rather like a jerky conveyor belt, with periods of storage separating episodes of sediment movement. Sediment deposition occurs as river landforms, e.g. sand bars, or on slopes, until a threshold is reached when the landform becomes unstable, e.g. slope failure or erosion of point bar deposits. During low river flows (baseflow), there may be little erosion or transfer of sediment and deposition may occur throughout the drainage basin. During high flows, sediment is eroded and transported throughout the system.

The effect of drainage basin size and discharge on sediment yield

Rainfall is the main vehicle by which sediment is delivered to a stream. Thus, we might expect that drainage basins with a large area or a high **discharge** will produce the greatest sediment yields. However, if we look at data for 18 of the world's large river basins (Table 5.1), we can clearly see the wide range of annual sediment loads and sediment yields produced by each basin. When we apply a statistical analysis, we find that the relationships for sediment yield are not significant (Table 5.2), i.e. the sediment yield of a drainage basin is *not* correlated with the discharge of a river or the size of the drainage basin. We therefore need to look at other factors if we are to understand the causes of sediment yields of drainage basins.

Table 5.2 Statistical analysis results for sediment yield using the Spearman rank correlation coefficient

Variable	Sediment yield correlation coefficient	Statistically significant at 0.05 significance level?
Drainage basin area	−0.14	No
Discharge	+0.137	No

Table 5.1 Catchment areas, water discharges and sediment yields of selected large rivers (*Source:* Cooke and Doornkamp, 1990)

River	Country	Drainage basin area (hundred km²)	Mean water discharge (m³/s)	Sediment yield (tonnes/km²/y)
Rhine	Netherlands	160	2200	17
Po	Italy	54	1550	280
Vistula	Poland	193	950	7
Danube	Romania	816	6 200	80
Don	Russian Federation	378	830	11
Ob	Russian Federation	2 430	12 200	6
Niger	Nigeria	1 081	4 900	19
Congo	Zaire	4 014	39 600	18
Mississippi	USA	3 269	24 000	91
Amazon	Brazil	6 100	172 000	139
Indus	Pakistan	969	5 500	450
Ganga (Ganges)	India/Bangladesh	955	11 800	1500
Brahmaputra	India/Bangladesh	666	12 200	1100
Irrawaddy	Myanmar	430	13 500	700
Red	North Vietnam	120	3 900	1100
Pearl	China	355	8 000	260
Yangtze	China	1 807	29 200	280
Yellow	China	752	1 370	2480

?

1a Use Table 5.1 to place the rivers in rank order for: • drainage basin size; • discharge; • sediment yield. Set your lists alongside each other.

b Name two rivers which fit each of the following descriptions:
• A large basin area and a low sediment yield.
• A small basin area and a high sediment yield.
• A high discharge and a low sediment yield.
• A small discharge basin and a high sediment yield.
• A small basin area and a low sediment yield.

2 Comment on the relationship between sediment yield, discharge and drainage basin area as shown by your answers to question 1 and the statistical analysis in Table 5.2.

3 The relationships shown in Table 5.2 have been devised using the Spearman rank correlation coefficient. Comment on the usefulness of these results. Suggest one other method of investigating the relationships of the data shown in Table 5.1.

4 Trace figure 5.4 and overlay it on to Figure 5.5.
a What are the sediment yields of areas with mountain climates?
b What are the climatic types of areas with sediment yields of less than 10 t/km²/y?
c What are the climatic types for areas with more than 1000 t/km²/y?

Figure 5.3 Seventeen of the world's large rivers

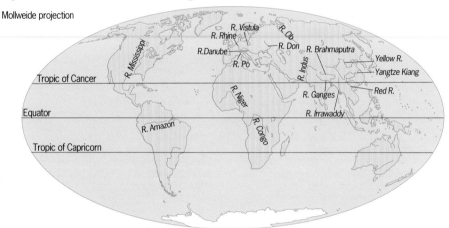

Mollweide projection

5.3 Natural factors affecting sediment yield

The natural processes which affect sediment yield are related to the climate, relief, rock and soil types of the area.

Climate and vegetation

Under natural conditions, the vegetation cover of an area is largely determined by the climatic characteristics, i.e. climate and vegetation are closely related. Water is the dominant factor in the delivery of sediment into rivers and we might, therefore, expect sediment yield to be related to the nature and total amount of the precipitation. However, as the precipitation input increases, so does the protective cover of the vegetation. Thus the highest sediment yields are obtained from semi-arid areas. In these areas rainfall is low on a world scale, but it occurs in intense downpours and there is little protective vegetation cover.

This conclusion is supported by the work of Fournier (1960) who used rainfall totals, monthly amounts and relief factors (height and slope) to calculate world suspended sediment yields (Fig. 5.4).

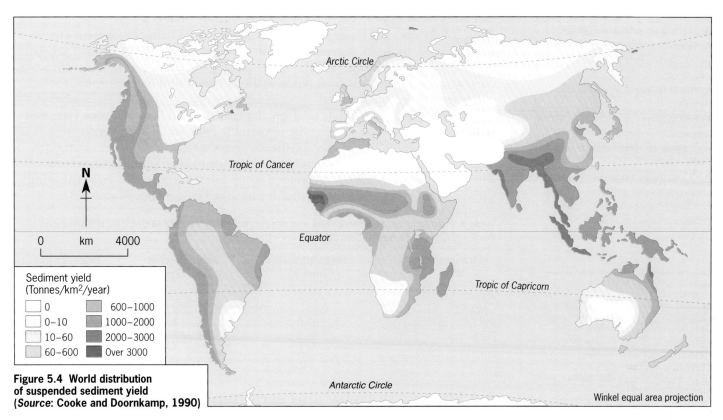

Figure 5.4 World distribution
of suspended sediment yield
(*Source*: Cooke and Doornkamp, 1990)

Sediment yield
(Tonnes/km^2/year)

☐ 0
☐ 0–10
☐ 10–60
☐ 60–600
▨ 600–1000
▨ 1000–2000
▨ 2000–3000
▨ Over 3000

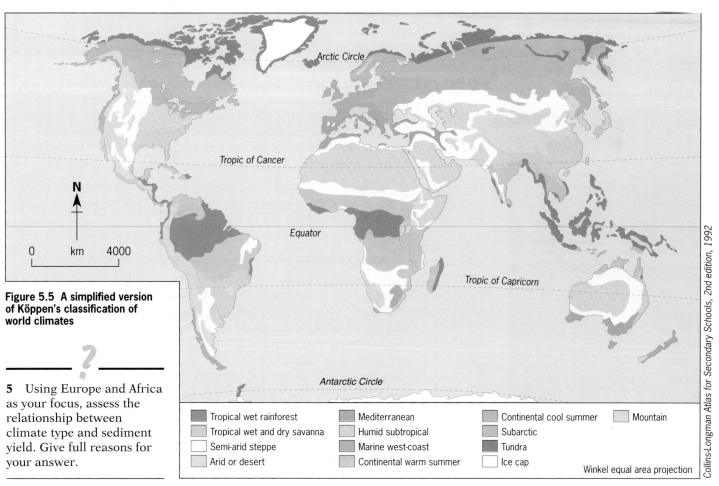

Figure 5.5 A simplified version
of Köppen's classification of
world climates

?

5 Using Europe and Africa
as your focus, assess the
relationship between
climate type and sediment
yield. Give full reasons for
your answer.

▨ Tropical wet rainforest
☐ Tropical wet and dry savanna
☐ Semi-arid steppe
☐ Arid or desert
▨ Mediterranean
☐ Humid subtropical
▨ Marine west-coast
▨ Continental warm summer
▨ Continental cool summer
▨ Subarctic
▨ Tundra
☐ Ice cap
☐ Mountain

Winkel equal area projection

Collins-Longman Atlas for Secondary Schools, 2nd edition, 1992

6 Using the data in Table 5.3:
a Plot two scattergraphs to investigate the relationship between:
- sediment yield and drainage density;
- sediment yield and infiltration rates.

Calculate the regression line in each case.
b Comment on the relationships shown by your graphs.
c Suggest reasons for any relationships identified.

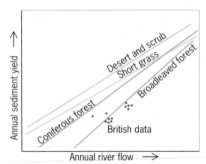

Figure 5.6 Annual sediment yield of world river basins by flow, stratified by vegetation type with British data shown for comparison (*Source*: Newson, 1992)

Figure 5.7 Gifford Pinchot National Forest and Skamania County private lands, Washington State, USA: unsustainable clear-cutting

Geology and soil type

The geology and soil types of the drainage basin will affect sediment yields. For example, loose, unconsolidated silts and sands are easily eroded, as with the fine loess soils in the middle of the Yellow River basin (Fig. 5.1). In contrast, hard, resistant rock types, such as basalt and metamorphic rocks, will give low sediment yields.

It is difficult for geologists to show the relationship between rock type and sediment yield, because rock type is variable over small areas. Also, weathering rates vary greatly for the same rock type in different climatic regions. However, work by Hadley and Schumm (1961) in the Cheyenne River, South Dakota, USA, produced some interesting results by comparing the sediment yield and other variables for five rock groups (Table 5.3).

Table 5.3 Infiltration, sediment yield and drainage density related to geological formations of the River Cheyenne basin (*Source*: Chorley et al, 1984)

Stratigraphic units	Mean infiltration (mm/h)	Sediment yield (km³/km²)	Drainage density (km/km²)
Wasatch formation	233.7	0.0619	3.4
Lance formation	127	0.238	4.4
Fort Union formation	33.0	0.619	7.1
Pierre Shale	25.4	0.667	10.0
White River group	4.6	0.857	160.0

5.4 Human activity and sediment yield

Increasing sediment yield

Deforestation

For the same annual river discharge in an area, a change of vegetation, e.g. by deforestation of broad-leaved forest and replacement with short grass, will produce an increase in annual sediment yield (Fig. 5.6). The removal of the protective vegetation cover will increase sediment yields from the soil surface (Fig. 5.7). It will also allow sediments in long-term storage on the hill slopes to be mobilised (Fig. 5.2). In the experiments of the Maracá Project (see Section 3.9), the sediment yields of the mid-slope sites increased from 200 to 7400 kg/ha after total clearance of the virgin rainforest.

Land use

Researchers have studied the effects of agricultural practices and land use on sediment yields in the USA (Figs 5.8 to 5.11).

Afforestation

Although the sediment yield from forested areas is lower than from similar areas under grassland or cultivated land, the process of afforestation can also increase sediment yields. In recent years there has been large-scale afforestation of British uplands. Peat and moorland catchments with high rainfall totals have been drained to plant coniferous trees. Work in Northumberland showed that, in the five years after drainage, soil erosion rates were equivalent to nearly 50 years of the natural sediment load. The drainage ditches are seen as the major cause of the increased erosion.

Research at Llanbrynmair in Wales showed that suspended stream sediment loads increased by between 246 per cent and 479 per cent after ploughing the moorland for forestry (Fig. 5.12). Tree felling and the construction of forestry roads have also added to the sediment yield. The increased yields may be short term only, associated with the early and harvest stages of the afforestation cycle.

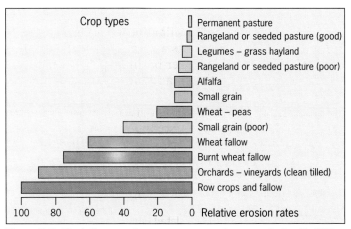

Figure 5.8 The influence of crop type on erosion rates in Pacific NW USA (*Source*: Gregory and Walling, 1973)

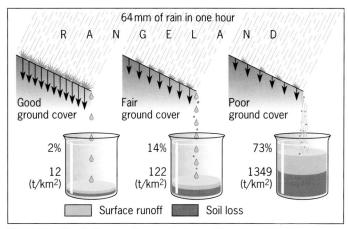

Figure 5.9 The influence of rangeland condition on runoff and sediment yield in Utah, USA (*Source*: Gregory and Walling, 1973)

Study Figures 5.8 to 5.11.

7 Which land uses would you recommend a farmer uses on farmland with:
a steep slopes?
b gentle slopes?
Explain your answers.

8 Use Figure 5.9 to describe and explain the importance of good management of rangeland pasture.

9 Describe and explain the relationships shown in Figures 5.10 and 5.11.

10 Draw two diagrams to show how sediment yield would be produced from the mature pine-hardwood catchments and cultivated watersheds. Include the amount of bare ground and the routes take by rainwater in your diagrams.

11 Study Figure 5.12.
a Describe the changes in sediment yield shown by the graph.
b Explain why forestry operations may not produce the low sediment yields of natural forests.

12 Describe the characteristics of mid-Wales which produce a naturally low sediment yield, but make the area susceptible to forestry operations.

13 Suggest what action forestry managers could take to reduce sediment yields.

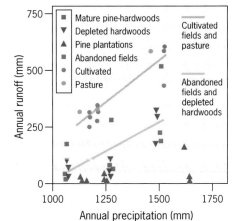

Figure 5.10 The influence of land use on annual runoff from watersheds in the hill land of the upper coastal plain in northern Mississippi, USA (*Source*: Gregory and Walling, 1973)

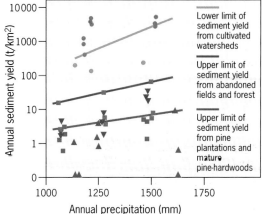

Figure 5.11 The influence of land use on sediment yield from watersheds in the hill land of the upper coastal plain in northern Mississippi, USA (*Source*: Gregory and Walling, 1973)

A Pre-afforestation stage
Low sediment yield in mid-Wales upland plateau. Sediment supplied by channel erosion rather than hillslope processes. Long-term storage of sediments under protective vegetation cover.

B Afforestation stage
A rapid rise in fine sediment outputs and bedload of streams. Drainage ditches and track building expose the highly erodible glacial drifts, screes and slope materials. The subsoil, as well as the soil surface, are exposed to erosion. Surface materials form suspended load. Subsurface sources produce bedload in the river channels.

C Mature forest stage
A long-term increase in sediment output over several decades in drained mature forested catchment. Yields are 3 to 5 times higher than nearby grassland catchments, e.g. the bedload yield of pastureland is 6.4 t/km^2/y compared to 38.4 t/km^2/y for mature forest; suspended load yields are 6.1 t/km^2/y for pasture and 12.1 – 35.3 t/km^2/y for mature forest.

D Felling stage
Sediments yields increase. Fine sediment yields increase rapidly; coarser sediment yields fall at first, as the sediment forms debris dams in the upper stream reaches and drainage ditches. Bedload yields up to five times the pre-felling rates as higher stream flows move the sediment downstream. The method of felling and the widening of roads are important in determining the sediment yield increases. Researchers observed short-lived pulses of suspended sediment during low flows associated with the movement of heavy machinery, drain clearance and road modifications.

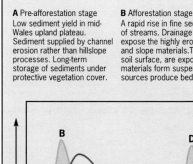

Figure 5.12 Forestry and sediment yields

Figure 5.13 Variation of sediment yield over time and with changing land use (*Source*: Gregory and Walling, 1973)

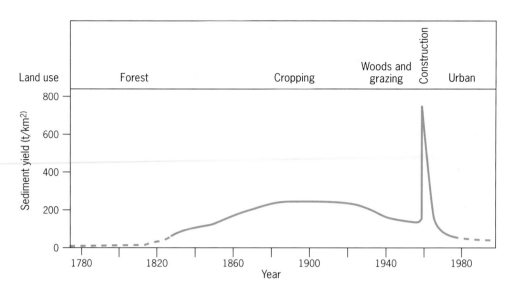

?

14 Describe and explain the changes shown in Figure 5.13. Use precise figures to illustrate your answer.

Mining and urbanisation

Mining and the early stages of urbanisation can increase sediment yields as the land is cleared. However, in urban areas, as building continues and the land is covered with impermeable surfaces, the sediment yield will decrease (Fig. 5.13).

Decreasing sediment yield

Human activity can affect the **streamflow** and channel processes which in turn will affect the ability of the river to transport its sediment load. Some soil fertility management and agricultural practices, such as contour ploughing and terracing (Fig. 3.29), will decrease the sediment yield and create sediment stores. River management too can have important impacts on sediment yields. Dams (Figs 4.40 and 5.14), reservoirs and irrigation systems provide new stores for the sediment. The building of the Aswan High Dam in Egypt has resulted in a dramatic reduction of sediment load downstream of the dam (Table 5.4). There have been other major consequences downstream (Fig. 5.15).

Figure 5.14 Natural and human factors which affect the sediment yield of a drainage basin

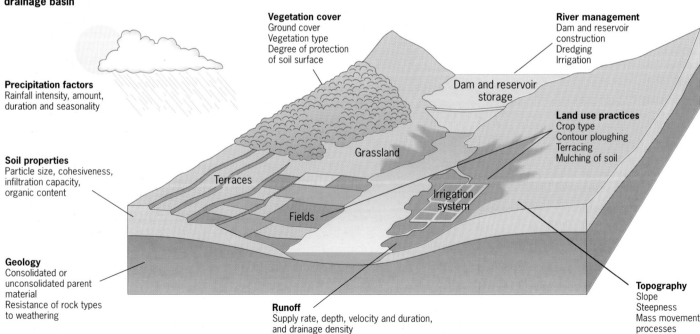

15 Read Figure 5.15. Draw a sediment inputs and outputs diagram for the Nile delta. Add notes to explain why the Nile delta is being eroded.

16 Represent the data in Table 5.4 graphically. Describe and explain the changes shown.

Figure 5.15 For thousands of years the Nile fertilised Egypt, but no longer (*Source: The Independent on Sunday,* 6 June 1993)

Table 5.4 Silt concentrations in the Nile at Gaafra before and after the construction of the Aswan High Dam (*Source*: Goudie, 1986)

Month	Sediment concentrations (ppm) before the dam, 1958–63	Sediment concentrations (ppm) after the dam	Ratio
Jan	64	44	1.5
Feb	50	47	1.1
Mar	45	45	1.0
Apr	42	50	0.8
May	43	51	0.8
Jun	85	49	1.7
Jul	674	48	14.0
Aug	2702	45	60.0
Sep	2422	41	59.1
Oct	925	43	21.5
Nov	124	48	2.58
Dec	77	47	1.63

Dammed to destruction

For thousands of years the Nile fertilised Egypt. No longer. **Fred Pearce** on a catastrophe in the making

THE NILE delta, granary of Egypt and still Africa's most productive farmland, is being eaten by the oceans and invaded by the desert. The Aswan dam, hailed in the 1960s as a triumph of engineering and water management, is now seen as a major cause of the region's impending devastation.

The delta is a wedge of highly fertile land the size of northern Ireland where the Nile reaches the Mediterranean. It is composed of layer upon layer of silt, most of it eroded from the highlands of Ethiopia over tens of thousands of years. Each year, 100 million tons of soil slips from the parched lands of Wollo and Tigre, and flows north in a muddy gush as the Blue Nile floods.

What was Ethiopia's loss was Egypt's gain. The silt raised the Nile delta by about one millimetre each year, fertilising it and counteracting natural subsidence and erosion by the sea. Until 1964, that is. That was the year when Colonel Gamal Abdel Nasser completed the Aswan dam. As planned, it trapped the Nile's fierce annual flood which rushed downstream each summer, and replaced it with near-constant flows designed to provide water all year round for irrigation canals.

But the dam also trapped 98 per cent of the Nile silt, which now drops uselessly to the bed of Lake Nasser, the reservoir which formed behind the dam. For Nasser, 'the largest lake ever shaped by human hand' would be 'a source of ever-lasting prosperity' for Egypt. But the prosperity looks set to be anything but everlasting. Denied the fertile silt that has sustained farms on the delta for more than 7,000 years (longer than anywhere else on Earth), Egypt already uses more fertiliser per hectare than any other nation.

And fertiliser won't protect the delta from the sea. Without a constant supply of silt, it faces eventual destruction as surely as a sandcastle meeting an incoming tide. As Egypt's population of 58 million grows by a further million every nine months, what future is there for Africa's second most populous state?

The bleakest prognosis yet for Egypt and the delta came in April in the journal *Science,* in a paper written by Daniel Stanley and Andrew Warne of the Smithsonian Institution in Washington DC. This 'vulnerable oasis in the vast inhospitable eastern Sahara desert', they wrote, is at risk from sea erosion. The coastal village of Borg-el-Borellos is now beneath the waves, two kilometres out to sea.

As the sea advances, the desert is also invading. Here again, mankind is to blame. Modern irrigation canals no longer bring silt to the fields with the waters of the Nile, but they do bring natural salts eroded upstream and dissolved in the water. In ancient times, when the river flooded fields, the ebbing flood flushed the salts away each year. But modern canal irrigation leaves the salt behind. It is gradually poisoning the soil of this, one of the world's leading cotton-producing regions, and turning it to desert.

Each year, one ton of salt accumulates on each hectare of delta fields. The country is spending tens of millions of dollars each year, laying the largest drainage network in the world in an attempt to flush out the salt. Even so, salt is already reducing crop yields on more than a third of the fields.

Once, much of the delta was composed of marshes and brackish lagoons, protected from the sea by sand bars. Today the lagoons have been reduced by drainage, and are increasingly poisoned by sewage and pesticides. Lake Maryut is now a cesspit for the metropolis of Alexandria. Fish catches there dropped by 85 per cent during the 1970s. The sewers of Cairo, a city of 10 million people, now empty into the equally fetid Manzala lagoon.

Even so, the four surviving lagoons supply 100,000 tons of fish (two-thirds of Egypt's catch) and employ 100,000 people. But soon the lagoons may disappear altogether. Deprived of silt, the sand bars are fast eroding and will collapse. They and the lagoons form the main defence against the sea for the entire delta. With them gone, the tides will rush inwards ever faster.

Another exacerbating factor is the greenhouse effect. Rising sea levels can only hasten the destruction of the delta. A rise of one metre over the next century could inundate the northern third of it, affecting 15 per cent of Egypt's farmland and 8 million of its people. Long before then, seawater would penetrate deep into the groundwaters beneath the delta, adding to the salt build-up.

Suspended sediment yields in the Baltic Sea drainage basin

The Baltic Sea is an inland shelf sea, divided into sub-basins with a total area of 415 266 km² (Fig. 5.16). As with all drainage basins, sediment output from the river systems into the Baltic Sea depends upon physical factors, especially climate, relief, geology and soils, as well as human activity.

We can divide the area draining into the Baltic Sea into seven morphological units (Table 5.5). A large part of the area is lowland, with low relief and large areas of forest and cultivation (Fig 5.18). Some of these lowlands have unconsolidated glacial and periglacial deposits. The highest relief area is the Carpathian Mountains with easily erodible soils, steep slopes and high precipitation.

Table 5.5 Physical and potential erosion conditions for the seven morphological units (*Source*: Lajczak and Jansson, 1993)

Main morphological units	Relief and slopes	Vegetation and soils	Gully erosion (1 = low; 4 = very high)	Mean annual precipitation (mm)	Number of months with mean temperatures >0°C	Runoff m³/s/km²	Lakes	Reservoirs	Swamp	Forest	Arable fields	Pasture	River
							(1 = low; 4 = very high)						
I Carpathian Mountains	600–2665 m steep slopes, often 15-60°	Forest with areas of deforestation on loess deposits. Sand, clay and stone soils	3	600–2000	9	0.3	2	2	2	2	2	2	1
II Carpathian Foreland	Gentle relief 300 m height Slopes 3-5°	Locally forested Silt and sandy soils	1	600	10	0.1	1	2	1	2	3	3	3
III Sudety Mountains	Up to 1605 m Slopes 5–25° Resistant bedrock	High areas forested Lower parts deforested	2	650	9	0.15	1	3	1	2	3	2	3
IV Middle Poland upland	Up to 600 m Slopes 5–25°	Some areas forested	3	700	10	0.10–0.15	1	2	1	1	4	2	2
V Lowland area	Many lakes and swamps Virtually flat Very low relief up to 250 m	Periglacial deposits Forested Cultivated areas	1	500	9–10	0.5	2	2	3	3	3	3	2
VI Scandinavian Mountains	Up to 2000 m Slopes 30–60°	Forested	1	400–1600	3–8	0.3	4	4	4	2	1	3	3
VII Norrland Plateau	Up to 1000 m Slopes 10–30°	Glacial deposits and forest	1	500	8	0.10	4	3	3	3	3	3	3

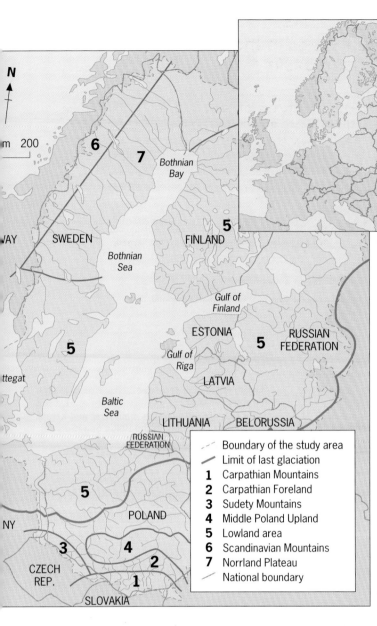

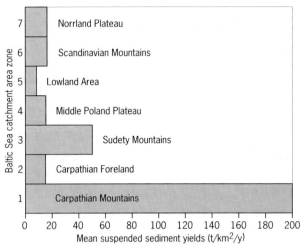

Boundary of the study area
Limit of last glaciation
1 Carpathian Mountains
2 Carpathian Foreland
3 Sudety Mountains
4 Middle Poland Upland
5 Lowland area
6 Scandinavian Mountains
7 Norrland Plateau
National boundary

Figure 5.17 Mean annual suspended sediment yield in the seven morphological units of the Baltic Sea drainage basin (*Source*: Lajczak and Jansson, 1993)

Sediment yields

The actual amount of sediment which enters the Baltic Sea and its sub-basin (Fig. 5.17) will depend upon erosion from each of the drainage basins feeding water and sediment into the sea. Some of the sediment will be deposited and stored in the drainage basin itself, either on the slopes, in lakes, or along the river channel and **floodplains** (Figs. 5.2 and 5.18). Reservoirs built along the course of the rivers will serve as further sediment stores. For the large rivers feeding the Baltic Sea, sediment deposition within the drainage basin represents a high percentage of the total sediment produced (Fig. 5.19).

17a For each of the physical and human potential erosion variables given in Table 5.5, explain how they would affect sediment yield.
b Give an estimate of the sediment yield for each of the seven morphological units of the Baltic Sea drainage basin. (Use the terms high, medium or low yields.)
c Compare the sediment yields of the seven morphological units given in Figure 5.17 with your estimate of the sediment yields.

18 List the most important variables which explain why sediment yields are low in the Scandinavian Mountains compared to the Carpathian Mountains.

19 Explain fully why the lowland area (5) has such a low sediment yield.

Figure 5.18 River Bug floodplain: a major sediment store

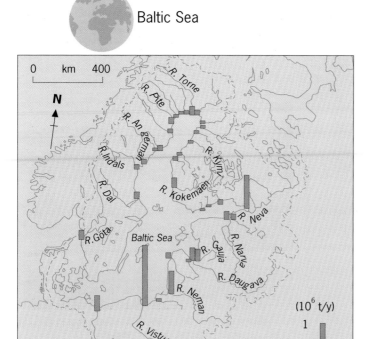

Baltic Sea

Figure 5.19 Mean annual inflow of suspended sediment to the Baltic Sea (*Source*: Lajczak and Jansson, 1993)

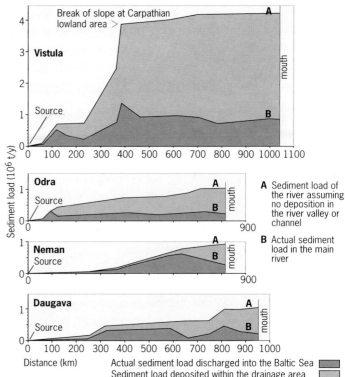

Figure 5.20 Hypothetical sediment inflow to the main river and actual sediment load for four large rivers draining to the Baltic Sea (*Source*: Lajczak and Jansson, 1993)

---

20 Using Figure 5.20:
a For the four rivers, calculate the percentage sediment load deposited within the drainage basin. Use the figures at the mouth of each river.
b Explain why there is a marked increase in sediment load and deposition 380 km along the course of the River Vistula.

21 Using Figures 5.19 and 5.20, describe and explain the sediment yield into the Baltic Sea and the amount of deposition in the drainage basin.

5.5 Sediment and drainage basin management

We have seen that human use of all or part of a drainage basin, e.g. land-use practices and soil conservation methods, as well as natural processes, will affect the sediment budget. In turn, a change in the sediment budget can have important impacts on landform processes, people and ecosystems. There is a need therefore for careful drainage basin management.

When HEP stations, reservoirs and dams are designed and planned, it is important for water managers to predict rates of sedimentation. This enables engineers to calculate costs and design life of the schemes. The Los Angeles area of southern California is drained by three major rivers – the Los Angeles, the San Gabriel and the Santa Ana. Dams built to manage these three rivers experienced problems of sediment accumulation as the vegetation on the watersheds was increasingly destroyed. There are now 80 debris dams which control the movement of sediment from the upstream canyons. These trap the sediment. Suitable sediment disposal sites have had to be found, because the dams must be emptied regularly.

Increased sedimentation in the river channel can affect the channel capacity and, thus, increase the likelihood of flooding. In areas of high or increasing sediment yields, expensive dredging of rivers is required to reduce flood risks (Fig. 5.21) or to keep channels navigable. For example, the Farakka Dam in India was built to divert millions of tonnes of water from the Ganges into the River Hooghly in order to flush out the sediment accumulation in the port of Calcutta.

Water quality

The amount of sediment in the channel affects water quality for domestic, industrial and agricultural uses, and assists in the transport of pollutants (see Chapter 10). In the USA, sediment accounts for 47 per cent of river pollution. In the southern Pennines, England, the erosion of dried-out peat after summer droughts is causing problems with water colour. There has been a rise in consumer complaints. Consequently, the number of water treatment plants has increased and water managers are now researching catchment management solutions as well as water treatment solutions.

A further problem caused by peat erosion is that the storage capacity of the reservoirs is reduced as the peat accumulates. On average, this is only four per cent of the total storage capacity, but can rise to, for example 93.5 per cent in the Tunnel End Reservoir. In the case of the Sanmenxia Dam on the Yellow River in China (Fig. 5.1), the storage capacity of the reservoir was reduced by 40 per cent in only four years.

Effects on the ecosystem

Changes in sediment yields can affect the stream ecosystem. Work on afforestation in the British uplands showed that high concentrations of suspended sediment limit the amount of light able to penetrate upland streams. This reduces photosynthesis by aquatic plants. In addition, sediment blanketing the stream bed can kill submerged vegetation and make conditions unsuitable for stream life adapted to clear water and gravelly stream beds. Filter-feeding molluscs are particularly affected, fish gills can become inflamed and fish egg survival impaired by the high concentration of sediment.

Figure 5.21 Bed-load excavation from a stream bed at Plynlimon

22 Essay: Using examples you have studied, show how land use and river management affect sediment yield.

Summary

- Sediment is a key output from the drainage basin system and an understanding of the processes involved is important for human management of the drainage basin system.
- The sediment yield of a drainage basin is the result of a complex set of variables related to key natural processes, e.g. climate, vegetation, rock type, and to human activity.
- Sediment is stored within the drainage basin for varying amounts of time as hillslope materials and depositional landforms.
- Human activity can increase the sediment yield of a drainage basin, e.g. land use change, deforestation, afforestation, mining and early urbanisation.
- Human activity can decrease the sediment yield of a drainage basin, e.g. by soil conservation measures, building dams and reservoirs, and the later stages of urban development.
- The mis-management of a drainage basin sediment budget can have important impacts on people, landform processes and ecosystems.
- The management of sediment load of rivers is important to human activity, e.g. for navigation and water supply purposes.
- There is a need for the management of sediment budgets and yields at the scale of the whole drainage basin.

6 Managing channels

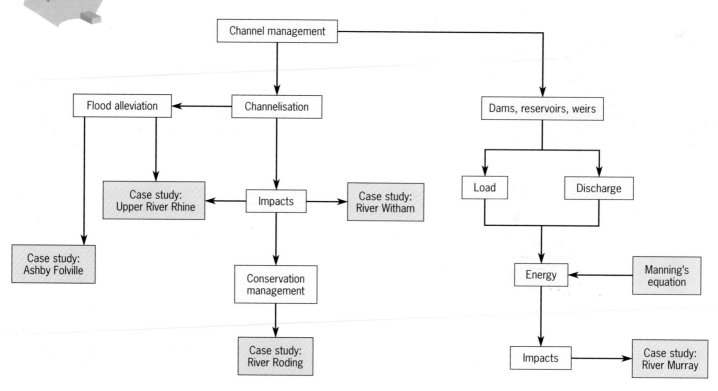

Channel management
→ Dams, reservoirs, weirs

Flood alleviation ← Channelisation

Case study: Upper River Rhine ← Impacts → Case study: River Witham

Case study: Ashby Folville

Conservation management

Case study: River Roding

Load   Discharge

Energy ← Manning's equation

Impacts → Case study: River Murray

6.1 Introduction

The characteristics of a river channel, e.g. channel width, depth and **sinuosity**, are adjusted to the natural flow **regime** and **bankfull discharge** of the river. There is a **dynamic equilibrium** among these variables, and a change in any one of them will cause changes elsewhere in the **drainage basin** system. People manage river channels by changing some or all of these variables and consequently altering the channel characteristics. For example, we deliberately and directly manage the channel form and sinuosity, or build dams, barrages and weirs, which will alter the flow regime and the **discharge**. The deliberate modification of the river channel for flood control, land drainage, navigation and prevention of erosion is called **channelisation.**

In this chapter we shall consider management of the channel itself, but river diversions as flood relief channels and embankments or artificial **levées** are also forms of channelisation (see Chapter 7).

6.2 Methods of river channelisation

Resectioning or enlarging

We can reduce or prevent flooding by deepening or widening the river channel to increase its cross-sectional area. The channel is often dredged to an energy-efficient trapezoidal cross-section, with a flat bottom and steep banks. This increase in area allows a larger discharge to be contained within the channel. Resectioning also lowers the **water table** on the **floodplain**, which allows wet floodplains to be used for agriculture.

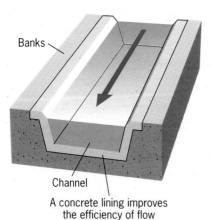

Banks

Channel

A concrete lining improves the efficiency of flow

Figure 6.1 Resectioning the channel (*Source*: Knapp et al, 1989)

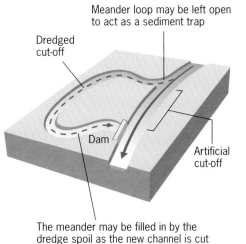

Meander loop may be left open to act as a sediment trap

Dredged cut-off

Dam

Artificial cut-off

The meander may be filled in by the dredge spoil as the new channel is cut

Figure 6.2 Realigning the channel (*Source*: Knapp et al, 1989)

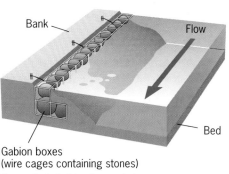

Bank

Flow

Bed

Gabion boxes (wire cages containing stones)

Figure 6.3 Gabion boxes (wire cages containing stones) strengthen the banks (*Source*: Knapp et al, 1989)

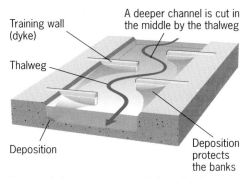

Training wall (dyke)

A deeper channel is cut in the middle by the thalweg

Thalweg

Deposition

Deposition protects the banks

Figure 6.4 Groynes or spurs deflect the thalweg, allowing the deposition of sediment in the lee of the groyne, thus protecting the banks from erosion (*Source*: Knapp et al, 1989)

Realignment or straightening

A **meandering** river can be straightened by means of artificial cut-offs (Fig. 6.2). This is known as realignment. The meander may be completely filled in with the dredge spoil as the new channel is cut. The aim is to increase the **long-profile** gradient of the channel in that reach of the river. An increase in gradient increases the flow velocity. Realignment, therefore, reduces the risk of flooding upstream and along the realigned stretch, because water is moved more quickly, helps river navigation and reduces journey times.

Bank protection

Erosion of banks and meander migration cause loss of land and may undermine structures, such as buildings and bridges. We can prevent this by protecting the banks with concrete blocks, steel **revetments**, gabion boxes (Fig. 6.3), **groynes** or spurs (Fig. 6.4).

Lined channels

Often a resectioned length of river is lined with concrete to improve the channel efficiency (Fig. 6.5). Concrete is smoother than the natural soil and pebble materials of the channel. This results in a reduction in energy loss through friction, and an increased flow velocity. The risk of flooding to the upstream and resectioned stretches is reduced because a greater amount of water is carried more quickly. Lined channels are often used in urban areas where access for maintenance is limited or other forms of management are not possible.

Figure 6.5 Twin concrete-lined channels formalised to act as a more effective conduit for flood flows, on the River Erewash at Stapleford, near Derby

Manning's equation

The most popular calculation to estimate velocity using the channel form and bed roughness variables is the **Manning equation**, often known as Manning's n:

Velocity $(v) = \dfrac{R^{2/3}\, s^{1/2}}{n}$.

Where: n = Manning roughness coefficient (based on variables such as the size and shape of bed material, the **wetted perimeter**, vegetation in and on the edge of the channel, and discharge)

R = **hydraulic radius**

s = channel gradient.

The Manning roughness coefficient ranges between 0.03 in straight, clean channels and 0.15 for densely vegetated channels. Table 6.1 gives some typical values for natural channels.

Table 6.1 Typical Manning roughness coefficient values (*Source*: Ven te Chow, 1959)

Channel type	Coefficient range
Small mountain stream, pebble and boulder bed	0.041–0.070
Small, clean, straight lowland stream	0.025–0.033
Small weedy stream with deep pools	0.075–0.150
Floodplain stream in pastureland	0.025–0.035
Floodplain stream in heavy woodland	0.100–0.150
Large streams (width > 33 m)	0.025–0.060

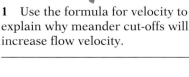

1 Use the formula for velocity to explain why meander cut-offs will increase flow velocity.

The Manning roughness coefficient (n) for a concrete-lined channel will be lower than that for a natural channel. If Manning's n in the velocity equation is reduced, the value of average velocity (*v*) will increase, even if the method of channelisation does not change the channel size or shape. Usually, however, the channel is resectioned to a larger trapezoidal shape. This increases the efficiency of the channel and the hydraulic radius (HR). The result is an increase in channel flow velocity, since the value of *R* multiplied by *s* will be higher.

Containment

Culverts are an extreme form of channelisation which contain the channel within concrete arches or pipes (Fig. 6.6). These structures are used where rivers flow under roads or built-up areas. They are more difficult to maintain because of access problems and are limited by a design flood level above which they will fail or cause ponding back of the water and possible floods upstream of the bridge.

Figure 6.6 East Goscote, Leicestershire: this was a major flood area before the culvert, under the A607, was built. Two tributaries of the R. Wreake join here. The Gaddesby Brook (behind the central wall) and the Queniborough Brook (in the foreground) are confined by concrete in the area where they meet, on the right of the photograph. The culverts carry the two streams under the road

Vegetation clearance

A smooth, regular channel can carry up to three times the discharge of a channel of similar size and gradient, which has its banks covered with extensive weed, reeds and other plants. Plants reduce the size of the channel and aid silt deposition, as well as increasing channel roughness (Fig. 6.7). The nature of the plants, e.g. whether they are clump-forming, or the flexibility of their stems, will be important in determining how much they influence channel roughness. In the River Yarrow in Lancashire, for example, there was a 58 per cent reduction in the value of Manning's n, from 0.1484 to 0.0627, following weed clearance. Following tree and debris clearance on the River Lostock in Lancashire, Manning's n was reduced by 23 per cent, from 0.0662 to 0.0152.

The seasonal cutting of vegetation can be ecologically beneficial, and is an established component in the management of streams. However, the removal

Figure 6.7 Plant growth is removed from channels to reduce roughness, and to prevent culverts and bridges from becoming obstructed or blocked. If they did become blocked, this would pose a serious flooding threat

Figure 6.8 Plant roots bind the soil and protect the banks. This structural protection can be lost by clearance schemes that remove trees and weeds

of vegetation is normally achieved with great ecological costs (see Section 6.4) and can lead to an increase in bank erosion (Fig. 6.8).

Dredging

Dredging involves the removal of **sediment** from the channel to enlarge its **capacity** (Fig. 5.21). Dredging machines are required and a suitable site must be found for the removed sediment. Alternatively, bed material is loosened and left in the channel to be entrained and transported by **streamflow**. The removal of sediment reduces the risk of flooding in the dredged section of the river, but it may increase the problem downstream, e.g. if the transferred sediment is deposited in the channel.

Flood alleviation: Ashby Folville, Leicestershire

Ashby Folville has experienced serious flooding on several occasions, most noticeably in 1975, 1979, 1992 and 1993. If you look at the flooded area for the 1993 flood (Fig. 6.9), you will note that the pattern of flooding is unusual. The main area of flooded land is not on either side of the Gaddesby Brook as you might expect, but is concentrated along the main street and around the Brook in the south-east of the village.

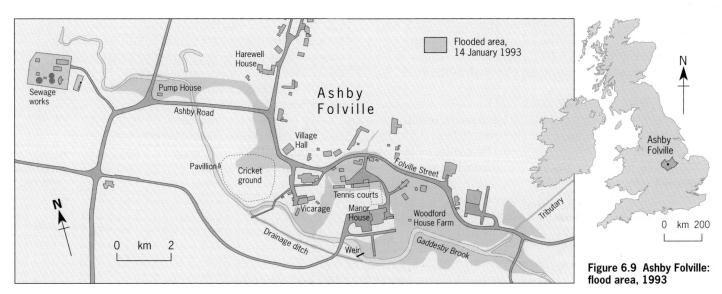

Figure 6.9 Ashby Folville: flood area, 1993

Ashby Folville

Figure 6.10 The channel near to Woodford House Farm. This section of the Gaddesby Brook was altered by a previous landowner. Water accumulates on the bend, which can cause flooding in the village

Figure 6.11 The channel near to Woodford House Farm, January 1994. Emergency dredging by the NRA prevented flooding in the village

This results from a diversion of the Gaddesby Brook around Manor House over 30 years ago. The artificial and unnaturally sharp meander near to Woodford House Farm causes water to build up under high-flow conditions (Figs 6.9–6.11). If the wall is overtopped, the flood waters flow on to the land near the farm and along the main street of the village. The flooding problem is therefore relatively recent and results from human mismanagement of the channel in the past.

A flood alleviation scheme

Flood events in Ashby Folville are frequent, and the costs in property damage are therefore high (Table 6.2). The National Rivers Authority (NRA) investigated four possibilities for a flood alleviation scheme:

Option 1 'Do nothing'. This would leave 32 properties at risk from flooding. A 1-in-100-year flood would create £550 000 of damage. A viable scheme exists, so this option was rejected.

Option 2 Construct floodwalls, raise an existing wall and regrade some of the channel. Ashby Folville is a conservation area, therefore this option was rejected.

Option 3 Regrade the Brook throughout the village; remove a weir and a short length of new cut; replace and underpin several bridges; and construct a short length of new floodwall and weir on the tributary (Fig. 6.12). This was the favoured scheme.

Option 4 Build a bypass (flood relief) channel in addition to the existing channel to convey the floodwater. Many trees would have to be removed in an area of tree preservation orders, therefore this option was rejected.

Table 6.2 Ashby Folville: flood frequency

Return period flow (years)	Gaddesby Brook (m³/s)	Tributary (m³/s)	Number of properties affected
2	10.7	2.48	15
5	16.37	4.01	–
10	19.82	4.90	–
50	28.03	7.00	31
100	31.88	7.99	31
150	40.00	9.00	32

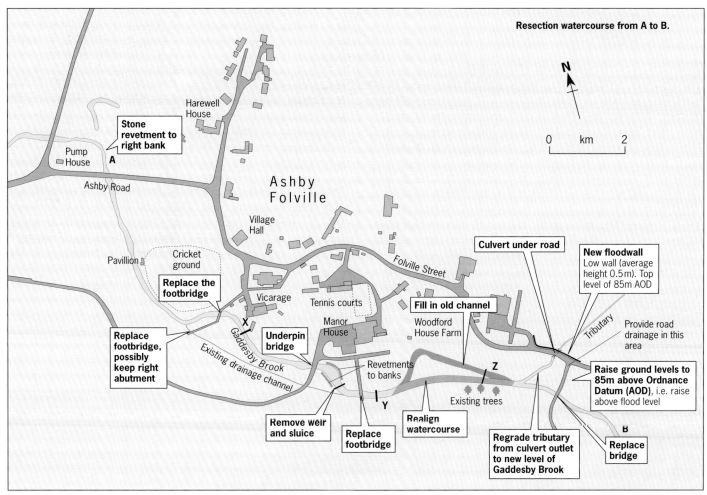

Figure 6.12 Ashby Folville: extent of the proposed flood alleviation works

The cost–benefit analysis

The proposed flood alleviation scheme (Option 3) was investigated for three standards of protection, corresponding to flood return periods of 50, 100 and 150 years. The preferred option from this **cost–benefit analysis** (see Section 7.8) was the 1-in-100-year standard of protection (Table 6.3).

The cost–benefit ratios for this scheme are relatively high because the properties involved are large, and even at the two-year event 15 properties are flooded (Table 6.2). Thus, the scheme would prevent much flooding with events at or below the 1-in-100-year level.

2a Describe the pattern of flooding in Ashby Folville for the January 1993 event. List the land uses affected.
b Suggest the main reason for this pattern of flooding.

3 Use Table 6.2 to draw a flood recurrence interval graph for Gaddesby Brook. Add the tributary to the same graph. Use semi-logarithmic graph paper. Use the logarithmic scale for the return periods and the arithmetic scale for the discharges.

4 Explain fully why the 1-in-100-year protection level was the preferred choice. Remember the cost–benefit analysis and the indicative standards of protection.

Table 6.3 Costs, benefits and the cost–benefit ratio of the flood alleviation scheme (Option 3) for the four standards of protection

	Do nothing	A	B	C
Standard years		50	100	150
Costs (£)	2 000 000	368 504	454 117	539 494
Benefits (£)		1 800 000	1 958 238	1 990 140
Average cost–benefit ratio		1:4.88	1:4.31	1:3.69

The 1-in-50-year protection scheme has the highest cost–benefit ratio and the highest net present value. However, this does not provide the indicative standard of protection for a medium density urban area where 32 properties are at risk (1-in-75-years).

The 1-in-100-year protection scheme has the next highest cost–benefit ratio and net present value. It also has the highest incremental cost–benefit ratio. This is therefore the preferred option.

Ashby Folville

Channel resectioning and realigning

The scheme is based upon resectioning and the removal of channel obstructions. The channel will be deepened by up to 2 m and consequently the bridges along the Brook will need underpinning or replacing. The artificial meander will be realigned to stop the floodwaters overspilling into the village.

?

5 The channel at X and Y is being resectioned, and the channel at Z is to be realigned. Using Table 6.4 and Figure 6.13:
a Calculate the hydraulic radius and the wetted perimeter for channel Z.
b Use the information to describe and fully explain how the new channels will reduce flooding. In your answer refer to channel size and efficiency.

Table 6.4 Channel characteristics before resectioning (original channel)

Cross-section	Width (m)	Average depth (m)	Cross-sectional area (m²)	Wetted perimeter (m)	Hydraulic radius
X	6.1	1.5	9.15	8.35	1.09
Y	7.0	0.8	5.6	7.3	0.77
Z	13.5	1.24	16.74	15.2	1.10

Note: Average depth measurements taken at 50 cm intervals across the channel and averaged.

Table 6.5 Channel characteristics after resectioning (original channel)

Cross-section	Width (m)	Average depth (m)	Cross-sectional area (m²)	Wetted perimeter (m)	Hydraulic radius
X	7.10	2.2	15.62	10.3	1.52
Y	8.4	1.36	11.42	10.0	1.142
Z	8.8	2.01	17.65	?	?

Note: Average depth measurements taken at 50 cm intervals across the channel and averaged.

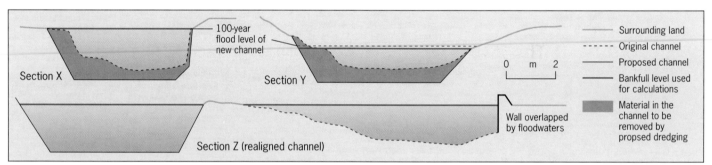

Figure 6.13 Ashby Folville: cross-sections before and after resectioning

?

6 Ashby Folville is an attractive conservation village, with many commuters. The work will be disruptive while the scheme is being implemented and the nature of the Brook will be changed. In pairs, one take the role of a resident whose property is affected by flooding, the other the role of a resident who lives above the flood levels. Discuss how your opinions about the scheme differ, giving reasons. Refer to the Environmental Impact Assessment, Appendix 5.

?

7a Draw a cross-section of a dredged trapezoidal-shaped channel to show low and high-flow levels.
b Comment on how the hydraulic radius and wetted perimeter of the low-flow levels in the channel will vary.
c Explain why the low flows result in deposition.

6.3 The impacts of channelisation

Resectioning

Researchers have studied the impacts of resectioning on channels at 57 sites in England and Wales. The schemes studied were aimed at enlarging channels by dredging to confine floodwaters within the rivers themselves.

Downstream adjustments

We have seen that resectioning increases streamflow. The studies showed that the higher velocities resulted in greater erosion rates downstream of the schemes. However, over a period of time a **negative feedback** mechanism operated to reduce stream velocity (Fig. 6.14). There was a state of adjustment and self-regulation by the river.

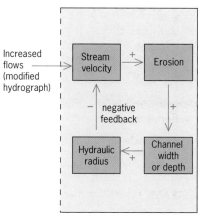

Figure 6.14 Feedback diagram for the adjustment of channel capacity following resectioning (*Source*: Brookes, 1985)

Not all rivers, however responded in the same way. Channel change is dependent on the energy of the river. For example, low-energy rivers in lowland Britain showed little or downstream channel change, while in high-energy upland rivers changes in width, rather than depth, were more common. This is explained by the **bed armouring** effect of the channel bedload compared to the smaller sediment and soil material of the banks. Channels which were cut into solid bedrock showed little downstream change.

The studies also showed that channel adjustment fell with distance downstream. Erosion was found to be selective, with reduced rates where trees and other vegetation protected the banks. Erosion was greatest on the outside of meander bends, with little **point bar** deposition on the inside of the bend. The length downstream affected did vary and ranged from a minimum of 120 m on Pickering Beck in North Yorkshire to a maximum of 1950 m for the River Caldew in Cumbria.

On-site adjustments
Resectioned reaches were found to adjust with time. For example, when the River Thame in Oxfordshire was enlarged as part of a flood alleviation scheme, the channel reverted to its original capacity in under 30 years without maintenance dredging. The enlarged channel was in equilibrium with higher flood flows, but not with the more common low flows. Reduced low-flow velocities and deposition occurred as a result.

The River Witham, Lincolnshire, England

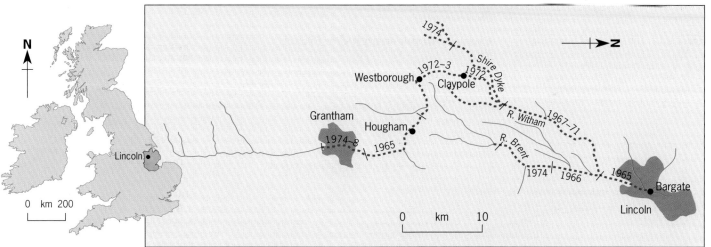

Figure 6.15 Location and timing of the River Witham channel works (*Source*: Institute of Hydrology)

During the late 1970s there were a number of high-flood flows in the city of Lincoln, and the River Witham came close to overtopping its flood embankments.

Much of the River Witham's catchment is quality agricultural land. During the late 1960s and early 1970s, extensive channelisation occurred to reduce flooding of this agricultural land (Fig. 6.15). The channel was dredged and the excavated material used to create flood embankments. Dredging increased the channel discharge capacity, e.g. from 13.2 to 31.4 m^3/s in the Shire Dyke reach. Consequently, rural flooding was reduced and resulted in the loss of floodplain storage upstream of Lincoln.

8 Describe the changes in lag times and peak discharges shown in Figure 6.16 and Table 6.6.

9 Draw a sketch map of Figure 6.15. Annotate the details of the channelisation scheme on your map. Add detailed notes on the changes in river processes and their impacts which occurred as a result of the scheme.

River Witham

Faster flows in the enlarged channels and the loss of floodplain storage resulted in more water moving at higher velocities downstream. This is shown by reduced time lags on the **hydrographs** (Fig. 6.16). The abrupt change in the lag times following channelisation provides evidence that the scheme has been a main factor in this change. Although the late 1970s were wetter than average, the reduced time lags were continued into the 1980s. A contributing factor might have been the change in agricultural practices, from ploughing to minimum cultivation, which would have resulted in the compaction of surface soil. However, the effect of this change on lag times would have been more gradual than those observed.

Readings from the Claypole **gauging station** (Table 6.6) show that since channelisation there has been an increase in the frequency and magnitude of floods, as well as the reduction in lag times. As a result, a new £8 million Washlands scheme has been designed to give additional flood protection for the city of Lincoln.

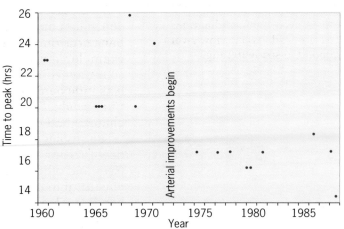

Figure 6.16 Unit hydrograph time to peak values at Claypole, for large events in the period 1960–88 (*Source*: Institute of Hydrology)

Table 6.6 Peak discharges of the River Witham at Claypole

Period	Mean discharge	Number per year over 8 m³/s	Number per year over 10 m³/s	Mean maximum discharge
1959–66	12.8	4.8	3.3	15.6
1974–83	15.4	5.3	4.3	27.2

Realigning

Figure 6.17 The impact of realigning

Changes in the straightened reach
The adjustments by rivers following realigning can be dramatic, especially in high-energy rivers or those with easily eroded sediments. Realigning increases the downstream slope of the channel by shortening the course (Fig. 6.17). The energy budget of the river increases with gradient, allowing more sediment to be transported. In the East and West Prairie Rivers in Alberta, Canada, researchers found that the higher energy available in the newly straightened reach resulted in erosion of the channel bed and encouraged bank collapse. A **knickpoint** was formed in the long profile which moved upstream.

c Channel adjustment following realigning of a river on erodible bedrock or deposits

Supply of sediment from upstream is insufficient for increased energy, and therefore erosion commences near X, and a knickpoint works progressively upstream.

UPSTREAM
Unmanaged reach – gentle long profile

Erosion, bank collapse and channel degradation

Increased gradient increases the river's energy to erode and transport material.

Erosion along straightened reach increases sediment input to downstream reach. The gradient of this unstraightened reach provides insufficient energy for the transport of all this extra sediment. Deposition and channel aggradation occur.

Loss of channel capacity may increase likelihood of flooding

STRAIGHTENED REACH
Channel length is shortened. Long profile is artificially steepened by this shorter channel path. Higher velocity and increased capacity and competence.

DOWNSTREAM
Unmanaged reach – a gentle long profile, reduced energy

Meander charcteristics are in equilibrium with the energy budget. Energy expenditure over the long profile is equalised by meandering. The system is in balance.

a Before channel realignment

Long profile

The straightening creates a period of disequilibrium in the system

Shorter, steeper long profile

b After channel realignment

10   Draw annotated diagrams to describe and explain how rivers respond to straightening.

Rivers do not flow in straight lines under natural conditions. If there is sufficient energy available they will try to re-establish their sinuous course by bank erosion. This is particularly the case with high-energy rivers. For example, a section of the River Severn at Llandinam, Wales, was straightened during the construction of a railway in the early 1850s. There was little bank protection to maintain this new course. Consequently, the river gradually recovered its sinuous course or plan form until, by 1982, the channel had returned to its original long-profile slope.

Schemes today, therefore, incorporate bank strengthening measures to prevent the river from re-meandering. For example, a 1.5 km stretch of the River Lune at Kelleth in Cumbria was realigned in 1975. The new channel was cut into bedrock rather than sediment, and the banks reinforced with gabions. There has been no channel adjustment.

Downstream changes
Downstream of the realigned reach, the channel retains its natural, lower gradient. Here, more sediment arrives than available stream energy can remove. The result is deposition and **aggrading** of the bed. Deposition can also result in the formation of large point bars.

The upper River Rhine, western Europe

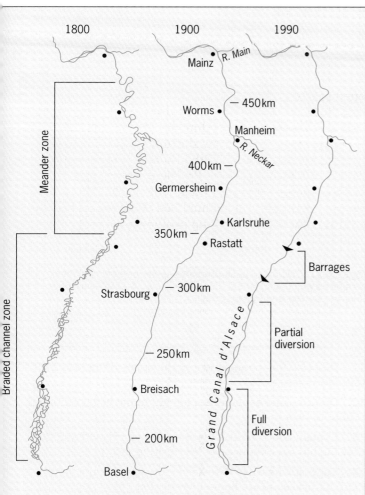

Figure 6.19 The historical development of the upper River Rhine (Source: Dister, 1985)

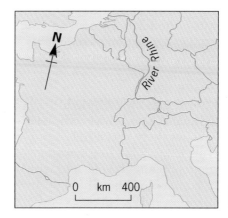

Figure 6.18 The River Rhine, western Europe

Early management

The upper River Rhine between Basel in Switzerland and Mannheim, Germany (Fig. 6.18), has had severe flooding problems which date back to 1306. The shifting channel caused problems with demarking the border with France. The nineteenth-century German engineer Tulla had the idea of concentrating the water flow of the upper **braided** reach (Fig. 6.19) into one channel. Bed level would be lowered by erosion and the flooding risk reduced. After his work, the river was 100 km shorter and 30 per cent faster in the former braided reach, and over 2000 islands had been removed. In the meandering section of the river, diversion structures were used to train the river to cut its meanders. The banks were stabilised to maintain this new structure.

This work protected against the severe flooding, but the river was still unsuitable for navigation due to

Upper River Rhine

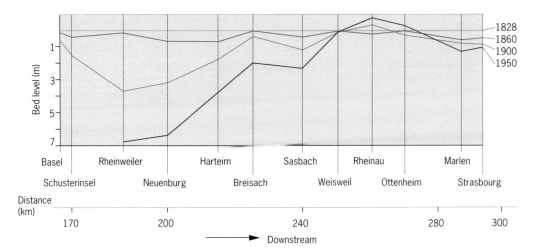

Figure 6.20 Bed level development of the River Rhine between Basel and Strasbourg since the beginning of river regulation up to the construction of the river diversions in 1959 (*Source*: Raabe, 1968)

irregular gravel bars, i.e. bars of sediment in the channel. Deflector groynes were used to reduce the channel width from 200–250 m to 75–150 m. Increased erosion in this narrower channel scoured the gravel bars. Levées were built for better flood protection. These early regulation works led to nearly 4 m of bed erosion at the beginning of the channelised section. By 1970 the bed levels had been cut down by 7 m. The eroded material was transported downstream and the bed showed aggradation, i.e. deposition of sediment built up the channel bed (Fig. 6.20).

Twentieth-century management

Major river works continued into the twentieth-century and the Grand Canal d'Alsace was completed in 1959. In the upper reaches there was a full diversion of the river. This led to a fall in the water table in the surrounding floodplain gravels, and with it came the loss of a large area of wetland habitat. In the partial diversion zone (Fig. 6.19), barrages and dams were built to feed power stations and for flow regulation. The downstream erosion effects are now reduced by artificial feeding of sediment into the river.

The diversion works reduced the active floodplain to 40 per cent of its former area. With the loss of this natural storage, the floodwaters built up downstream, giving higher flood peaks. The flood protection defences of Karlsruhe and Mannheim were reduced from the 1-in-200-year flood to the 1-in-50-year flood event. Calculations show that a repeat of the major flood of 1883 under today's conditions would show a clear reduction in lag times and an increase in the flood peak at the city of Worms (Fig. 6.21).

The upper Rhine, therefore, has been subjected to much management. This has had an effect on the natural flow patterns and ecosystems of the river and its floodplain. Efforts to restore the upper Rhine to a more natural state are now taking place.

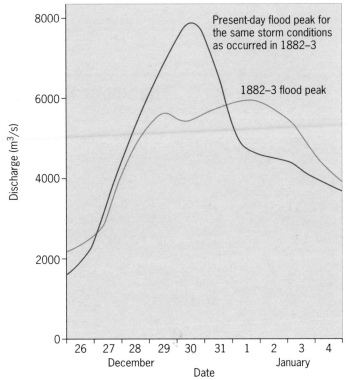

Figure 6.21 Calculated peak discharge under present conditions compared with the historical Rhine flood peak of 1882 and 1883 (*Source*: Carling and Petts, 1992)

?

11 Describe the management of the upper Rhine using the text and Figure 6.19.

12 Describe and explain the changes in the bed level (long profile) shown in Figure 6.20.

13 Explain why the peak discharge has increased and the time lag has been reduced at Worms (Fig. 6.21).

14 Suggest why ways of restoring the upper Rhine to a more natural state are being investigated.

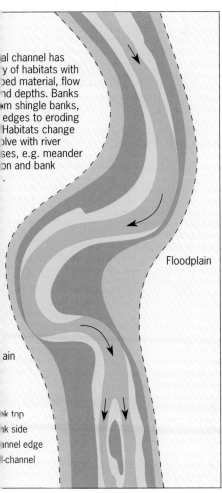

al channel has
y of habitats with
ed material, flow
nd depths. Banks
m shingle banks,
edges to eroding
Habitats change
olve with river
es, e.g. meander
on and bank

ain

k top
k side
nnel edge
-channel

Figure 6.22 Plan diagram of the habitat types of a typical lowland river (*After*: Lewis and Williams, 1984)

Transition zone between floodplain and channel gradation of soil water content. Supports a wide range of plant types and animal life, e.g. otters, water voles, kingfishers and sand martins.

Low velocities encourage broad-leaved and floating-leaved species, e.g. lilies and pondweed. There are different habitats on riffle-and-pool sequences. Turbulent rivers have mainly mosses, algae and lichen. Fish habitats vary with channel bed materials and water velocities; the wider the variety, the wider the range of fish species found. Wide variety of invertebrates, e.g. stony riffles support mayfly nymphs and river limpets. Pools have a smaller variety of invertebrates.

Figure 6.23 Habitat types of a typical UK lowland river (*After*: Lewis and Williams, 1984)

6.4 The ecological impacts of channelisation

River channels and floodplains provide a wide variety of natural habitats (Figs 6.22 and 6.23). Engineered channels lack many of these natural characteristics because there is little flow variability or habitat diversity. Some managed rivers, with high-energy flows or easily eroded sediments, can recover structural and habitat diversity, but engineered reaches in bedrock or in low-energy rivers can not.

We should remember that some rivers are managed with the intention of preventing structural diversity from returning, for example with constant dredging and weed clearance. However, concern about the environmental consequences of channelisation is increasing. Water managers are beginning to value the ecological diversity of natural channels, and modern engineering schemes are more sympathetic to environmental considerations. Most schemes today require an Environment Impact Assessment (EIA) (see Appendix A5) as well as a cost–benefit analysis before implementation.

Plants may be woodland or field edge. Trees and other plants provide shade and nutrients to support the river ecosystem.

Bank top   Bank side   Channel edge

Dry   **Damp**   **Waterlogged**

Rich habitat for plants due to low velocities in shoals or shelter by robust plants. Pond-like conditions in the summer low flows. Perennial plants are common, e.g. watercress, reeds. Amphibians, such as newts and toads, breed here. Many birds, e.g. reed warblers, sedge warblers, little grebes, swans, coots. Dragonflies and damselflies.

Floodplain

?

15a Using Figure 6.24, describe how the River Witham meander was retained.
b Suggest the ecological advantages of retaining this meander.
c Describe how channelisation has affected the ecological structure and diversity of the new channel.

The impact of realigning

Many river channelisation schemes involve the removal of meanders which can have major impacts on the stream ecology. Meanders provide a wide range of habitats: eroding river cliffs; pools and riffles; turbulent and still water; sun and shade; and sheltered and exposed sites. In the channelisation scheme on the River Witham, Lincolnshire, we saw that the main channel was deepened and slightly widened into a trapezoidal shape. The dredge spoil was used to infill the meanders along the straightened reach. However, one meander was retained at Westborough because of the landowner's objections (Fig. 6.24).

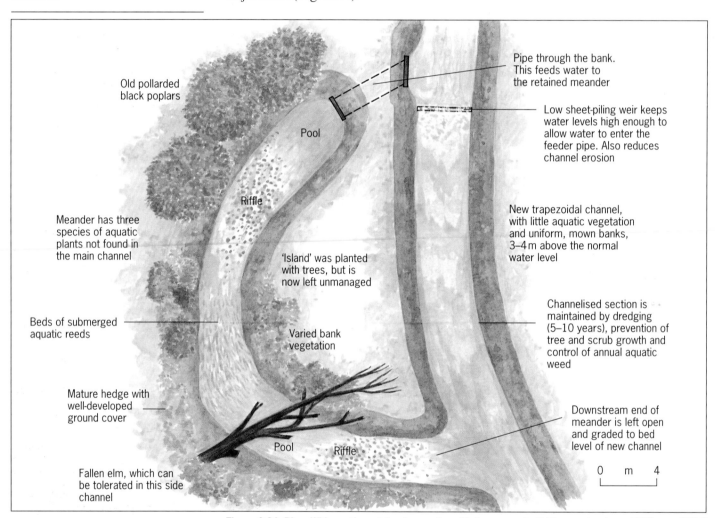

Old pollarded black poplars

Pool

Riffle

Meander has three species of aquatic plants not found in the main channel

'Island' was planted with trees, but is now left unmanaged

Beds of submerged aquatic reeds

Varied bank vegetation

Mature hedge with well-developed ground cover

Pool

Riffle

Fallen elm, which can be tolerated in this side channel

Pipe through the bank. This feeds water to the retained meander

Low sheet-piling weir keeps water levels high enough to allow water to enter the feeder pipe. Also reduces channel erosion

New trapezoidal channel, with little aquatic vegetation and uniform, mown banks, 3–4 m above the normal water level

Channelised section is maintained by dredging (5–10 years), prevention of tree and scrub growth and control of annual aquatic weed

Downstream end of meander is left open and graded to bed level of new channel

0   m   4

Figure 6.24 River Witham: the retained meander with the new cut-off (*Source*: Lewis and Williams, 1984)

Managing the River Roding, England

The River Roding in Essex drains a small narrow catchment which is agricultural in its upper reaches and heavily urbanised in the lower reaches as it flows into the River Thames (Fig. 6.25, Table 6.7). The river has a characteristic lowland meandering pattern, with riffles and pools providing ideal conditions for fish. However, urban development has resulted in changes to the river, and flood control has been necessary.

Flood control management of the river has involved various forms of channelisation, i.e. straightening, dredging, training walls with gabion boxes, sheet piling and concrete blocks, and realignment. The older schemes have had significant adverse impacts on the river system. However, recent schemes, from 1979 to 1980, have attempted to restore environmental diversity to former channelised reaches.

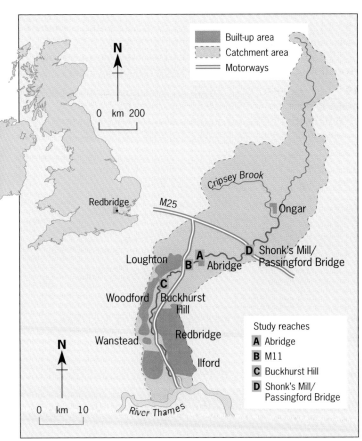

Figure 6.25 The River Roding and its catchment (*Source*: Lewis and Williams, 1984)

Table 6.7 River Roding: key facts

Catchment area	342 km²
Length	80 km
Channel width	5.5–8.5 m
Banks	Naturally high and steep, cut 1.5–2 m into the floodplain
Long profile	Average gradient 0.001
Low level flow	2 m³/s
Geology and land use:	
Upper reaches	Glacial clay deposits, arable agricultural area with many villages
Lower reaches	Alluvial deposits on active floodplain. Urban development and transport routes

Management near Abridge (Reach 1)

Between 1979 and 1980 a flood alleviation scheme was needed for the village of Abridge, the B172 road (1-in-70-year flood protection) and the improved pastureland between Abridge and Loughton further downstream (1-in-10-year protection). The scheme involved building a two-stage channel along 3.5 km of the River Roding (Fig. 6.26). The method of channel management chosen allowed the natural channel to remain as undisturbed as possible. The scheme left more than 90 per cent of the river bed untouched to conserve the chub fishery. Nevertheless, the loss of the

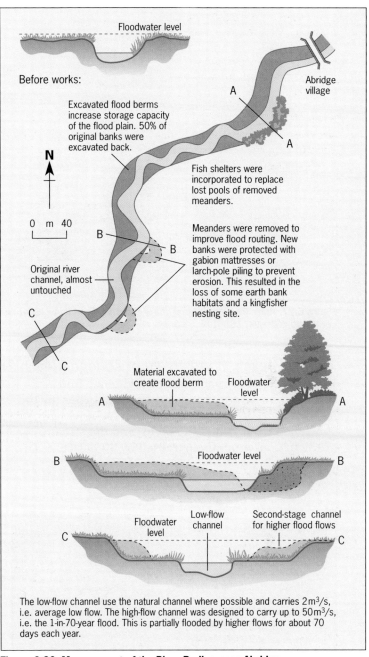

Figure 6.26 Management of the River Roding near Abridge

two meanders removed deep pool habitats. To compensate, fish shelters were incorporated into the scheme. Overall, habitat diversity has been retained and new habitats created in the higher level channel.

?

16 Explain why a two-stage channel was developed near Abridge.

17 Explain why the flood engineers decided to remove the two meanders as part of the flood alleviation scheme.

River Roding

18 In the newly straightened sections where the meanders were removed, it was thought that bank protection was needed. Use Figure 6.28 to explain why the nature of the river flow during flood flows proved this unnecessary.

19 List the features of this flood alleviation scheme which make it more environmentally sensitive than simple channelisation with a straightened trapezoidal channel.

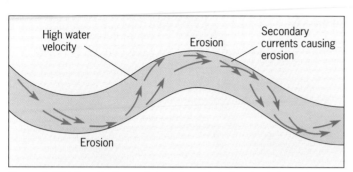

Figure 6.27 River Roding: original channel during flood flows (*Source*: Lewis and Williams, 1984)

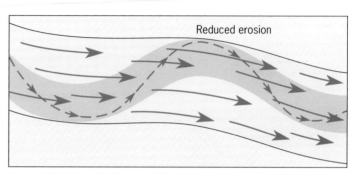

Figure 6.28 River Roding: modified channel during flood flows (*Source*: Lewis and Williams, 1984)

The M11 reach, downstream of Abridge (Reach 2)

In 1973, the M11 reach was straightened and reshaped into a trapezoidal channel in order for the motorway to be built. The length of channel was shortened from 700 m to 500 m, and the stream gradient consequently increased by 40 per cent. The channel was lined with concrete blocks and river flow became shallow, fast and uniform.

Water managers took the new 1979–80 flood alleviation scheme as an opportunity to upgrade this reach and introduce a more environmentally sensitive scheme (Figs 6.29 and 6.30).

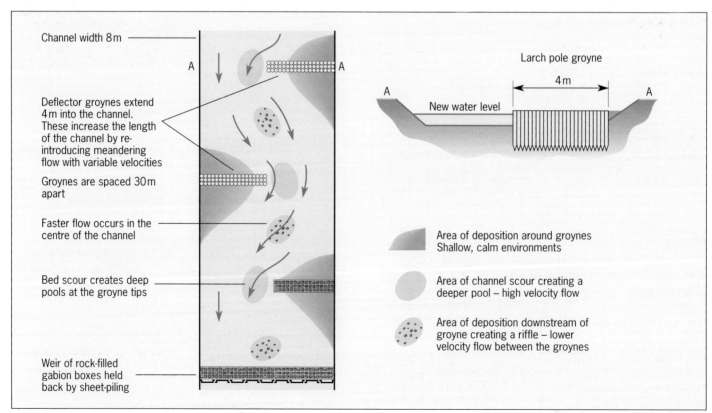

Figure 6.29 The 1979–80 upgrading of the M11 reach

20 Study Figures 6.29 and 6.30. Explain how the deflector groynes give areas of variable velocities and erosion and deposition in the channel.

21 Draw two annotated diagrams of the channel cross-sections in Figure 6.29, one at the site of the groynes and one between the groynes to show the changes in channel profile which result from the scheme.

The effect of the management schemes on habitat diversity

Figures 6.31 to 6.33 show in-channel vegetation in straightened reaches.

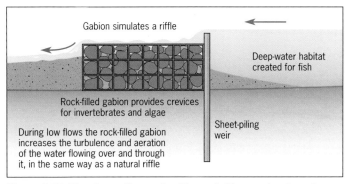

Figure 6.30 The sheet piling and gabion weir (*Source*: Lewis and Williams, 1984)

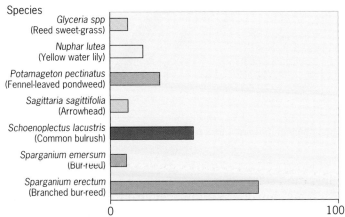

Figure 6.31 At Shonk's Mill (reach 4) 880 m of river was straightened in 1750 to provide power for a mill. The reach was shortened by 330 m, its gradient increased by 60 per cent and the channel was cut as straight and narrow as possible. There is a gently meandering thalweg, but due to the resistant clay river bed there has been little morphological recovery

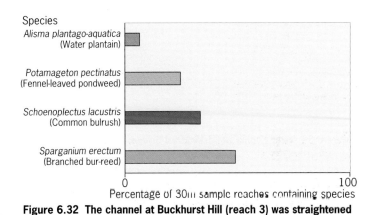

Figure 6.32 The channel at Buckhurst Hill (reach 3) was straightened in 1975 to allow people to extract gravel from the floodplain. The river was shortened by 250 m, the gradient increased by 25 per cent and the width by 6.75 m. The river flow is shallow, fast and uniform. There has been bed erosion upstream, resulting in bank collapse and lateral instability. This upstream section has had to be dredged to prevent deposition of the newly eroded sediment. Downstream, increased sedimentation means that maintenance dredging has become necessary

22a Compare the in-channel vegetation for the three reaches of the Roding shown in Figures 6.31 to 6.33. Comment on changes in biomass and ecosystem diversity.
b What implications do the three vegetation surveys have for the fluvial ecosystems?

23 In what other ways has the channel upgrading improved opportunities for wildlife in the area?

24a Describe the upstream and downstream effects of channelisation in the Buckhurst Hill reach.
b Explain why maintenance dredging became necessary.

Figure 6.33 In the M11 reach (reach 2) deflector groynes and a weir have had a major impact on the quantity and diversity of fish species and the vegetation. In 1978 a survey showed that there were large numbers of small fish, such as stone loach, typical of shallow streams. A year after the groynes were installed, the fish population showed a wider variety, with more medium and large-sized species, such as chub, dace, roach, gudgeon, pike and large eels

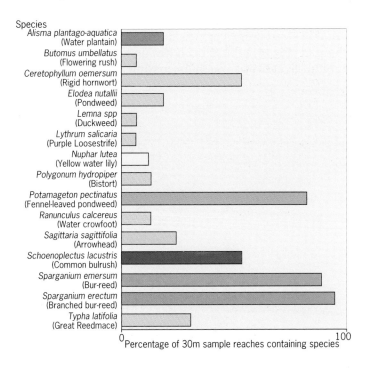

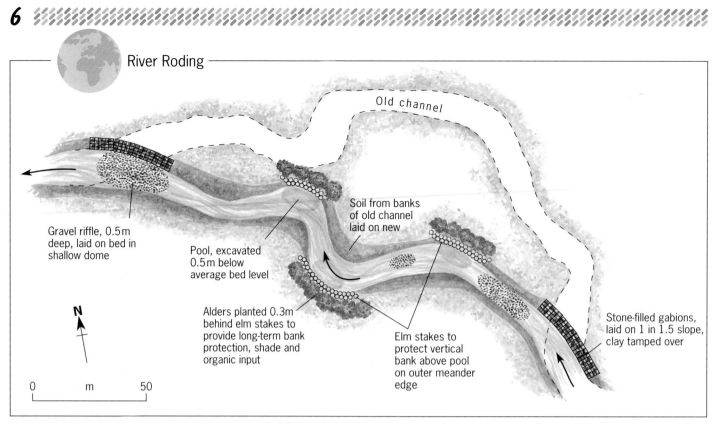

River Roding

Old channel

Gravel riffle, 0.5m deep, laid on bed in shallow dome

Pool, excavated 0.5m below average bed level

Soil from banks of old channel laid on new

Alders planted 0.3m behind elm stakes to provide long-term bank protection, shade and organic input

Elm stakes to protect vertical bank above pool on outer meander edge

Stone-filled gabions, laid on 1 in 1.5 slope, clay tamped over

N

0   m   50

Figure 6.34 River Roding at Passingford Bridge: detailed design of the realigned channel (*Source*: Lewis and Williams, 1984)

Management of Shonk's Mill, Passingford Bridge (reach 4)

In 1982, the River Roding at Passingford Bridge required a similar diversion to that which had taken place for the M11 in 1973. This time it was for the building of the M25. The impacts on the river ecosystems from the 1973 scheme and the necessary upgrading were considered when planning this work. A whole channel realignment was needed. Four kilometres downstream of Passingford Bridge a suitable stretch of river was found. The realigned channel (Fig. 6.34) has been designed to maintain habitat diversity as much as possible.

?

25 Use Figure 6.34 to describe how the engineers have designed the realigned channel to simulate a natural river and its ecosystems.

26 Essay: A major debate taking place in many countries, e.g. the UK, the USA and Germany, is whether to restore rivers to a more unmanaged state which maintains wetlands and other habitats and enhances their amenity value. Suggest why early river management schemes have been so damaging to rivers and examine how future management can preserve, restore or enhance the natural environment. Use a range of examples which you have studied to exemplify the points you make.

6.5 Dams and channel processes

In Chapter 4 we saw that dams and storage reservoirs have important impacts on the flow regime and discharge of rivers. In Chapter 5 we learned that reservoirs provide a new store for the river's sediment. Consequently, water emerging from a dam has a changed regime, discharge, sediment load and hence available energy.

Upstream effects

As a river with high capacity and **competence** opens into a reservoir, the available energy is abruptly reduced. The reservoir acts like a natural lake and the sediment builds out as a delta-like deposit. The reduced flow velocity results in reduced capacity and competence upstream. Sediment is deposited, the river bed is aggraded and the risk of flooding is likely to increase.

Figure 6.35 The upstream and downstream effects of a dam on the long and cross profiles (*After:* Goudie, 1990)

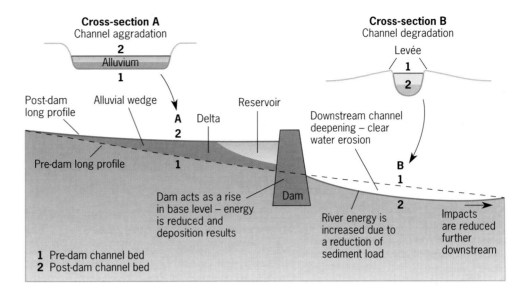

27 Draw a large copy of Figure 6.35. Add detailed notes on the upstream and downstream effects of a dam.

Downstream effects

Clear water erosion

Downstream of the dam, water emerges with a reduced sediment load of 8–50 per cent. The Aswan High Dam (Fig. 4.40) traps 98 per cent of the Nile silt. The river has increased energy as a result of this reduction, and erosion of the channel results. This channel incision is called **clear water erosion**. In the case of the Hoover Dam on the River Colorado, USA, vertical incision has lowered the river bed by 6.1 m over an 11 km stretch in four years. Rivers with a naturally high sediment load show dramatic results. The Sanmenxia Dam on the Yellow River in China (Fig. 5.1) has caused 4 m of bed degrading over 68 km in only four years.

Clear water erosion can cause **rejuvenation** of tributary channels as they adjust their long profiles to the newly degraded main channel. Continued vertical down-cutting can undermine bridges and other structures along the river. To reduce these effects, some river engineers artificially feed channels with sediment. However, the increased erosion is not all bad. In northern China, the incision of the river channel has reduced the strain on levées and consequently reduced the need for increasing levée heights.

Increasing sediment load

One of the main reasons for building dams is to regulate the flow regime. Thus, the discharge of the river downstream has changed from the pre-dam flow. Water abstraction for irrigation and municipal use will reduce the discharge of the river. As a result, the river may have a reduced flow which has insufficient energy to carry any sediment load supplied by undammed tributary rivers. The effect is the opposite to clear water erosion. For example, downstream of the Glen Canyon Dam on the River Colorado, USA, the extremes of flow have been reduced. The main channel is no longer capable of removing the sediment supplied by flash-flooding tributaries. As a result, deposits of up to 2.6 m thick have accumulated in the upper Grand Canyon (the opposite effect to the clear water erosion downstream of the Hoover Dam).

Reducing channel size

The decreased maximum discharges downstream of dams result in reduced channel sizes, especially if the river is not competent to carry the sediment load supplied by tributaries. Reductions of 30–70 per cent have been recorded. For example, the Elephant Butte Dam on the Rio Grande in the

?

Study Figure 6.36.

28 Describe and explain the terrace development in the Grand Canyon before the Glen Canyon Dam was built.

29 Describe and explain how the changed regime of the river has affected the terraces.

30 You are a water engineer advising a planning authority on the feasibility of building a dam. Outline a programme of fieldwork and other data that you would need before you could assess the likely impacts of the dam on the river system.

USA, has resulted in a 50 per cent channel capacity loss; the Ladybower Reservoir on the River Derwent in Derbyshire has caused a 40 per cent loss. Discharge reductions of 10–30 per cent in the North and South Platte Rivers in the USA resulted in changes in channel form. The North Platte River was 760–1220 m wide in 1890 and today has a reduced width of 60 m. Both rivers had a braided course before dam construction, but today the river flows in one narrow, well-defined channel. When channel slope stays the same but discharge reduces, the channel is more likely to meander than be braided. Indeed, sinuosity of the North and South Platte rivers has increased. The channel forms have adjusted to a new dynamic equilibrium with the new conditions.

The impact on landform development

Our study of the Aswan High Dam in Chapter 5 looked at the consequences of controlling flooding. Without flooding, there will be no further deposition of sediment on the floodplain or building of natural levées. The lack of sediment transport downstream means that delta regions are not supplied with sediment. Erosion by the sea continues and the delta is eroded away. There is a reduction in soil fertility and an increase in **salinisation.** Channel and floodplain morphology will have to reach a new equilibrium with the changed sediment and discharge conditions. The Glen Canyon Dam on the Colorado River has reduced the flood peaks and water is now released through the dam to generate HEP. This reduction in flood flows and sediment load has led to changes in the **alluvial morphology** of the channel (Fig. 6.36).

The effects of channel morphology change downstream are reduced as distance from the dam increases and the human management variables of flow regulation and sediment loss are reduced by tributary rivers. There is also a reduction in impacts over time, for two reasons:

1 Downstream degrading flattens the channel slope so much that there is insufficient energy to transport the available sediment.

2 Reduced peak flows lessen the competence of the river. Thus, only the finer particles are transported, leaving behind a larger bedload. This eventually forms a protective armour on the river bed, which reduces further erosion.

Figure 6.36 The effects of the Glen Canyon Dam on the alluvial morphology and ecology of the Grand Canyon

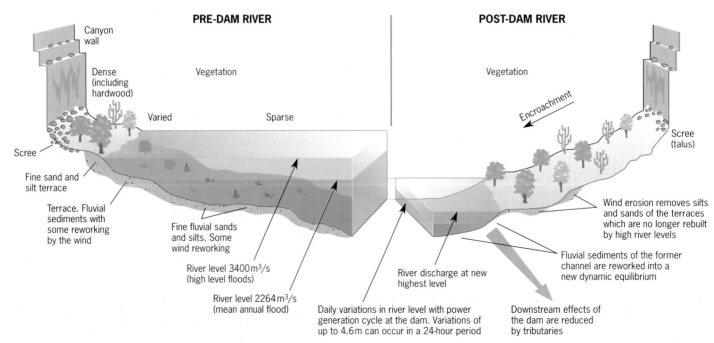

The River Murray, South Australia

The River Murray has its source in the Snowy Mountains and flows north-west to South Australia (Fig. 6.37). It has an extended long profile due to the low gradients downstream of the Snowy Mountains.

River regulation

Regulation of the Lower Murray began in 1929. Weirs were built (Fig. 6.38) which reduced floods, but increased flows to near channel capacity. Today the weirs are used to maintain flows for irrigation. They provide a steady flow of water upstream, but downstream water levels vary erratically with changes of up to 2.6 m recorded in one day. Estimates suggest that up to 73 per cent of the river's sediment load is retained by the dams and weirs along its course.

Changes in channel form

The lower Murray is a low-energy river due to its gentle gradient (55 mm/km) and there have been no changes in channel planform as a result of regulation. However, fluctuating water levels from weir operations have increased bank erosion downstream, even in relatively cohesive sediment (Fig. 6.39). As the water levels fall with the operation of the weir, the banks are left saturated and there is collapse. The small, but frequent changes in water level may undermine the bottom of the bank, making it more vulnerable to collapse. Immediately below weir 4, bank slopes increased from 65 to 81 degrees between 1988 and 1989.

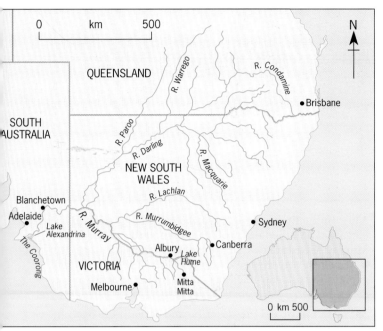

Figure 6.37 The River Murray channel has a low-energy and meandering form. Flow is controlled by upstream dams and reservoirs. The river receives no major tributaries downstream of the River Darling junction (*Source*: Carling and Potts, 1992)

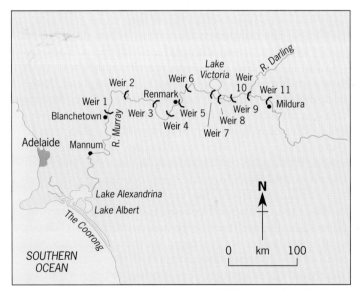

Figure 6.38 Eleven weirs were built in the 830 km stretch of the River Murray, initially for navigation purposes (*Source*: Carling and Petts, 1992)

?

31a Use Figure 6.39 to describe the effects of the weirs on bank erosion.
b Explain why increased bank erosion occurs and describe the impacts on bank slope.

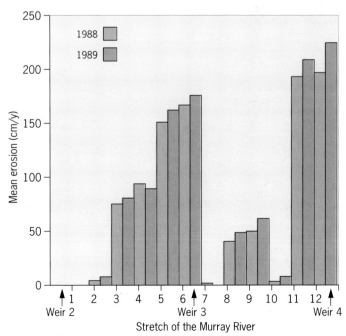

Figure 6.39 Bank erosion at twelve sites on the River Murray between weirs 2 and 4, 1988–9 (*Source*: Thoms and Walker, 1992)

River Murray

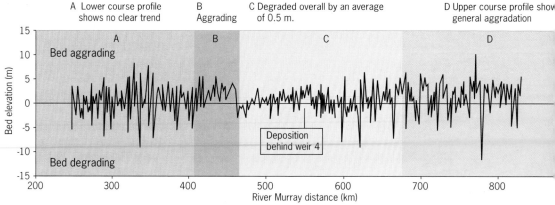

A Lower course profile shows no clear trend B Aggrading C Degraded overall by an average of 0.5 m. D Upper course profile show general aggradation

Bed elevation (m)

Bed aggrading

Deposition behind weir 4

Bed degrading

River Murray distance (km)

Figure 6.40 Changes in bed elevation of the lower River Murray, 1906–88 (*Source*: Thoms and Walker, 1992)

Changes to the long profile

The long profile has shown significant changes which are similar to those downstream of dams. There is an increased gradient due to aggrading in the upper region of the profile. The long profile has become stepped in form, with the individual steps corresponding to the weirs. These changes are shown by mean bed elevation (i.e. height above sea level). Four regions of response have been distinguished, as shown in Figure 6.40.

On a local scale, the impacts of the weirs on the long profile can be identified (Fig. 6.41). Degrading of the bed has occurred below each weir varying from 4–19 km. The downcutting below the weir 5 occurred within 18 km of the weir. In the first kilometre downstream the bed was lowered by 2.4 m, but by only 0.8 m in the next 9 km. Upstream of each weir, there has been aggrading of the bed. The material deposited behind the weirs builds up into a delta-type feature and then migrates downstream towards the next weir.

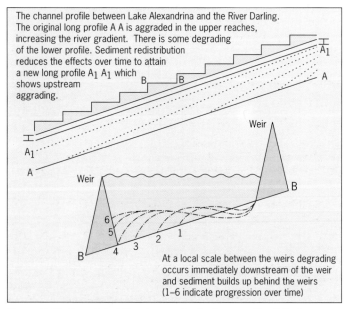

The channel profile between Lake Alexandrina and the River Darling. The original long profile A A is aggraded in the upper reaches, increasing the river gradient. There is some degrading of the lower profile. Sediment redistribution reduces the effects over time to attain a new long profile A₁ A₁ which shows upstream aggrading.

Weir

Weir

At a local scale between the weirs degrading occurs immediately downstream of the weir and sediment builds up behind the weirs (1–6 indicate progression over time)

Figure 6.41 A model of the changes to the long profile of the Lower River Murray over time (*Source*: Thoms and Walker, 1992)

32a Study Figure 6.40. Describe the changes in bed elevation (i.e. the long profile) shown in the lower River Murray. Give reasons for your observations.
b Suggest why the low-energy budget of the river might explain the unclear response in the lowest reaches (Section A).

33 Use Figure 6.41 to describe and explain the overall changes in the long profile of the River Murray.

34 Draw an annotated long profile of the River Murray to describe and explain the changes in bed level observed between the weirs.

Changes in cross-sectional area

Earlier in the chapter we saw that below dams clear water erosion causes channel enlargement. This erosion is rapid at first and then slows down until a new equilibrium is reached with the managed flow and sediment regime. The weirs on the River Murray cause a similar response. There is channel enlargement, which is then followed by reduction in channel size as the new equilibrium is reached. The managed section of the Murray is near the mouth of the river and therefore receives a constant supply of fresh sediment from upstream. However, coarse sediments are trapped behind the upland weirs and, consequently, sediment size has decreased by 32 per cent overall. Recent research on the cross-sectional area of the channel downstream of the weirs has identified three groups of responses (Figs 6.42 to 6.44).

35a Using Figures 6.42 to 6.44, list the changes which have occurred in the size of the river channel. Explain the three types of response shown by the river.
b What changes would you expect to occur in the eroding and fluctuating channels in the future? Explain your answer.

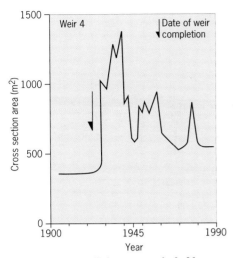

Figure 6.42 Stabilising, e.g. weir 4. After an initial period of erosion and fluctuation, the channel cross-section reaches a new dynamic equilibrium, 30–40 years after the building of the weir, with channels larger than before regulation. After initial clear water erosion, there is infilling or aggrading as sediment deposits behind each weir are reworked by the river

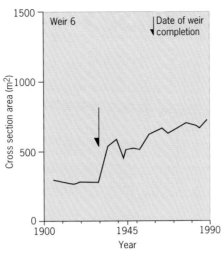

Figure 6.43 Eroding, e.g. weir 6. After initial fluctuations, erosion has continued to enlarge the cross-sectional area since the 1950s

Figures 6.42–6.44

(*Source*: Thoms and Walker, 1992)

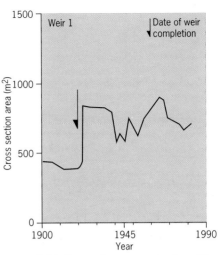

Figure 6.44 Fluctuating, e.g. weirs 1 and 2. There is no clear pattern of adjustment and the changes do not appear to be related to discharge. It is interesting that the two weirs in this group are located the furthest downstream. Possibly the impacts of management have not resulted in any new dynamic equilibrium in the lowest reaches, because the time scales are insufficient for this low-energy river environment

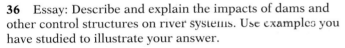

36 Essay: Describe and explain the impacts of dams and other control structures on river systems. Use examples you have studied to illustrate your answer.

37 Essay: The key to successful river management is an understanding of river processes and channel dynamics. Discuss with reference to examples you have studied.

38 Describe and explain each of the four human activity impacts, bulleted below, in terms of:
a sediment supply to the channel;
b erosion (degrading) or deposition (aggrading) in the channel;
c channel size;

d likelihood of increased flooding;
e changes in landform development, e.g. floodplains and meander development.
(Think about channel form and discharge-sediment relationships.)
• Urbanisation causes an increase in discharge and a reduction in sediment load.
• Deforestation causes an increase in discharge and sediment load.
• Mining activity can lead to a large input of additional sediment to the channel.
• Soil conservation measures reduce the discharge and sediment load of a river.

Note: Flood alleviation, Ashby Folville. In late 1994, the road bridge was found to be unsuitable for underpinning (Option 3). The value of the trees was reassessed as lower quality species which could be replaced. Hence, Option 4 is now the proposed option.

Summary

• People manage river channels by the deliberate action of channelisation for flood control, land drainage, erosion prevention and navigation.

• Channelisation involves resectioning, realignment, bank protection, lining channels and containment, vegetation clearance and dredging, as well as flood relief channels, embankments and levées.

• Channelisation aims to increase channel efficiency, size or gradient, so that flow velocities are increased in the channelised reach.

• Channelisation can have major impacts on channel processes and form, both in the altered reach and downstream.

• Channelisation can have major ecological impacts. Many modern schemes try to reduce the adverse effects and restore channels to a more natural state.

• Dams have important impacts on river channel forms and processes, both upstream and downstream of the dam site.

7 Flooding and human responses

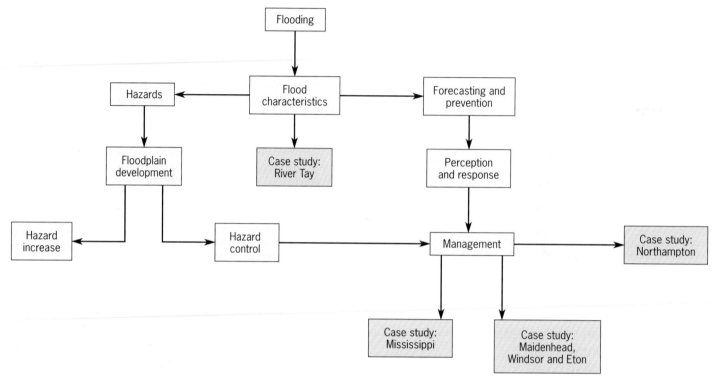

7.1 Introduction

Most of the time, a river's water and **sediment** load are transported in the river channel itself. The function of the **floodplain** is to act as a temporary store at times of higher flows. Floods occur with similar frequency in different environments, with **bankfull discharges** occurring on average every 1.5 years, with a range of 0.5–2 years. Overspill is therefore a normal event, and the floodplain and river channel are closely linked parts of the same **fluvial system**. In semi-arid areas, **alluvial fans** have a similar function.

Most floods are caused by a large input of water to the river by **quickflow processes**. Although there are rare events, such as landslides or dam failures, most river floods result from a downpour of very heavy rainfall, or prolonged rainfall giving high antecedent soil moisture conditions or rapid snowmelt. The severity of the flooding is related to the degree of quickflow-forming processes (see Chapter 3).

Floods as hazards

Floods are the cause of 40 per cent of all deaths due to natural disasters and, throughout the world, this figure is increasing. Between 1965 and 1990, 100 000 deaths worldwide were caused by flooding, and three-quarters of a billion people were distressed or had their lives disrupted in some way. Since floods are a frequent natural process in fluvial systems, we might ask why they are also the most common environmental or natural hazard.

Floods become a hazard when they interact with human activity. It is this interaction which distinguishes a natural process from a natural hazard.

?

1 Read Figure 7.1.
a Suggest why floods are described as disasters which are people's own fault.
b Explain why Professor Thorne suggests that rivers should be allowed to flood.
c Give reasons why it would be difficult to restore floodplain and water meadows to their water storage function.
d Explain why the National Rivers Authority (NRA) is in a difficult position regarding flooding.

Who's soggy now?

Much of Britain is a sodden sponge. A hundred rivers or more have asserted their ancient rights, defied man's arrogance, and rampaged across countryside long denied them. Neglect and greed for land have made such floods inevitable. And now, as **John Vidal** reports, the soak's on us.

After a decade of dryish winters broken by occasional severe downpours in a few regions, the British weather has gone back to basics. And it is still only January, the start of the usual wet season.

The Severn, Britain's longest river by a short head from the Thames, meets the Avon at Tewkesbury. Normally it's a quiet affair conducted below serious riverbanks but for 37 of the last 39 days it's been a passionate, public mingling of juices collected from as far away as the Black Country and Stratford.

What excites Jim Bourton, the former mayor of Tewkesbury, and many old timers is that these rains are nothing unusual. They're very widespread, yes, but not *really* severe.

'We've built on everything,' Jim says. 'One reason for all the floods now is that we've built so much on the flood plains. Water has to go somewhere. You stop one area getting flooded and another one floods.'

Last year Tewkesbury built a Safeway's hypermarket on many acres of the Severn flood plain; it built on St John's Island, it built new roads and over the years it has partly filled in the 'ham', all areas that used to flood. 'And they haven't maintained their sluices,' Jim says. 'I've warned them. Nothing a river likes more than flooding. It's nature's drainage. Can't stop it. Sometimes shouldn't try.'

But it's worse than that. Floods are more likely even in moderate rains these days, he says, because we've grubbed up the hedges, felled the trees, filled the ditches and turned the water meadows to cereal growing. 'The water runs off more now than it used to, see?'

A mature tree, Jim says, takes up 150 gallons of water a day and Dutch elm disease took out thousands near the town.

Colin Thorne, professor of geography at Nottingham University, a flood man who has advised the Bangladeshis on how to mitigate the monsoons and the Brahmaputra river says: 'We can put a man on the Moon but science has found no way to describe adequately the dynamics of a river. There are so many variables, it just goes its own way. It's much better to work with nature and where possible leave rivers to overflow.'

Study after study shows that urbanisation is directly linked to flooding. 'Floods are becoming more peaked,' Thorne says. 'Rivers are rising faster, their periods of concentration are becoming reduced and they fall back more quickly — even if the volume of water is the same.'

A river is not just water, he says. 'It's full of sediment, too, and we've become much better at managing the water than the sediment. But if you disturb the dynamics between water and landscape, things start happening and it becomes very unpredictable. Your channels will start naturally to silt in and the only way to stop that is to dredge. Thousands of miles of river dredging take place each year.'

Not only that, we've tried to manage some of our rivers almost to death. Massively expensive, heavy-handed concrete drainage works along many British rivers are testament everywhere to people's arrogance over nature, developers' profit motives and farmers' desires to drain every last inch of lowland ground in the name of subsidies. Some British rivers are today little more than concrete drainage channels designed to take water away as quickly as possible.

A British river, along with its flood plain, is nature's supermarket, its shoppers the voles, the birds and small mammals, their food the damselflies and nature's lesser creatures stacked high as at any Sainsbury's. Continually dredging rivers destroys the very base of the food chain, partly explaining the massive decline in British river fishing. And building or intensively farming to the edge of rivers leaves nature little to survive on. 'All you do is impoverish the floodplain.'

Thorne advocates not quite a tearing down of the river flood defences (we spend some £250 million a year on them) but a gradual compensating of farmers and others and a grand taking back of the floodplains and restoration of the water meadows.

'Rivers are meant to flood,' he says. 'They must have room to move. Ideally it should be three times as wide as their lowest channels.'

Meanwhile, on the south coast, Chichester is still reeling after a week or more of red alerts. Small clay dams have been built, roads dug up and miles of pipes now lead from river to reservoir, to culverts, gravel pits and harbour and, it seems, back again.

Peter Midgeley, a Sussex National Rivers Authority man who loves his rivers like children ('They're all important to me'), is astonished: 'Groundwater levels usually peak in April or May, but the land is completely saturated already. There are wells actually gushing water out their tops.'

Midgeley, like all river men, faintly approves of rivers overflowing: 'You can't tame nature. There comes a point when no drainage system can cope. Developments tend to increase the rate of runoff. You get bigger impermeable areas. There's great pressure to drain land and to accelerate flows into rivers. There's arable farming now in the bottom of valleys.' And in Chichester there are some huge developments on areas which used to soak up the waters.

The NRA, however, is young and suffering from endless reorganisations, but it is gradually leaning towards mimicking nature rather than trying to restrict it. The old idea of massive engineering solutions and the concreting over of rivers to control their flow is falling gradually into disfavour as the benefits of just trying to buffer nature are appreciated.

'There may be a connection between the fact that we have droughts one year in Britain, followed by floods,' says Lianna Stupples, of Friends of the Earth. 'If you try to get water away as fast as possible, which has been the basic strategy for years, you deny the land the chance to take in water and let it out at a natural speed.'

'Floods are not a natural disaster,' says Jim Crabbe, a senior water engineer in the NRA emergency room at Tewkesbury. Computers flash out the height and flow of the Severn all along its length, but Jim is full of little home-grown homilies: 'If they become disasters it's entirely people's fault. Those who've lived here a long time know and accept floods and see them as part of the price of living here. If you tinker with nature you don't know where you'll end up. I say keep it simple, just try and minimise what nature's trying to do.

'We exist to protect rivers from nature and nature from people. Trouble is, we don't learn.'

Figure 7.1 UK floods, January 1994 (*Source:* The *Guardian*, 10 January 1994)

2 Study Figure 7.2.
a Describe the trends shown in damage and loss of life in the USA from 1925 to 1989.
b Suggest reasons for the wide yearly variations.

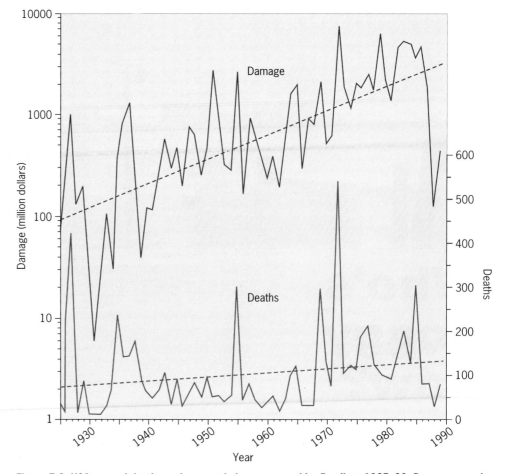

Figure 7.2 USA: annual deaths and economic losses caused by flooding, 1925–89. Damages are in millions of US$, adjusted to 1990 values. (*Source*: Smith, 1993)

Countries in the economically developing world typically experience the greatest loss of life and damage to crops and property, but the trend is clear even in developed nations such as the USA (Fig. 7.2). Research suggests that developed nations suffer only 5 per cent of fatalities from floods, but 75 per cent of the costs from natural hazards, whereas the economically developing world suffers 95 per cent of the deaths but 25 per cent of the costs.

The reasons for this increasing damage to life and property are inter-related, but they can be divided into three factors:

1 Changing agricultural activity on floodplains which is not compatible with flooding.
2 Development of floodplain areas with urban uses. This is called floodplain encroachment.
3 Human activity changing the location, magnitude, frequency and duration of flooding.

7.2 Increasing the hazard: changing agricultural activity

Flooding can sustain agricultural productivity by renewing soil fertility. Silt is deposited on the floodplain, and floodwaters wash away any salt build-up in the soil. In semi-arid areas, people develop irrigated agriculture along the courses of **perennial streams** which provide a vital water supply.

Many of the world's river floodplains have high population densities on the fertile agricultural land. Examples are the Nile in Egypt, the Mississippi in

Figure 7.3 A historic view of flooding

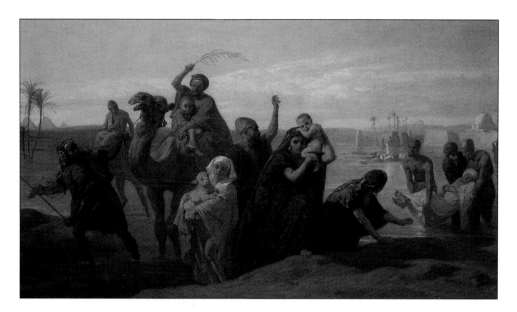

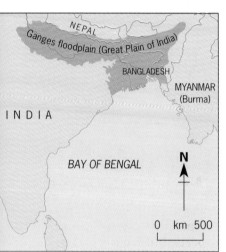

Figure 7.4 The Great Plain of India

the USA, the Ganges in India, the Yellow River (Huang He) in China, the Tigris–Euphrates in the Middle East and the Rhine in Europe. It is not by chance that many of these rivers form the areas of development of our earliest civilisations. In some of these areas, the seasonal agricultural processes are linked with the flooding pattern and the society has adjusted to the flooding **regime**, as with the River Nile before the Aswan Dam and in Bangladesh today. It is the extreme events in these increasingly densely populated areas which result in loss of life and property. Increasing population pressure and economic development mean that people need to reduce river flooding over time, because the hazard increases as the traditional economic and social systems which work with the river begin to break down.

The Great Plain of India

The Great Plain of India is 650 000 km² of alluvium which has been deposited on the Ganges floodplain (Fig. 7.4). The area supports a population of over 100 million people. The land nearest to the river was traditionally used as pasture, so that at times of flood the area could be easily evacuated. After 1947, these areas were occupied by Hindu refugees from the newly created Islamic West Pakistan and used for subsistance and commercial arable farming. Although homes on the floodplain have raised platforms, flooding has become a hazard to people's lives, homes and property, including crops. Increasing population pressure has changed the balance in the area. Even the normal, seasonal floods are now a hazard rather than a benefit, and extreme events could result in a disaster.

7.3 Increasing the hazard: floodplain encroachment

Floodplains provide areas of flat land with a ready water supply and are, therefore, ideal locations for urban development. In upland areas, river valleys provide a natural routeway for roads and railways. However, as development increases, the flooding hazard also increases. The flood risk varies among individual countries.

The United Kingdom

In England and Wales, less than 2 per cent of the population live in floodplain areas, compared to 10 per cent in the USA. Many areas in Britain

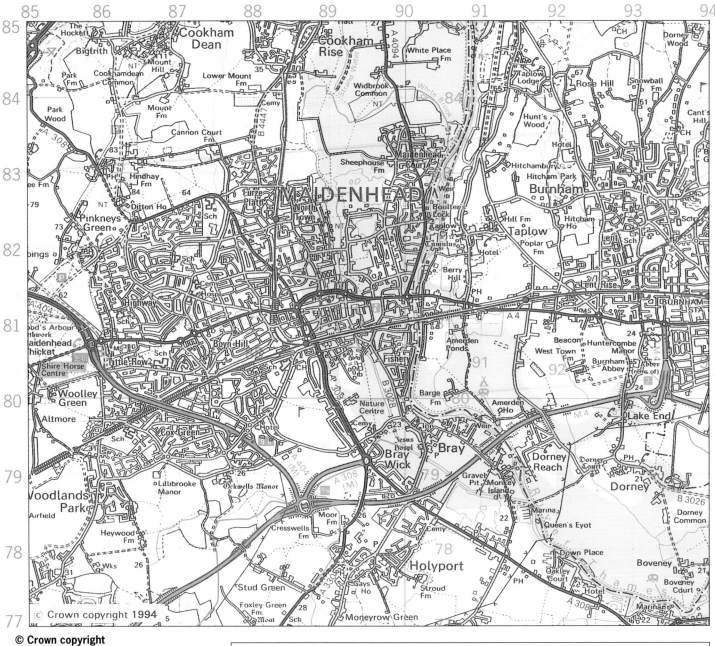

© Crown copyright 1994

© Crown copyright

_____ ? _____

3 Using Figure 7.5, draw an annotated sketch map to show the land uses liable to flooding in the Maidenhead area.

4 Use the map to explain why flooding at Maidenhead is more extensive to the west of the River Thames than to the east.

5 Draw a cross-section from Pinkneys Green (860820) to Burnham (920825). Label the floodplain area liable to flooding and the land uses.

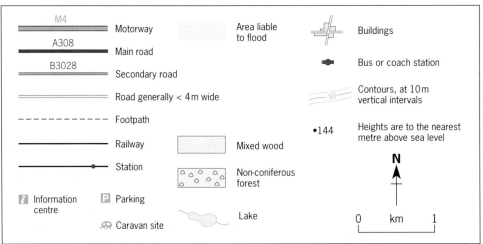

M4 — Motorway	Area liable to flood
A308 — Main road	Buildings
B3028 — Secondary road	Bus or coach station
— Road generally < 4m wide	Contours, at 10m vertical intervals
– – – – Footpath	•144 Heights are to the nearest metre above sea level
—— Railway	Mixed wood
—•— Station	Non-coniferous forest
ℹ Information centre	Lake
P Parking	N
🚐 Caravan site	0 km 1

Figure 7.5 1:50 000 Ordnance Survey extract of the Maidenhead, Reading and Windsor area

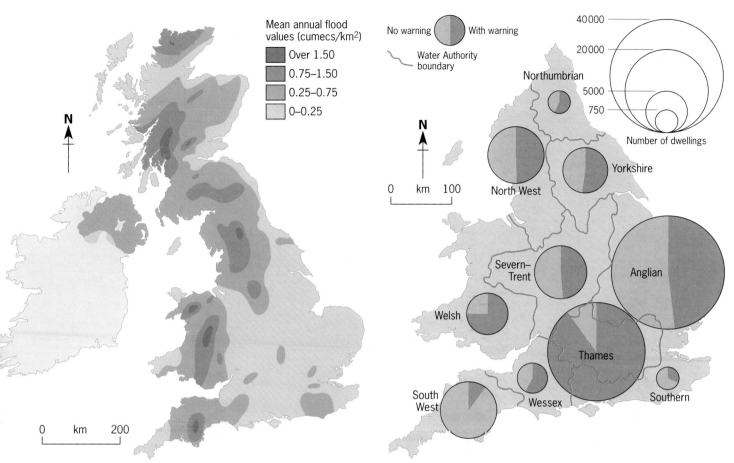

Figure 7.6 UK: best estimate of mean annual flood values (*Source*: Ward and Robinson, 1990)

Figure 7.7 England and Wales: dwellings within the 1-in-50-year to 1-in-100-year floodplain (*Source*: Penning-Rowsell and Handmer, 1988)

?

6a Using Figure 7.5, list the arguments for and against the further development of floodplain areas around Maidenhead, e.g. along the M4 motorway between the A308 and Lake End.
b Would you allow further development in the area? Explain your answer.

7 Study Figure 7.6. Describe and explain the pattern of mean annual flood values for the UK.

8 Using Figures 7.6 and 7.7, give reasons for the contradiction in the pattern of number of dwellings at serious risk from flooding and the flood runoff.

9 Describe and suggest reasons for the regional variations in the availability of flood warning systems shown on Figure 7.7.

which were affected by widespread flooding in 1947 have since seen further, substantial urbanisation. Much of the lower Thames floodplain has become developed, especially at Maidenhead (Fig. 7.5), and between Windsor and London, despite opposition from the NRA and its predecessors. In Nottingham, the floodplain of the River Trent has been developed behind embankments which are now considered to provide a lower standard of protection than when they were built.

It is this floodplain enroachment which is the crucial factor in determining the flood hazard from extreme events, since most urban land uses are not compatible with flooding (Figs 7.6 and 7.7).

7.4 Increasing the hazard: human-induced flooding

Within an individual drainage basin there are a number of flood-intensifying factors or conditions which are stable over time, e.g. rock type, slope, altitude and drainage network, which will make some river basins more likely to flood than others. However, there are also key *variable* flood-intensifying conditions, such as vegetation cover, fires, urban development, channel load and shape, soil **porosity** and land drainage. The variable conditions are subject to change as a result of human activity. If change results in increased quickflow processes, there is consequently an increase in the size and frequency of flooding (Fig. 7.1). Human activity can, therefore, result in flooding in areas which were not previously threatened, or increase the size and frequency of flood events.

113

10 Study Figures 7.8 and 7.9.

a Describe the pattern of river floods for these two examples.

b Explain the seasonal pattern of UK flooding.

11 Suggest why small drainage basins with a high degree of urban development respond with a distinctive seasonal pattern of flooding, e.g. Beverley Brook (Fig.7.9).

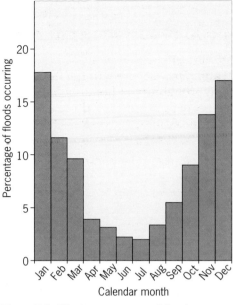

Figure 7.8 UK: the percentage of floods occurring in each calendar month (*Source*: Institute of Hydrology)

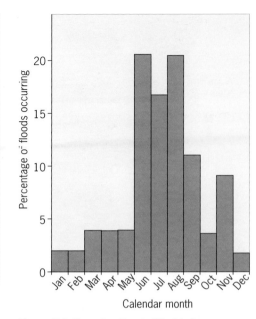

Figure 7.9 Beverley Brook, Wimbledon: percentage of floods occurring in each calendar month (*Source*: Institute of Hydrology)

Changing the seasonality of flooding

In addition to changing the location, magnitude and frequency of floods, human activity can also result in a change in the seasonality of flooding. Using data from 77 000 flood records held on a database at the Institute of Hydrology, hydrologists have shown that the north and west of the UK have a dominant flood season in the autumn, when soils become **saturated** earlier. Further to the south and east, the dominant flood season is winter, because lower rainfall than in the north and west of the country means that soil saturation is delayed.

Hydrologists have also shown that, in central and south-east England, there are a low number of catchments with a summer modal month of flooding (MMF). These catchments are small with a predominantly urban land use, e.g. Beverley Brook at Wimbledon, which has 81 per cent of its catchment area urbanised (Fig 7.9). The catchments respond to localised high-intensity summer rainfall. Urban development increases the likelihood and intensity of convection storms. As drainage basin size increases, the proportion under urban use is likely to decrease and the diversity of other land uses is likely to increase.

Dam failure

Other human-induced causes of flooding include the rare but dramatic effects of dam failure. In 1928, the St Francis Dam in California, USA, collapsed, killing 500 people. In 1963, the Vaiont Dam disaster in northern Italy was caused by a landslide into the reservoir behind the dam, destroying several villages and killing 2000 people. In 1972, 238 deaths occurred in Rapid City, South Dakota, where a dam failure resulted in catastrophic flooding.

7.5 Physical characteristics of floods

Every flood event is the result of a unique set of variables which result in eleven critical characteristics of floods (Table 7.1). These are important in evaluating flooding in terms of the magnitude, frequency and duration of the flood event. There are two key flood documents: the flood **hydrograph** (see Section 3.3) and the flood frequency or flood recurrence interval graph.

Table 7.1 Critical physical characteristics of floods (*After*: Cooke and Doornkamp, 1990)

1 How deep is the flood water? (Magnitude)
2 What area is flooded?
3 How long does the flooding last? (Duration)
4 What is the velocity of flow?
5 How often does the flooding occur? (Recurrence interval)
6 What is the lag time between the flooding over the banks and the peak flow?
7 When does flooding occur during the year? (Seasonality)
8 What is the peak flow? (Magnitude)
9 How fast does the river flow rise and fall? (Time lag and recession limb)
10 What is the sediment load?
11 How much water is stored on the floodplain? (Flood runoff)

The flood recurrence interval graph

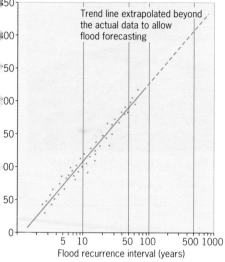

Figure 7.10 Flood recurrence intervals and discharge (*Source*: Clowes and Comfort, 1987)

Two vital questions that water managers ask are, 'How often can we expect a flood?' and 'How severe will the flood be?'. We can calculate the likelihood or statistical probability of flooding from flood frequency graphs (Fig. 7.10). We rank the records of a river's **discharge** over the longest time available, from the largest peak to the lowest discharge recorded. We then calculate the **recurrence interval** as follows:

$$\text{Recurrence interval (years)}\atop\text{of discharge } z \text{ m}^3/\text{s} = \frac{\text{number of peaks in the list} +1}{\text{ranked position of discharge } z}$$

If we plot the recurrence intervals, or return periods of a number of discharges, against discharge as a graph on semi-logarithmic graph paper, it is possible to extrapolate the data to give recurrence intervals for floods which have not been recorded. Using these graphs, we can make statements about the statistical probability of flood events. The longer and fuller the flood records, the more confidence we can place in this extrapolation. Thus, in Figure 7.10, a discharge of 110 m³/s or more is likely to recur on average every 10 years. Another way of putting this is to say that there is a 10 per cent chance of a discharge of 110 m³/s or more occurring in any given year.

You must remember that the statistical prediction of flood recurrence intervals is only an indication of probability based upon *past* records. As events happen, the statistical prediction will change. It is therefore important for hydrologists to update records as events happen. You should also remember that this information does not forecast a flood for a particular year.

River Tay, Scotland

The River Tay at Ballathie (Fig. 7.11) provides an illustration of how flood records used by water managers must be constantly updated. In the period 1989–93, events in Scotland have caused a reassessment of the River Tay's flood recurrence intervals.

In mid-January 1993, the River Tay and its tributaries were in flood with a record flow of 2200 m³/s. This surpassed the previous highest flow on the National River Flow Archive. Hundreds of properties in Perth were flooded and there was severe disruption of the transport network (Fig. 7.13). What surprised hydrologists was that only 3 years had passed since the last major flood on the River Tay, in February 1990 (maximum discharge of 1043 m³/s). Both the 1990 and 1993 floods were greater in magnitude than the previous highest record from 1952, and the expected flood return periods have consequently had to be reduced (Table 7.2).

The short time between such extreme events raises the question of climatic change or whether these events are just part of our 'normal' changeable climate. The River Tay example shows clearly the need for continued monitoring and research by institutions such as the Institute of Hydrology.

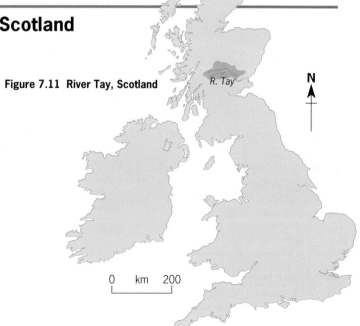

Figure 7.11 River Tay, Scotland

Table 7.2 Variation in flood quantities for the River Tay

Period of record (Ballathie gauging station)	Number of annual maxima	100-year flood (m³/s)	Return period for 2000 m³/s flood (y)
1952–89	38	1540	>1000
1952–93	42	1990	105

River Tay

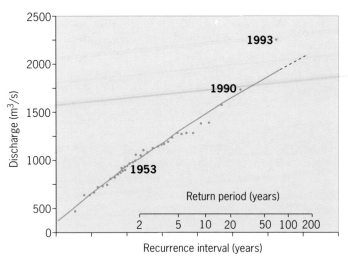

Figure 7.12 River Tay: revised flood recurrence intervals, 1953–93, and the extreme 1990 and 1993 events (*Source*: Institute of Hydrology, 1993)

Figure 7.13 Flood damage near Dalguise, Tayside, January 1993

?

12   Use Table 7.2 and Figure 7.13 to describe the significance of the 1990 and 1993 floods to flood forecasting on the River Tay.

7.6 Flood forecasting and prevention

Water managers use flood recurrence interval graphs as a key tool to assess the flood hazard and, thus, the nature and cost of possible flood prevention measures. Flood prevention is expensive. It is related to the degree of risk, and also to the land uses involved, i.e. the potential costs of the flood event in terms of the risk to life and property. The design flood is the flood recurrence that defence measures are designed to cope with. The Ministry of Agriculture, Fisheries and Food (MAFF) issue guidelines to organisations, such as the National Rivers Authority and local councils, on the degree of protection to be considered for different land uses (Table 7.3). MAFF recommends, for example, that a high-density urban area is protected against the 1-in-100-year flood event where possible, but that there should be a lesser degree of protection against the 1-in-10-year flood for arable farming with isolated properties. Grassland and low-productivity agricultural land with few properties should not protected from flooding.

?

13   Study Table 7.3.
a   Why do MAFF recommend that high-density urban areas and areas subjected to tidal flooding should have a higher degree of protection than rural areas?
b   Suggest what may happen to the degree of protection recommended for rural land uses if there was a shortage of food production in the future.

Table 7.3 Indicative standards of protection (*Source*: MAFF, © Crown copyright, 1994)

Current land use	Indicative standard of protection (return period in years)	
	Tidal	Non-tidal
High-density urban area containing significant amount of both residential and non-residential property.	200	100
Medium-density urban area. Lower density than above, may also include some agricultural land.	150	75
Low-density or rural communities with limited number of properties at risk. Highly-productive agricultural land.	50	25
Generally arable farming with isolated properties Medium-productivity agricultural land.	20	10
Predominantly extensive grass with very few properties at risk. Low-productivity agricultural land.	5	1

Forecasting the timing and location of flooding

Water managers also use hydrological data to calculate the likelihood of a river flooding at a particular time of year. This can be useful in the planning and allocation of resources for flood protection or in the timing of repairs and maintenance. They relate the flood recurrence interval and the discharges involved to the area likely to be flooded (Fig. 7.14). Smaller floods will only affect the area near to the river channel itself. However, the larger, rare events will flood a greater area of the floodplain.

The **floodway** is that area of the floodplain needed to transmit a selected flood. This area will experience a high degree of flooding and thus potential loss of life and property damage. The flood fringe is only affected by the rare, higher floods. Although the fringe is still within the flood hazard area, the degree of risk is lower. This difference can be used for land-use zoning of the floodplain.

Figure 7.14 Hazard zones on the floodplain (*Source:* Knapp et al, 1989)

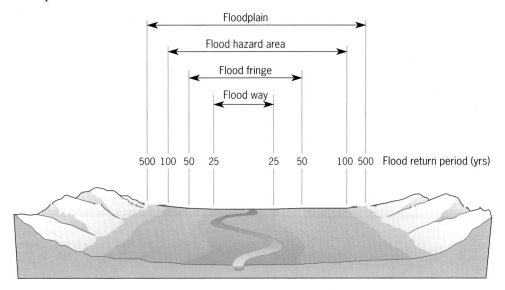

7.7 Flood perception and response

A key factor determining how a society responds to floods depends upon how the hazard is perceived. The frequency of flooding is a vital factor. Human behaviour is more likely to adjust to flood events if they are frequent occurrences. This adjustment can vary depending upon how people use the area of flooding, the nature of the flood event and how the flood is perceived. Cultural influences are important. Some groups of people are more likely to see floods as 'Acts of God' and as a result are more prepared to endure them and bear the loss. Other societies, especially the more technically advanced societies of western Europe and the USA, are more likely to wish to control floods.

Perceptions of floodplain occupants and water managers

Individual perceptions of the flood hazard vary from those directly affected by flooding (the floodplain occupants), to the water managers involved in decision-making (Fig. 7.15). The water manager's view is more objective, but still incomplete, because most decisions are made using past flow records and hydrological data. The floodplain occupant's perception of the hazard is based on direct experience. Research suggests that public expectations in the UK are rising, and even very occasional flooding is considered unacceptable. This is especially so when the floodwaters are polluted, e.g. with discharges from sewage treatment works and urban storm drains.

Figure 7.15 Information sets, perception and human responses to the flood hazard (*After*: Park, 1983)

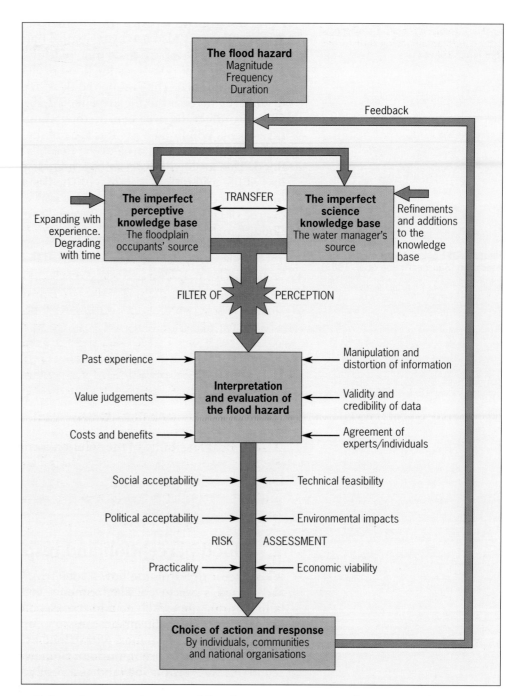

Although economic costs of floods are important in decision-making and influence the manager's actions and responses, the intangible damages caused to floodplain occupants are of the greatest importance. In Southgate, London, people were asked to rate the impacts of a flood event on a scale of 1 to 10 (Fig. 7.16). Economic losses received a lower score than the effects on mental health and physical well-being. At Tooting and Ruislip in London, people affected by flooding showed continuing anxiety or a feeling of helplessness several years after their flood experience. Other research links longer-term adverse health effects with major flood events. Following the 1986 floods in Bristol, researchers found a 50 per cent increase in the number of deaths from homes that had been flooded, with cancer forming a significant element in this increase. There was also an increase in doctor's surgery attendances and hospital admissions.

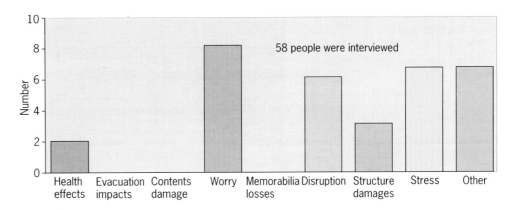

Figure 7.16 Southgate, Enfield, England: rating scale for the effects of flooding (*Source*: Penning-Rowsell and Handmer, 1988)

7.8 Evaluating responses to the flood hazard

Cost–benefit analysis
A common method of assessing the feasibility of a public flood control programme or hard engineering structure, such as a dam, is a **cost–benefit analysis**. Water managers compare the options available using the costs involved and the benefits to be gained by the alternative flood control measures. The costs are essentially the engineering costs and are relatively straightforward. The project benefits are more difficult to measure. They are the same as the expected flood damage in the 'without project' situation, minus the expected annual damage in the 'with project' situation.

Criteria for choosing flood management options (see Appendix A3)
1 The economic cost–benefit analysis.
2 Technical feasibility of the solution available.
3 The environmental impacts of the schemes.

7.9 Managing the flood

Water and land-use control measures
The aim of this method of flood abatement is to modify the cause of the flooding within the drainage basin itself. Land-use practices which minimise the quickflow processes in the catchment area aim to slow or reduce the delivery of water to the river channel. Soil conservation measures, especially afforestation, generally help to reduce runoff (see Section 4.2). However, there are problems in establishing forests in areas of grassland cover. In the initial stages, at least, there may be increased flooding, because preafforestation ditching is required to drain the land before planting.

Flood abatement involves widespread planning and it may not be possible to control land uses effectively. Whole-catchment planning is hampered by administrative and political difficulties, because many river catchments are international in scale or cross local authority boundaries. Two other limitations with this approach are that the flood risk is only likely to be reduced for smaller scale floods and that these measures are slow to take effect.

Non-structural control measures
This group of measures involves a variety of responses, with the overall aim of redistributing the losses. The responses vary: simply bearing the loss; public relief from family and friends, to government and international aid; or emergency action, where people and property are removed from the flood hazard area. Emergency action relies on an adequate flood warning system if it is to be effective. The effectiveness of emergency action improves with increased warning time.

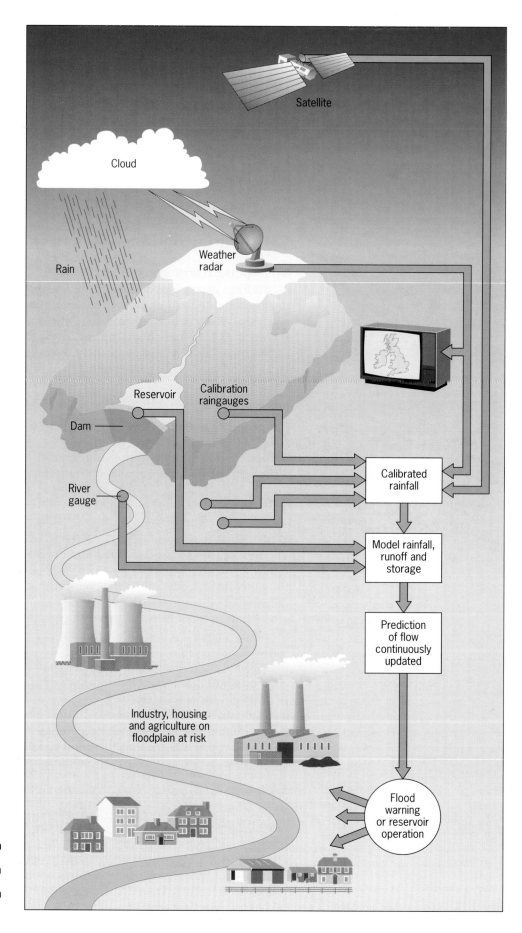

Figure 7.17 The structure of a flood forecasting system. Continued research is taking place to try to provide more realistic models of how drainage basins respond to rainfall, runoff and storage in order to increase the accuracy of flood warnings and the length of time between the warning and the flood event. (*Source*: National Environment Research Council, 1994)

Read Figure 7.18.

14 In which ways did European governments and authorities act to reduce injury and loss of life?

15 State two reasons why people did not have flood insurance. Give an example in each case, and explain why there was no insurance cover.

16 Explain why it was necessary for European governments and the European Commission to release emergency aid.

17 Describe the causes of economic losses for businesses in the flooded area.

18 List the arguments for and against insurance and government aid as a flood hazard response.

Insurance

Flood insurance is another possible response, where a premium is paid over time to spread the costs. An issue with flood insurance as a stategy is that it may encourage people to live on the floodplain rather than developing land elsewhere. In areas of above-average chance of flooding, the financial risk for insurance companies is too high and flood insurance may not be available. Government and international action is likely to be needed in such circumstances, e.g. in northern Europe during December 1993 and January 1994 (Fig. 7.18).

Zoning

Floodplain zoning involves dividing the floodplain into areas (Fig. 7.14) which experience different degrees of flood risk. It also involves regulating land use to take account of the nature of the flood hazard. In the highest-risk areas, development is excluded, except for land uses which have a low damage potential. Land uses which retain the floodplain as a natural floodwater storage area and wetland also help to reduce the flood risk downstream. In urban areas, recreational uses allow the valuable provision of open space which maintains wetland habitats but allows use by residents for most of the time. An example of such a development is the Watermead Country Park to the north of Leicester city centre. This retains wetland open space on the floodplain of the River Soar.

States prepare to pick up bill for flood chaos

Businesses face ruin and thousands are homeless, write **Michael Bond** and **Lucy Walker**

GOVERNMENTS across northern Europe are preparing to pay out millions of dollars in compensation following the devastation of thousands of homes and businesses in the worst flooding northern Europe has seen for more than 50 years.

The deluge, in which at least 20 people died, has been doubly hard for the thousands of families left homeless at Christmas as almost none are insured.

It will be weeks before the true extent of the devastation is known as businesses in France, Germany, Belgium and the Netherlands begin to assess the damage.

As a result, governments are stepping in to fund clean-up costs after disaster zones were declared across the four countries.

In the Netherlands, where 12 000 people were evacuated from their homes in the province of Limburg over Christmas weekend, the government offered an initial aid package of 20m guilders.

Dutch insurers have refused flood cover ever since thousands died in the worst floods in living memory when the sea engulfed Zeeland in 1953. 'With half the country below sea level, insurers maintain that it is too expensive to insure against flooding,' said Gert Kloosterboer, spokesman for the Dutch insurers' association, VVV.

Ironically, VVV proposed to issue policies for freshwater damage, but has not yet made cover available.

The European Commission released emergency aid worth $565 000 for the four worst-hit countries and is expected to approve top-up aid soon following pleas for assistance from member state governments.

Ulrich Bockrath, spokesman for Colonia Versicherung, a German insurer, said: 'We introduced insurance against natural disasters but the number of policies is small. Most people are not insured against flood damage.'

This is a severe blow for small businesses now facing bankruptcy as the toll of cleaning up adds to lost sales.

In Belgium, Sun Alliance is the only insurer to offer flood cover, but is notoriously choosy in its policies. The government has opened a disaster fund to compensate families, farmers and businesses after damage was estimated to have exceeded well over Bfr50m ($1.4m) — the government minimum for declaring a disaster area.

Figure 7.18 Flood damage, northern Europe, 1994 (*Source: The European*, 31 December 1993)

In the outer areas of the floodplain which are at a reduced risk of flooding there would be regulations to minimise flood problems, e.g. flood-proofing of buildings, flood insurance and contingency planning (Fig. 7.19).

Floodplain zoning is a successful management technique because it is cheap and effective. Unfortunately it is not realistic for existing urban areas. Relocation of structures would be effective, but might be resisted by owners who lose the advantages of a floodplain location. Also, the cost is prohibitive because people will need compensation payments as well as the expense of re-building. Thus, in reality zoning is only appropriate for new developments.

Structural control measures

Structural measures aim to control the flood and prevent floodwaters from reaching developed or sensitive areas. These hard engineering solutions can centre on the flood site or on upstream storage of floodwaters. They can be divided into four main groups:

1 Storage of floodwaters in reservoirs behind dams or flood storage basins. Dams provide the advantage of multi-purpose water uses, e.g. a public water supply, irrigation potential, HEP and recreational uses. There are, however, some serious environmental implications (see Sections 4.5, 5.4 and 6.5). Flood relief channels and flood storage basins are used as temporary stores for excessive flows.

Figure 7.19 Floodplain zoning management approach as applied in New Zealand (*Source*: Eriksen, 1986)

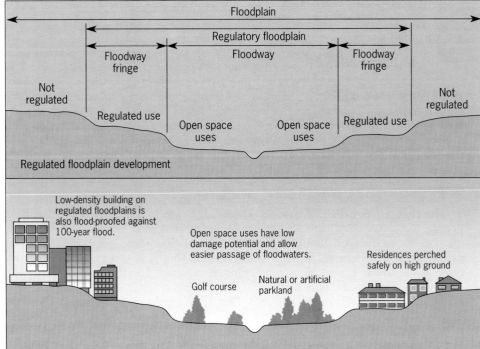

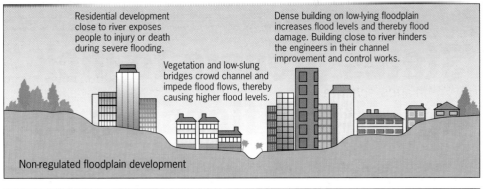

19 Using Figure 7.19, define:
a the floodway,
b the floodway fringe,
c the regulatory floodplain.

20 Explain how the development of the non-regulated floodplain increases the flood hazard.

21 Describe how floodplain land use is regulated.

22 List the advantages and disadvantages of this method of flood control for flood managers and urban land users.

2 Changing the channel by cutting a new channel for the excess water while leaving the original channel for the 'normal' flow, or by modifying the channel by realigning, resectioning or smoothing it (see Section 6.2).
3 Building defences such as floodbanks or heightened **levées** along the channel (Figs 7.25 and 7.26).
4 Flood-proofing the area at risk of flooding, e.g. constructing buildings on stilts, sealing walls or having flood control gates on underground structures.

Flood defences in Northampton, England

Northampton is situated on the River Nene. The town suffered serious flooding in 1937, 1939 and 1947. The New Towns Act, 1965, designated Northampton as a growth area, with a planned population increase from 30 000 to 230 000 by 1981. This urban expansion, with much new development on the floodplains of the Nene and its tributaries, meant that flood defences in the town were unlikely to be adequate. The increased flood risk results from two factors. First, the new development would cover a larger area with impermeable surfaces. Secondly, there would be a loss of storage water capacity on the floodplains as the area was developed. Three main problem areas were identified (Fig. 7.20).

The Washlands scheme

The Washlands storage basin on the River Nene floodplain covers 103 ha within curved earth embankments, varying in height from 2 m to 5 m. The scheme was completed in 1980 at a cost of nearly £3.5 million (Fig. 7.21). In their calculations, water managers had to consider three factors:
1 The water generated by extra runoff from the new urban development (1.1 million cubic metres).
2 A high-intensity storm over the area (Table 7.4) (up to 0.96 million cubic metres).
3 The loss of storage capacity of floodwaters on the floodplain itself after development (1.29 million cubic metres).
The storage capacity of the Washlands scheme needed to be sufficient to cope with a combination of factor 3 with either factor 1 or 2, i.e. a maximum capacity of 2.39 million cubic metres of water. The Washlands actual storage capacity is 2.34 million cubic metres. However, this is adequate because the channel has storage space and the sluices can release water from the reservoir.

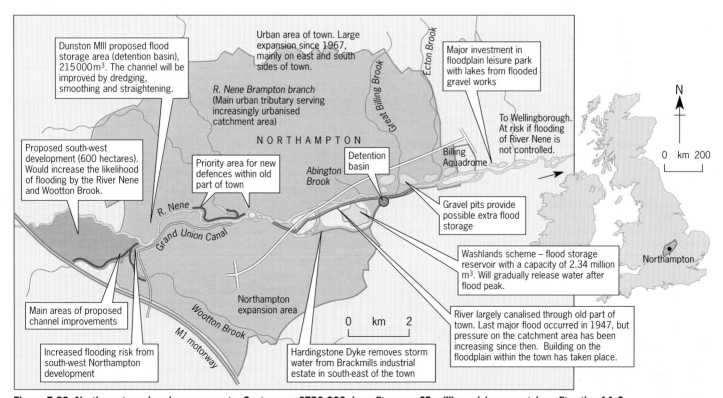

Figure 7.20 Northampton: river improvements. Costs were £750 000, benefits were £5 million, giving a cost–benefit ratio of 1:6

Northampton

Figure 7.21 Aerial view of the Washlands

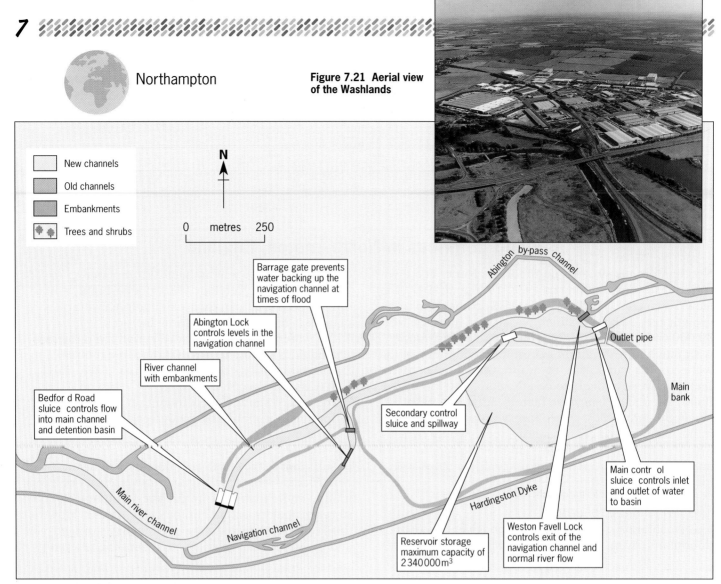

New channels

Old channels

Embankments

Trees and shrubs

N

0   metres   250

Barrage gate prevents water backing up the navigation channel at times of flood

Abington Lock controls levels in the navigation channel

River channel with embankments

Bedford Road sluice controls flow into main channel and detention basin

Main river channel

Navigation channel

Abington by-pass channel

Outlet pipe

Main bank

Secondary control sluice and spillway

Main control sluice controls inlet and outlet of water to basin

Hardingston Dyke

Reservoir storage maximum capacity of 2 340 000 m³

Weston Favell Lock controls exit of the navigation channel and normal river flow

Figure 7.22 Northampton Washlands scheme. Water enters the Washlands through the new Bedford Road Sluice. Under non-flood conditions, the water flows west to east along a new embanked channel to leave via the outlet control at Weston Favell Lock. At times of flood, the Bedford Road Sluice diverts water into the Washlands and the water is released slowly by the main control sluice. If the storage volume of the reservoir is effective, the outflow can be reduced to 82.5 m³/s instead of the 170 m³/s of the 1-in-50-year flood. The main sluice and emergency spillway could discharge 620 m³/s in an emergency. Navigation rights are maintained through the Washlands scheme.

Table 7.4 Storage demand due to an intense urban storm

Storm duration (hours)	Storage demand pre-development (million m³)	Storage demand post-development (million m³)	Increase in storage demand (million m³)
4	0.82	1.38	0.56
8	0.87	1.54	0.67
12	0.81	1.55	0.74
15	0.73	1.52	0.79
20	0.56	1.41	0.85
24	0.40	1.29	0.89
30	0.14	1.08	0.94
33	0	0.96	0.96
34	0	0.92	0.92

?

23 Draw an annotated sketch map to show the flood prevention measures employed by Anglian Water (now NRA Anglian region).

24 Using Figure 7.22, describe how the Washlands scheme works.

25a Draw a graph to illustrate the information in Table 7.4. Plot storm duration on the *x* axis and storage demand on the *y* axis. Draw two lines: one to show storage demand *before* the development and one to show storage demand *after* the development.
b Shade the area between the two lines and label it, 'Increase in storage demand after development'.
c Give your graph a key and annotate it with details of why there was an increase in storage demand.
26 Explain how the water managers calculated the size requirements for the Washlands.

27a How was the scheme paid for?
b Do you consider that this scheme is an appropriate way to use public money? Explain your answer.

The Maidenhead, Windsor and Eton flood alleviation scheme, England

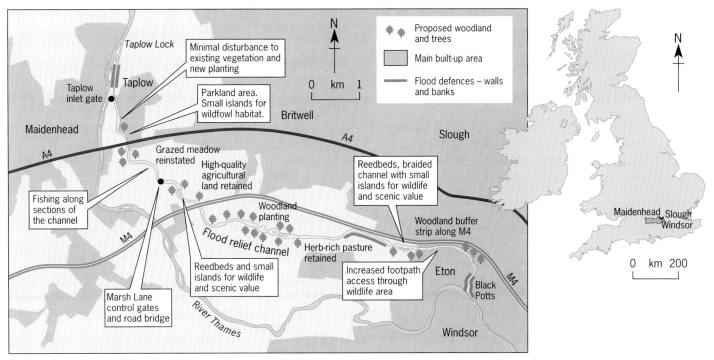

Figure 7.23 The flood alleviation scheme

The towns of Maidenhead, Eton and Windsor, and nearby villages (Fig. 7.23) have a long history of flooding by the River Thames. Major flooding occurred in 1894, 1947, 1979 and 1990. The 1947 flood was particularly severe, widespread and lasted for many weeks. A repeat of a flood of this scale today would affect more than 5500 properties and severely disrupt services and communications. Extreme conditions would close the M4 motorway.

To reduce the flood risk, Thames Water considered 492 combinations of options, some of which included widening the River Thames. The preferred option was an 11.8 km flood relief channel (Fig. 7.23). Planning proposals were submitted in January 1991 and approval was given in November 1994, following a public inquiry in 1992.

The flood relief channel scheme

The flood relief channel leaves the Thames upstream of Taplow Lock, Maidenhead, and rejoins it downstream of Black Potts Viaduct, Windsor. It will look like a natural river. Water levels will be maintained by six low weirs. The scheme is designed to contain flows of 515 m^3/s, i.e. the 1-in-65-year flood. At flows over 515 m^3/s, there is the risk of flooding from the Thames, but its magnitude would be much reduced by the scheme. There is no risk of

flooding from the flood relief channel.

The flood relief channel has been designed with wider aims than simply flood relief. The scheme also aims to enhance the local environment and provide increased amenity for residents, e.g. with public-access common land, new woodland, club fishing, cycleways and footpaths. In some areas, low flood banks and walls are required to ensure flood protection.

The construction costs of the scheme are estimated at £45 million. The costs of flooding over the 65-year life of the scheme lie between £41 million and £69 million. These flooding costs, which would not be incurred if the scheme were built, become the benefits in the cost–benefit ratio. The average cost–benefit ratio has been calculated at 1:1.2.

28 Using Figure 7.23, describe the route of the flood relief channel.

29 How has the scheme been designed to enhance the area's environmental and amenity value?

30 Suggest why flood defences (walls and embankments) are needed in some locations.

The Mississippi floods, USA, July 1993

Flood damage

In July 1993, the Mississippi floodplain was affected by a catastrophic flood which was over the 1-in-100-year flood event (Fig. 7.24). Towns and seven million hectares of farmland were flooded, communications disrupted and the River Mississippi closed to shipping for two months upstream of St Louis.

The timing and location (Fig. 7.24) of this flood were unusual. Normally, flood flows occur in spring and in the lower course of the river south of Cairo, Illinois. Unusual weather conditions caused a change in this pattern and resulted in an estimated US$10 billion worth of damages. Although 50 lives were lost, the death toll was prevented from being higher by good warning systems.

Flood defences

Flood defences along the Mississippi are the responsibility of the US Army Corps of Engineers. Defences have centred upon building levées with dams, reservoirs and barrages, i.e. hard engineering solutions. The 1993 flood has started a debate about these solutions, even though the defences were not built to cope with such a catastrophic flood.

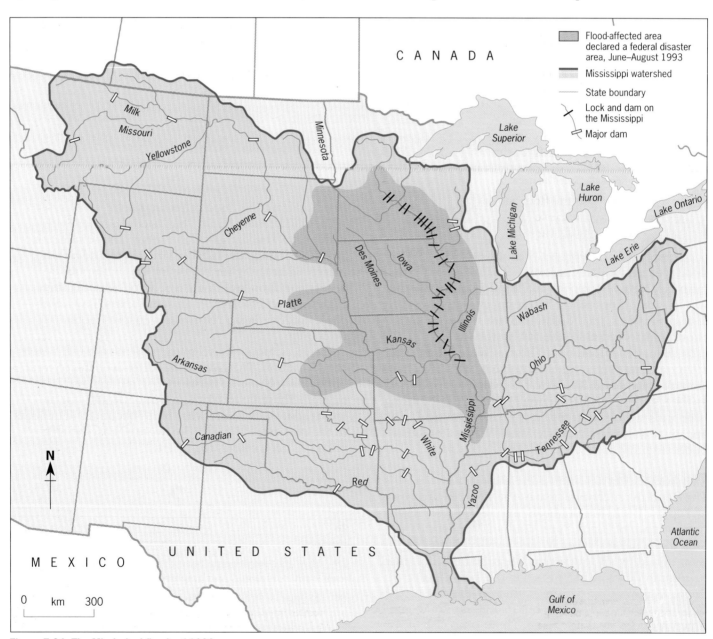

Figure 7.24 The Mississippi floods of 1993

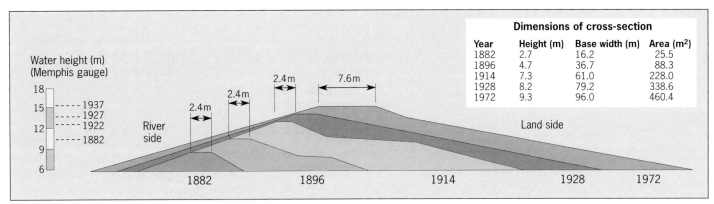

Dimensions of cross-section			
Year	Height (m)	Base width (m)	Area (m²)
1882	2.7	16.2	25.5
1896	4.7	36.7	88.3
1914	7.3	61.0	228.0
1928	8.2	79.2	338.6
1972	9.3	96.0	460.4

7.25 How the Mississippi levées have grown, 1882–1972 (*Source: The Independent*, 27 July 1993)

Water managers hoped that the levée defences would confine the river channel into artificial 'canyons'. Some are set back from the river to provide a larger storage capacity. The policy of levée-building has undoubtedly been effective up until 1993, but there are three main problems with this strategy:

1 With each successive flood, the levées grow higher and wider (Fig. 7.25), increasing the land required and the costs involved.
2 The river flow confined by the levées rises above the level of the surrounding floodplain at times of flood flows. This increases the damage by floods if the levées are breached.
3 The levées increase the flood peaks because water is channelled between the levées and there are higher flow velocities. The storage capacity of the natural floodplain is lost.

Future plans

The debate taking place in the USA is similar to that following the 1994 floods in the UK. Should rivers be allowed to flood and floodplain wetland environments be maintained as natural water storage areas, or should the levées be rebuilt and reinforced to continue the hard engineering flood protection policy? Hard engineering solutions have been relatively successful along the Mississippi and have allowed major urban and agricultural development to occur along the river. Nevertheless, the 1993 flood illustrates the effects of a flood above the design level of the hard engineering structure, with the associated human misery and economic cost.

?

31a Using Figure 7.25, describe how the levées along the Mississippi have grown.
b What have been the advantages of the levées?

32a List the arguments for and against rebuilding and reinforcing the Mississippi levées.
b Would you advise the US government to rebuild the levées? Justify your answer.

Figure 7.26 Many levées were reinforced by local people building them higher as the floodwaters rose

Choosing a method of flood control

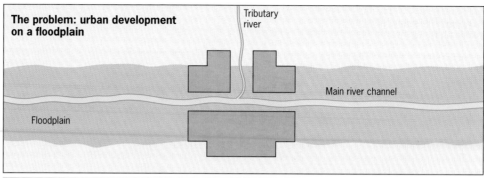

Figure 7.27 The main methods of flood control in the UK (*After:* Cooke and Dornkamp, 1990)

The problem: urban development on a floodplain

Tributary river

Main river channel

Floodplain

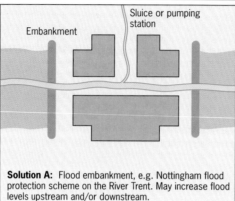

Solution A: Flood embankment, e.g. Nottingham flood protection scheme on the River Trent. May increase flood levels upstream and/or downstream.

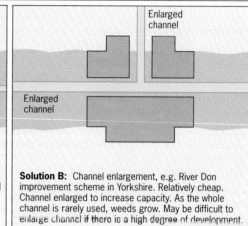

Solution B: Channel enlargement, e.g. River Don improvement scheme in Yorkshire. Relatively cheap. Channel enlarged to increase capacity. As the whole channel is rarely used, weeds grow. May be difficult to enlarge channel if there is a high degree of development.

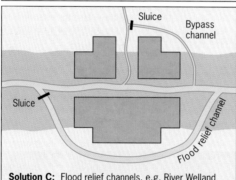

Solution C: Flood relief channels, e.g. River Welland improvement scheme which bypasses Spalding. Excess flood waters are diverted from the urban area. Very expensive.

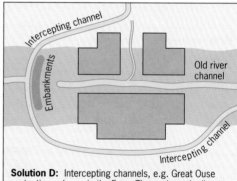

Solution D: Intercepting channels, e.g. Great Ouse protection scheme in the Fens. These channels divert part of the flow from the urban area but retain some river flow. May have commercial impacts if the economic activity is based on river traffic.

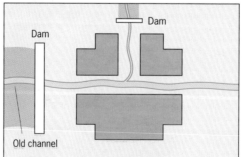

Solution E: Flood storage. Dams and reservoirs may have multiple uses, e.g. for water supply and recreation as with the Bala Lake scheme. Expensive to implement, may be loss of homes and high-quality land behind the dam. Other important environmental impacts.

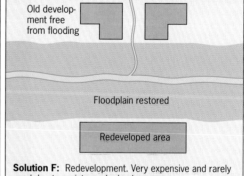

Solution F: Redevelopment. Very expensive and rarely used due to resistance by land owners.

?

33 Study Figure 7.27. Explain how each method of flood control works. Evaluate each method.

34a Which scheme would you choose for:
• a large urban area with a high amount of industrial and residential development close to the river channel?
• a small market town with little industrial development and low-density housing along the floodplain?
b Justify your choice in each case.
c What other information would be helpful in making your choice?

35 For each of the flood hazard adjustments in Table 7.5, draw up a matrix to evaluate their appropriateness to:
a a Thames floodplain area in Greater London;
b an agricultural area on the floodplain of the Ganges in India.

Table 7.5 Flood management solutions with their advantages and disadvantages

Method	Advantages	Disadvantages
A Water and land-use control measures	Promote soil and water conservation. Reduce flood levels without affecting river ecosystems. Floodplain development could continue.	May be very expensive. Only affect minor floods. Needs co-operation of many groups and organisations. Drainage basins may be international in scale – need international planning. Slow to take effect.
B Non-structural control measures		
Bearing the loss	Cheap. Allows floodplain development.	Individuals bear the burden of flooding. Applicability depends upon society's perception of the flood hazard.
Public relief/emergency action	Costs only involved if there is a flood event.	Costs may be very high if there is a catastrophic flood or large numbers of people involved.
Flood warnings	Relatively cheap. Prevent loss of life. Reduce damages if warning time is insufficient. Floodplain can continue in use.	Community response is uncertain. Require accurate and continuous information. Damage potential to property remains high. Effectiveness may diminish over time.
Floodplain zoning	Low cost for undeveloped areas of floodplain. Prevents/reduces future damage effectively. Some land uses require floodplain location/large water supply.	Existing floodplain damages are not reduced. May reduce development in the area – located elsewhere.
Flood insurance	Helps promote community involvement. Inexpensive to policy holders. Raises an awareness of the flood hazard. May encourage floodplain development.	Flood damages are not reduced. May not be available in high-risk areas. Insurance cover may be limited in cost/property.
C Structural measures		
Storage of floodwaters, e.g. dams, basins and relief channels	Reduce flood losses. Protect property already in the risk area. Dams etc. may be multi-purpose. Increase development in the area. Some harmful environmental impacts. Flood may be worse if defences fail.	High cost to build and maintain. Proper site needs to be available. Have a design level – may encourage a false sense of security.
Change the channel	Relatively cheap. Does not affect existing land uses. Suitable site not required. Channel enlargement requires room – not suitable for highly-developed areas.	Needs to be maintained. Harmful environmental impacts to channel and bank ecosystems.
Flood proofing	Reduces damages. Can remain at site. Lowers flood insurance costs.	Damage is still likely/possible. Only applicable to certain types of structures. May be costly with a false sense of security.

Summary

- The floodplain acts as a temporary store for runoff at times of higher streamflow.
- The floodplain and river channel are closely linked parts of the same fluvial system.
- Flooding is a natural event and can be beneficial, e.g. it renews soil fertility, washes away any salt build-up from the floodplain.
- Human activity, such as changing agricultural practices and urban development, can cause a change in the location, magnitude and frequency of flooding. The flood event can consequently become a disaster.
- Water managers forecast flood events using past hydrological data and flood characteristics, such as the hydrograph and recurrence interval graph. Information must be continually updated.
- A range of flood control and management strategies are now used.

8 Water supply and the control of groundwater

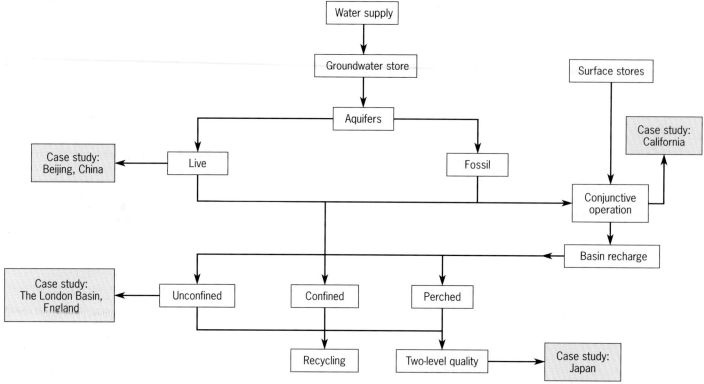

8.1 Introduction

Water is a fundamental resource for all forms of life – without it, we die. Throughout the world, people's demand for water is increasing and is pressing against the limits of supply. An aim of every government is to achieve a reliable water supply which is sufficient in both volume and quality. For example, in the 1994 peace negotiations between Israel and the Palestinian communities, access to water resources was an important item on the agenda (Fig. 8.2). Water conservation, i.e. the more efficient storage and usage of water, is a high-profile issue for environmental, economic and political reasons (Fig. 8.1).

Water stores

Water resource managers organise supply by drawing upon surface water stores – rivers, lakes, reservoirs – and subsurface stores. The balance between the two stores varies from one environment to another, but all management systems integrate both sources. In its broadest sense, 'groundwater' refers to all water below the ground surface. However, hydrologists divide this subsurface water into four zones (Fig. 8.3). In this chapter we shall concentrate on the zone below the **water table**. Water managers call this zone the **groundwater store**. First, we shall illustrate the growing importance of the groundwater store in water supply. In later sections we shall examine how the groundwater store works, and how it is both managed and mismanaged as a water resource.

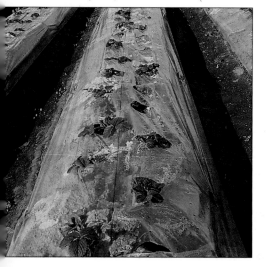

Figure 8.1 Florida has a water shortage. Irrigation water to this huge vegetable field is expensive and is metered. Only the minimum amount required by the plants is fed into the shallow channels. Plastic covers are used to reduce water loss by evaporation

Peace pact promises unity in the desert

Fred Pearce

WATER as well as land is at the heart of this week's Middle East agreements. The first fruits of the deals announced in Washington DC are expected to include a large dam on the River Yarmuk, a tributary of the River Jordan, to relieve a worsening water crisis in Jordan.

The first, half-completed, Yarmuk dam was destroyed by Israeli soldiers in 1967, and Israel said it would do the same to any replacement. The agreement between Israel and Jordan, which sets out an agenda for future negotiations, lifts that threat, allowing talks to begin with the World Bank and the US government to finance construction of the Wahda, or Unity, dam.

According to Ishan Moustafa of the Open University, Ramallah, a leading Palestinian expert on the region's water conflicts, 'the dam could provide Jordan with 80 million cubic metres of water a year', enough to supply the capital Amman.

This week's agreements also open the way for a resolution of wider water conflicts, especially over apportioning water from the River Jordan. Most of the Jordan's flow was redirected by Israel in 1964, when it linked the sea of Galilee to its water grid, the National Water Carrier.

According to Moustafa, the basis for negotiations on the river is likely to be the 'Johnson plan', drawn up by a US envoy, Edward Johnson, in 1955. This plan, which was never implemented, allocated almost two-fifths of the water in the rivers Jordan and Yarmuk to Israel, half to Jordan and the rest to Syria and Lebanon.

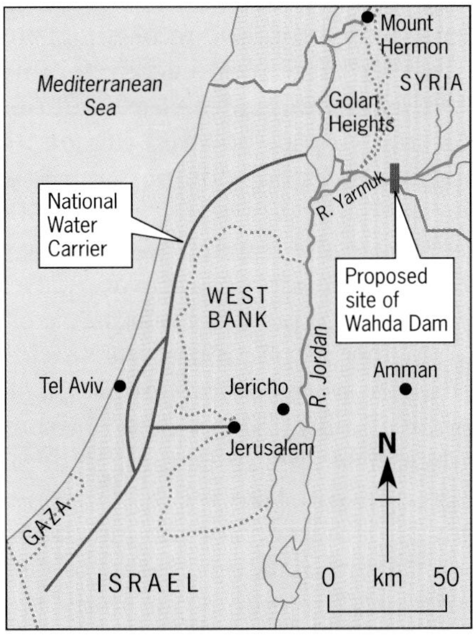

The drawback to the plan is that it makes no special provision for Palestinians. 'In talks up to now, Israel has said that Jordan has taken the Palestinians' share,' says Moustafa. 'But we say our share must come from Israel.'

British water experts who are advising negotiators in the Middle East talks say Israel is unlikely to agree to such a plan before it reaches agreement with Syria to secure rights to the River Jordan's water after its forces withdraw from the Golan Heights. These hills contain the springs around Mount Hermon, the principal source of the Jordan. A Syrian threat to divert these waters is often cited as a prime reason for the 1967 war between Israel and its neighbours.

According to Hillel Shuval of the Hebrew University of Jerusalem, Israel regards Syria and Lebanon as having 'considerable excess water resources' and that they have the 'main obligation to help the Palestinians and Jordanians'.

For the Palestinians, the more immediate need is to secure rights to underground water beneath the West Bank and Gaza Strip. Since 1967, Israel has prevented Palestinians sinking new wells in these occupied territories. Moustafa says that talks on apportioning the West Bank's water must wait until there is independent data on how much is available. 'We don't trust the Israeli data,' he says.

According to Ibrahim Matar, a Palestinian water engineer based in Jerusalem, his people receive less than 20 per cent of the water extracted from the West Bank aquifer. He says that water for Jericho, which will be one of the first Palestinian areas to be given some autonomy, has become saline because of overabstraction through new boreholes dug by Israelis.

In the Gaza Strip, so much underground water has been taken that seawater is flowing into the aquifer. Last year, the UN Development Programme reported that: 'Gaza's aquifer is being severely overexploited and salinated to the extent that wells are going out of operation and water is becoming unpalatable.'

Figure 8.2 Access to water in the Middle East (*Source*: Pearce, 1993)

?

1a Using the headings 'store', 'inputs' and 'outputs', draw systems diagrams for the two environments in Figures 8.1 and 8.2.

b Use your diagrams to compare the differences between these environments.

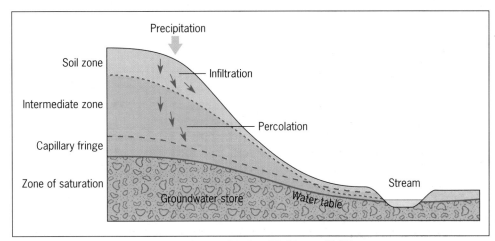

Figure 8.3 Subsurface water zones (*Source*: Ward and Robinson, 1990)

?

2 In south-east England groundwater provides 70 per cent of the water supply. In Wales and Scotland the figure drops to 10 per cent. With the help of your atlas, suggest reasons for this contrast. (Compare rainfall, temperature, land use, relief and population distribution maps.)

8.2 The global store

Groundwater is the earth's largest accessible store of fresh water (Fig. 1.1), accounting for over 90 per cent of the total. (The volume locked up as ice is excluded because it is not regarded as being readily accessible.) One-half of this store lies within 800 m of the ground surface and is, therefore, relatively accessible for human and **ecosystem** use. It is difficult for us to grasp the scale of this groundwater store, but one way is to visualise the whole of the world's land surface covered to a depth of 60 m by water.

Groundwater is one component of the global **hydrological cycle** (Fig. 1.4). On average, a drop of water spends 300 years in the groundwater store, and so may reduce the impacts of climatic change. For instance, today's arid regions may contain groundwater reserves from wetter periods. Under the Sahara there are reserves which are estimated at 500 000 km^3 of water.

A surprising proportion of the world's human population depends on groundwater stores. For example, in south-east England, which has a moist, temperate climate, 70 per cent of urban water supplies are drawn from groundwater stores. In Denmark the proportion reaches 90 per cent.

The groundwater store is a component of the **drainage basin** system (see Chapter 2). However, for the purposes of this chapter, we shall regard it as an open system in its own right. It has inputs, a main store, several pathways and outputs. Throughout our study, we should keep the key questions of Figure 8.4 in mind.

Figure 8.4 Groundwater: key questions we should ask

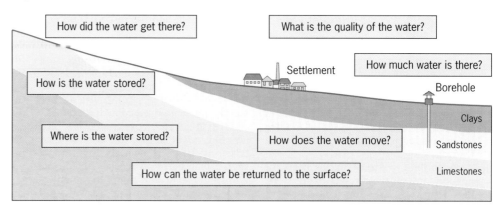

How did the water get there?
What is the quality of the water?
Settlement
How much water is there?
How is the water stored?
Borehole
Clays
Where is the water stored?
How does the water move?
Sandstones
How can the water be returned to the surface?
Limestones

California: an example of a conjunctive operation strategy

The State Water Plan

The issue facing California's water resource managers is straightforward but immense. Seventy-five per cent of the population live in those regions with only 25 per cent of the rainfall (Fig. 8.5). The combination of Californian life-style (Fig 8.6) and intensive irrigated agriculture produces very thirsty consumers. Water managers have integrated surface and groundwater stores in their State Water Plan. The Plan is based upon massive inter-basin surface water transfers (Fig. 8.7), and maximum use of the groundwater capacity. It is an example of a **conjunctive operation strategy**.

Groundwater stores

California's groundwater potential looks impressive. Forty per cent of the area consists of basins containing water-bearing strata. There are 450 water basins which give a total store of 1.6 million cubic hectometres (hm^3) (one hectometre = one hectare covered by a one-metre depth of water). However, only 11 per cent of this water is classified as 'usable'. The rest is either inaccessible or too saline.

About 40 per cent of California's water supply comes from the groundwater sources and, consequently, many of the usable water basins are being overdrawn. It is crucial to understand that only 34 per cent of the usage is being replenished by natural and deliberate recharge. A further 50 per cent is made up by **percolation** losses from canals and infiltration of excess irrigation water. (You should note that this 'wasted' water is therefore not actually lost, but re-enters the groundwater store.) In consequence, during the 1980s, overdraft of the groundwater stores was providing 16 per cent of the water supply.

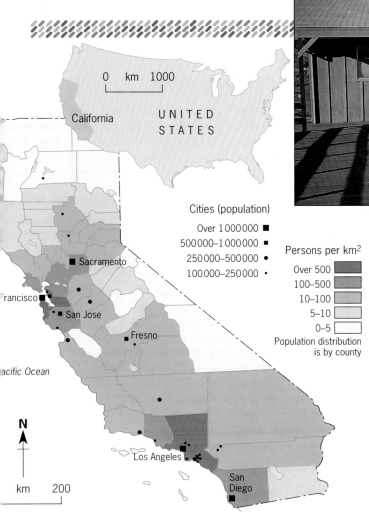

Figure 8.5 California: population (*Source*: Collins–Longman Atlas, 1989)

Cities (population)
- Over 1 000 000 ■
- 500 000–1 000 000 ■
- 250 000–500 000 ●
- 100 000–250 000 ·

Persons per km²
- Over 500
- 100–500
- 10–100
- 5–10
- 0–5

Population distribution is by county

Figure 8.6 The Californian life-style: typical water consumption

?

3 Using Figure 8.8, construct a systems diagram of the conjunctive operation technique. Label the inputs, stores, throughputs and output.

Deliberate recharge

California is making increasing use of the deliberate recharge technique (Fig 8.8). This is a good example of the conjunctive operation strategy at work and emphasises that hydrology functions as an integrated system. Surface water is transferred to spare capacity in the groundwater store. Approximately 65 000 hm³ are available in California's water basins. By 1990, more than 20 such replenishment schemes were in operation.

There are advantages of using groundwater storage space:

- There is less impact on the environment and the costs of surface **dams** and reservoirs are reduced.
- **Evaporation** losses are reduced.
- Pollution risks are reduced.
- Water is maintained at low and constant temperatures.

Alternatively, we could keep the groundwater stores as emergency stores for use during periods of drought. They would be recharged in unusually wet years.

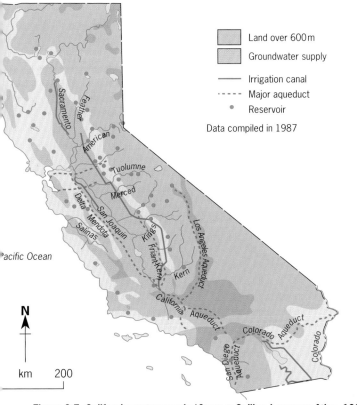

Land over 600 m
Groundwater supply

— Irrigation canal
---- Major aqueduct
· Reservoir

Data compiled in 1987

Figure 8.7 California: water supply (*Source*: Collins–Longman Atlas, 1989)

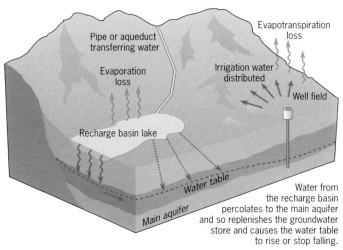

Figure 8.8 The recharge basin technique

133

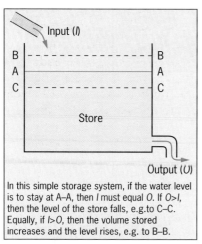

In this simple storage system, if the water level is to stay at A–A, then *I* must equal *O*. If *O>I*, then the level of the store falls, e.g. to C–C. Equally, if *I>O*, then the volume stored increases and the level rises, e.g. to B–B.

Figure 8.9 A simple storage system

8.3 Understanding the groundwater store

Wherever and whenever a groundwater reservoir is used, the most important message should always be, 'You can't take out more than is put in'. The groundwater store works like any other reservoir (Fig. 8.9). In economic terms, if demand continues to exceed supply, the reserve will shrink.

Aquifers and aquitards

Geological formations vary in their water-holding capability. Rock formations or layers of unconsolidated deposits which hold substantial volumes of water are known as **aquifers**, i.e. water bearing materials. They are permeable and can transmit and store water effectively. Rock formations which are less permeable and transmit water more slowly are known as **aquitards** (Figs 8.10 and 8.11). Notice from Figures 8.10 and 8.11 that these terms are relative. In Figure 8.10 the fine-grained silt beds are the aquitards and in Figure 8.11 they act as the aquifers.

Most aquifers are composed of **sedimentary deposits** which have well-developed systems of interconnected pore spaces (gaps between the rock particles) of a range of sizes. For example, the groundwater reservoir for Beijing, in China, is made up of an alternating series of sands and clays (see Fig. 8.14). Notice too, that the depth and size of this groundwater store vary, because of the uneven surface of the impermeable bedrock.

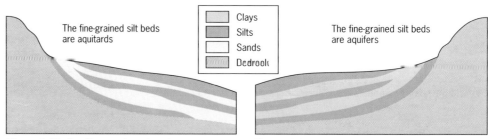

The fine-grained silt beds are aquitards

	Clays
	Silts
	Sands
	Bedrock

The fine-grained silt beds are aquifers

Figure 8.10 Aquifers and aquitards   **Figure 8.11 Aquifers and aquitards**

Aquifers in Beijing, China

The population of Beijing, China's capital city, doubled to six million between 1961 and 1981. Because Beijing lies at the junction between mountains and sedimentary plains, the city draws its water supplies from both groundwater and surface reservoirs (Figs 8.12 and 8.13). The groundwater store is a series of alternating sands and clays (Fig. 8.14). Until recently, it was the dominant water store. However, as demand has grown, the balance has been shifting.

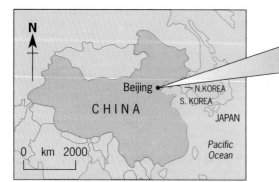

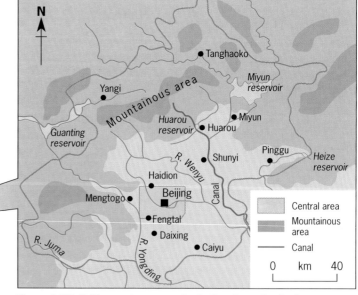

Figure 8.12 Beijing: water reservoirs in the city and suburban area (*Source*: Volker and Henry, 1988)

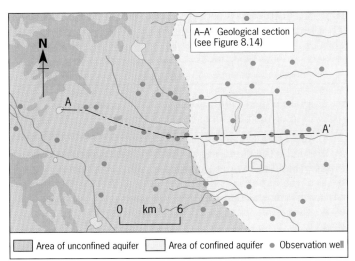

Figure 8.13 Distribution of observation wells around Beijing (*Source*: Volker and Henry, 1988)

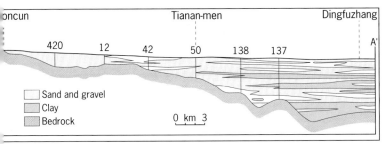

Figure 8.14 Quaternary aquifers in the Beijing area (*Source*: Volker and Henry, 1988)

?

4 Study Figure 8.13. In which parts of the city would wells:
a dry up first?
b last longest?
Give reasons in each case.

5 In Figure 8.14, which beds would be the aquifers and which the aquitards? Give your reasons.

Water demand exceeding supply

Table 8.1 Beijing: increase in groundwater use, 1961–81 (*Source*: Volker and Henry, 1988)

	Increase in groundwater use (million cubic metres per year)			
Year	Domestic	Industry	Agriculture	Total
1961	157	161	106	424
1971	191	343	747	1281
1981	388	650	1671	2709

Table 8.2 Beijing: input and output relationships of the groundwater store (*Source*: Volker and Henry, 1988)

Number of years when:	1951–60	1961–70	1971–80
R > W	6	3	1
R = W	2	3	1
R < W	2	4	8

Note: R = the rainfall input; W = the water abstracted

Demands on Beijing's groundwater store have been increasing (Table 8.1). By the early 1980s, over 2700 million cubic metres of water a year were being abstracted (drawn out) from 40 000 wells spread across the city. Annual abstraction was exceeding recharge by more than 300 million cubic metres a year and, consequently, water table levels were falling across an area of at least 1000 km² (Figs 8.15 and 8.16). Between 1961 and 1981, the fall in groundwater levels in some places exceeded 40 m. This is an excellent example of output (demand) exceeding input (supply), and so depleting the store (reserve).

Apart from two unusually wet years in the 1950s, the annual rainfall input for Beijing has remained at between 400 mm and 800 mm (Fig. 8.17). Yet, when we examine Table 8.2, we can see that the **water budget** of the aquifers has become increasingly negative over time.

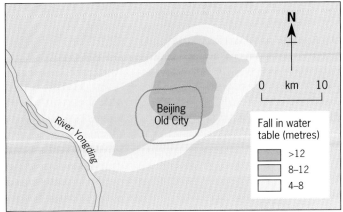

Figure 8.15 Beijing: drop in groundwater levels, 1970–80 (*After*: Volker and Henry, 1988)

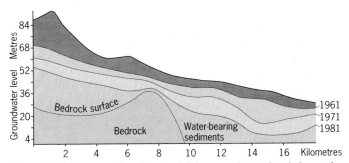

Figure 8.16 Cross-section showing fall in groundwater levels beneath Beijing City (*After*: Volker and Henry, 1988)

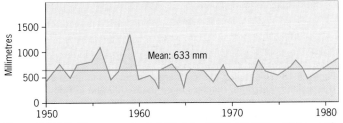

Figure 8.17 Beijing: annual rainfall totals, 1950–80 (*After*: Volker and Henry, 1988)

Beijing

Water management

During the 1980s, the population of Beijing grew by a further one million. In response, the city authorities were forced to control the drilling of new wells and the **abstraction** rates from the existing network. By 1994 two methods were being used to create an additional water supply:

1 Dams built in the mountains to enlarge the surface reservoir supply.

2 Water transferred from the mountains and pumped into the aquifers to recharge the groundwater store. This has the additional benefit of reducing ground subsidence, caused by the fall in groundwater levels.

6 Explain why a falling water table increases the likelihood of surface subsidence.

7 Using Table 8.2 and Figure 8.17:
a Describe the changing relationships between the rainfall input (R) and the water abstracted (W).
b Test the hypothesis that the changing R–W relationship is caused by increased output, i.e. demand from wells, and not by a change in recharge, i.e. the rainfall input.

8 Define the terms 'live' and 'fossil' groundwater.

9 Explain to what extent live groundwater may be defined as a renewable resource. For example, at what level of usage would such live water become non-renewable? (Think of a system with inputs and outputs.)

Live and fossil aquifers

An essential piece of information which we need to have for any **sustainable** water management policy is whether a groundwater store is 'live' or 'fossil'. Where the store is being replenished regularly by water inputs from the recharge surface area, the groundwater is said to be 'live' (Fig. 8.18). Many present-day arid regions enjoyed moister climates in the past, e.g. the northern Sahara of Africa, during which times groundwater stores were filled. Today, however, the recharge surfaces no longer receive much rainfall and the groundwater stores are not being replenished. The groundwater stores are therefore said to be 'fossil' – a relic of former times (Fig. 8.19).

Fossil groundwater is a non-renewable resource and, consequently, water levels in wells which tap fossil aquifers fall rapidly. In the basins of Arizona, 25 per cent of irrigated farmland has gone out of production since 1980 because wells have dried up. This is why the Central Arizona Project, which moves water from the Colorado River through a system of surface transfer basins, is so vital for the state's economy.

Figure 8.18 This region of the Atherton tablelands in north-east Queensland, Australia, receives more than 2000 mm of rain a year. The sedimentary formations beneath this rainforest dip westwards under the increasingly dry interior plains, and are the sole source of the water supply. This is a live groundwater store because it is being constantly recharged from the recharge surface

Figure 8.19 In late Pleistocene times rainfall in Arizona, USA, was heavy and the aquifers of the sedimentary basins were filled. Today, however, Arizona is an arid state. Groundwater stores are no longer being replenished – it is fossil water

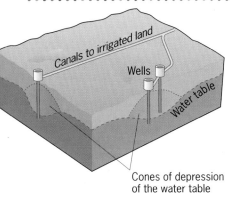

Figure 8.20 Water table draw-down by well abstraction

10 In hot, arid environments, the transfer of water from the basin to surface reservoirs is a common technique. A key problem, however, is high water loss by evaporation.

a Suggest how aquifers might be used to manage the water resource more efficiently.

b Would your suggested strategy work for both live and fossil groundwater stores? Explain your answer using annotated sketches and systems diagrams.

11 Suggest what factors will influence:

a the development of a cone of depression;

b the infilling of a cone of depression after water abstraction.

Figure 8.21 Canyon de Chelly National Park, Arizona. These thick-bedded and well-jointed sandstones are excellent aquifers

Cones of depression

The draw-down (lowering) of the water table is likely to be greatest around a well or a cluster of wells (Fig. 8.20). It is rather like the hollow around the straw as you drink a thick milkshake! These **cones of depression** are a common feature of exploited aquifers, and gradually refill when water abstraction stops.

Lower limits

The lower limit of groundwater occurs at a depth where the pore spaces are so few and so small that further downward transmission and storage of water virtually stops. In dense rocks, such as granites, this may be at a shallow depth. However, porous sandstones may permit a deep groundwater store (Fig. 8.21). At depths of more than 10 km we can say that *all* rocks are impermeable.

Confined and unconfined aquifers

We subdivide aquifers into three main types according to their position within the surrounding geology and their hydraulic characteristics. There are **unconfined aquifers**, **confined aquifers** and **perched aquifers** (Fig. 8.22). Each type behaves quite differently when wells are drilled into them, and each has a different water-yielding potential. For example, on Figure 8.22, engineers have drilled three wells (W_1, W_2 and W_3) and the water level in each is different.

The water level in wells sunk into an unconfined aquifer is controlled by the position of the water table, as shown by Well W_3 on Figure 8.22 which has been drilled into the unconfined aquifer A. The upper limit of the saturation zone is the water table (T_1), and it is therefore under atmospheric pressure.

On the other hand, the water level in a well bored through to a confined aquifer depends upon the **hydrostatic pressure** in the aquifer. For example, Well W_2, on Figure 8.22, has been sunk into the confined aquifer B. In this

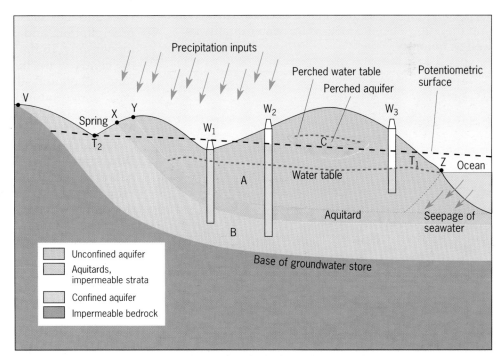

Figure 8.22 Unconfined (A) and confined (B) aquifers are distinguished by whether or not they have an overlying, i.e. confining, impermeable aquitard. Perched aquifers (C) are generally smaller and are created above an isolated impermeable layer

?

12 Explain why water would have to be pumped to the surface from Wells W_2 and W_3 on Figure 8.22, but would flow freely to the surface from Well W_1.

13a Which of the three wells on Figure 8.22 are artesian wells? Justify your choice.
b Describe what will happen to the potentiometric surface of an artesian well as more water is abstracted.
c Under what circumstances would pumping become necessary at Well W_1?

14 Suggest why a well sunk into a perched aquifer might be relatively cheap to drill, but have a limited water supply potential.

15 Explain why an increase in water abstraction and a fall in the water table make subsurface infiltration into the aquifer by saline seawater more likely.

case the upper limit of the saturation zone (T_2) is maintained under pressure by the overlying impermeable strata (aquitards), perhaps thick clays. Thus, the water level in Well W_2 will rise to the level allowed by this hydrostatic pressure. This is determined by the shape and especially the elevation of the aquifer's recharge area. This is the area of land surface through which rainwater **infiltrates** to refill, i.e. to recharge the aquifer (surface area V–X on Figure 8.22). The level to which the hydrostatic pressure allows the water to rise is known as the **potentiometric surface** (T_2 on Figure 8.22). (Some older books use the term piezometric surface.) The potentiometric surface is the equivalent of the water table for an unconfined aquifer. The recharge area for the unconfined aquifer B on Figure 8.22 extends between Y and Z.

Artesian basins

Basins containing confined aquifers which are fed from recharge areas in mountains, perhaps hundreds of kilometres away, are known as **artesian basins**. The wells sustained by the associated hydrostatic pressure are known as **artesian wells**. Over time, as more water is abstracted from the confined aquifers, the hydrostatic pressure tends to decrease.

The London basin, England

The London basin (Fig. 8.23) is the most intensively used artesian basin in the UK. This gently curved bowl is made of an alternating sequence of sedimentary formations which vary in permeability and which are exposed around the rim (Fig. 8.24). More than 10 million people live within this basin. It is therefore not surprising that the aquifers have been overdrawn and that there have been concerns for water quality as well as quantity.

Supply – the aquifers

The principal aquifer is the Cretaceous chalk, with substantial amounts of water also stored in the Lower London Tertiary Series (Fig. 8.24). The chalk behaves as an unconfined aquifer in those areas where the series outcrops (see Fig. 8.27). Here, the water table rises and falls seasonally with natural recharge from precipitation, and generally reflects the surface topography. In the confined zone of the aquifer – in the centre of the basin where the chalk is overlain by sands, clays and silts – the fluctuation in the water table under natural conditions is not great and is mainly caused by well abstractions.

The average annual precipitation over the exposed chalk catchment across the Chiltern Hills, Berkshire Downs and North Downs is 720 mm. Approximately half of this total infiltrates, while the rest is lost by evaporation or transferred by surface runoff. Most of the water which infiltrates moves laterally and emerges eventually as springs and as river discharge. Only perhaps 25 per cent of the subsurface water percolates deeply enough to become part of the 'reservoir' below London. Before people tapped this reservoir, the slowly migrating groundwater eventually discharged into the River Thames.

Figure 8.23 The London basin, England: Hampton Reservoirs, Middlesex, from the south-west

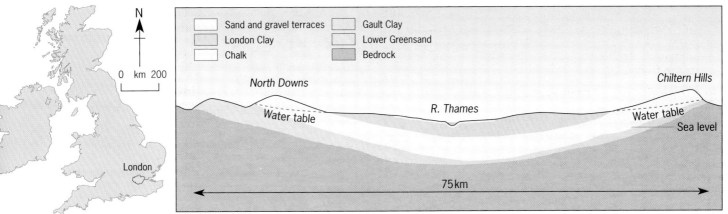

Figure 8.24 The London basin as a groundwater store

?

16 Make a copy of Figure 8.24.
a Colour and name the two main aquifers.
b In a second colour, mark and name the main aquitards.
c Use a heavy line to mark the recharge surfaces of the main aquifers.

d The cross-section runs in a north–south line. Mark north and south at the correct end points of your section.

17 Describe briefly how the London basin illustrates the definitions of: **a** an artesian basin,
b a confined aquifer.

Demand history

Under natural conditions the London basin has a shallow potentiometric (piezometric) head. Thus, the water level in any wells should be near the surface. However, the number of wells tapping the aquifer expanded rapidly after 1820 and, consequently, the water table fell (Figs 8.25 and 8.26). During the second half of the nineteenth century, the water table was falling at an average rate of 0.7 m/y.

As the built-up area of London spread, an increasing proportion of the water was removed as direct surface runoff from the urban surfaces into the River Thames and its tributaries. This contributed to the lowering of the water table. Between 1850 and 1965, the water table had fallen by at least 50 m across an area of 200 km^2 (Figs 8.27–8.30), causing a range of impacts (Table 8.3).

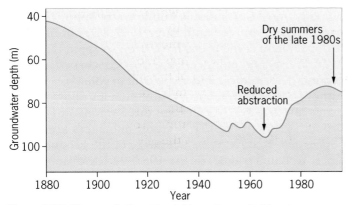

Figure 8.25 Changes in the water table under central London
(*Source*: Institute of Hydrology, 1990)

Table 8.3 The effects of the depletion of the groundwater store beneath London

Effect

1 Boreholes give a reduced yield as water pressures drop. They eventually fail as the water table sinks.

2 Drilling of boreholes becomes more expensive and less economic.

3 The deeper, lower Chalk series is less well fissured than the upper beds. Therefore, yields from the deeper, more costly wells are poorer. (Water transmission through chalk is largely via the fissure and joint system.)

4 Salt water penetrates the aquifers by induced recharge from the lower Thames where it flows over exposed chalk, e.g. by 1965 a zone of saline intrusion up to 8 km wide extended as far west as Lambeth.

5 Land subsidence occurs as artesian pressures decline. This is accentuated by the ever-increasing weight of buildings, roads etc. Most importantly, this settling – up to 1 m in places – is uneven, causing structural problems.

6 A reduction of river flows, an increasing failure of springs and a falling water table reduce the in-flow into headwaters, e.g. in 1965 the River Colne was estimated to be losing 45 000 m^3 per day.

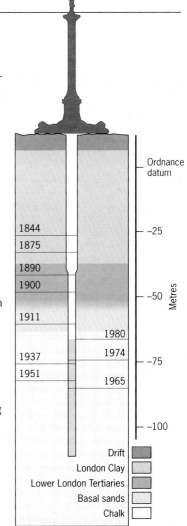

Figure 8.26 Trends below Trafalgar Square (*Source*: Marsh, 1983)

139

London

Figures 8.27–8.30 The increasing extent and scale of the impact. The figures on the isolines are heights above or below Ordnance datum (OD), i.e. sea level

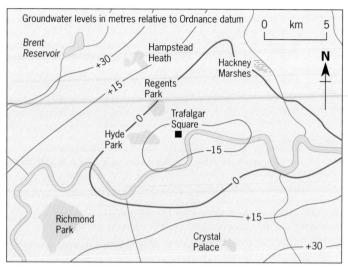

Figure 8.27 Groundwater levels below London, 1850 (*Source*: Marsh and Davies, 1983)

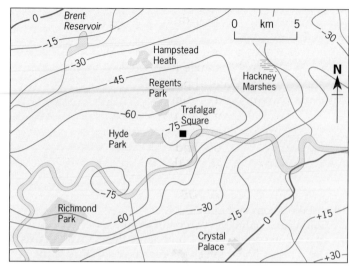

Figure 8.28 Groundwater levels below London, 1950 (*Source*: Marsh and Davies, 1983)

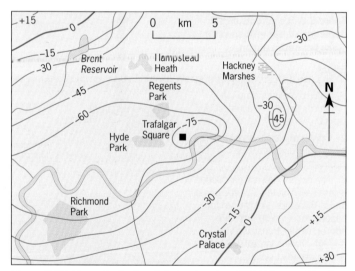

Figure 8.29 Groundwater levels below London, 1965 (*Source*: Marsh and Davies, 1983)

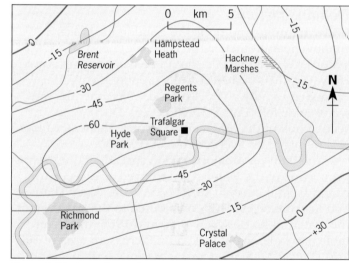

Figure 8.30 Groundwater levels below London, 1980 (*Source*: Marsh and Davies, 1983)

Management responses

By 1945, water engineers had fully understood the problems of falling water levels. A new national Water Act was passed in that year and further exploitation of the London basin aquifer virtually stopped. Since the early 1950s, few new wells have been sunk. Water abstraction continued at about 75 per cent of the pre-1945 level. An increasing proportion of the water supply came from the Thames and Lea surface reservoirs. The result was that by 1980 there were signs of water table recovery (Fig. 8.25). Recovery was also helped by a halving of the water abstraction from the central basin between 1965 and 1980, and by seepage from London's ageing water supply network.

Today, most of London's public water supply is met from surface sources and, since 1992, rises in the water table in some areas have been so rapid that hydrologists and engineers are now concerned about ground deformation and structural problems. Although the above conservation policies allowed water levels to recover despite three significant drought years in the 1970s, water managers are still concerned. Recovery, i.e. recharge of the groundwater store, remains fragile, as the 1988–92 UK drought revealed. Furthermore, abstraction rates across the outer basin in both the confined and unconfined zones continued to increase through the 1980s. This was triggered by the housing and industrial boom in

Hertfordshire and Berkshire. Extraction from the chalk outcrop areas increased by more than 40 per cent between 1950 and 1990. Consequently, catchments such as the Darent, Ver and Misbourne have shown significant reductions in their groundwater levels.

Increased abstraction from the surface recharge areas is worrying, because it reduces the water available for slow lateral percolation to the confined aquifers. One method of maintaining water levels, which water managers are introducing, is by flow and groundwater augmentation. Water is added to rivers, which sustains the flow and maintains some groundwater recharge via the stream bed and banks.

Technological solutions

?

18 Using the London basin as an example:
a Illustrate the idea that a groundwater basin works as an open system.
b Explain how the abstraction capacity of a confined aquifer is determined by the nature and use of the surface recharge area of the aquifer. (Use an annotated diagram in your answer.)

19 Outline the methods being used today to balance the water budget of the confined chalk aquifer beneath the central London Basin.

Figure 8.31 Newspaper article on how Britain's longest tunnel supplies London's water (*Source*: © Times Newspapers Ltd 1994)

Ring main cleans up water's act

UTILITIES

The completion of a £250m pipe around London will bring huge savings, writes **Christopher Lloyd**

WHEN the Queen officially opens the 50-mile-long Thames Water Ring Main on Friday, she will be inaugurating what the company claims is 'the most advanced drinking-water supply system in any capital city in the world'.

That bold claim stems from nearly 10 years of design, construction and development at a cost of £250m. Delivered two years ahead of schedule and incorporating the fastest ever tunnelling work, Thames Water says the ring means that, except in the most extreme drought conditions — such as the summer of 1976 — London should never again be subject to hosepipe bans.

The ring main has 12 extraction shafts and five inputs from reservoirs — four of which are situated west of the capital near Heathrow airport; the fifth is at Coppermills, north-east London.

The ring incorporates a wealth of technical innovation. Ian Bensted, Chief planning manager at Thames Water, developed the idea of constructing a main, 2.54 metres in diameter, in such a way that pumps would not be needed to drive water around the capital. Instead, the ring main would rely purely on gravity.

One of the big advantages of this type of system is huge cost savings in electricity usage and staff, formerly needed to man numerous pump stations to keep the water flowing.

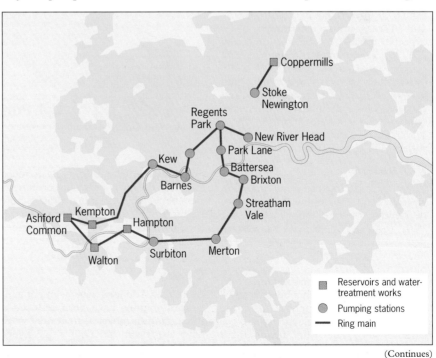

Reservoirs and water-treatment works
Pumping stations
Ring main

(Continues)

London

Reservoirs are situated at either side of the ring main and extraction shafts puncture the tunnel throughout its length to feed London's arterial water mains, some of which date back as far as 1838. As water is pumped out of the extraction shafts, a siphon effect is created — gravity forces water from the input reservoirs along the ring main towards the shafts from which the water is being extracted.

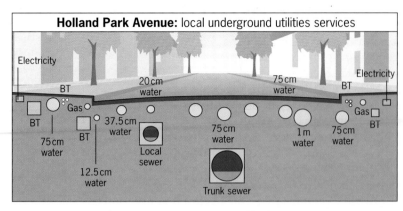

Holland Park Avenue: local underground utilities services

Electricity — BT — Gas — 75cm water — BT — 37.5cm water — 12.5cm water — Local sewer — 75cm water — Trunk sewer — 75cm water — 1m water — 75cm water — Electricity — Gas — BT — 20cm water — 75cm water

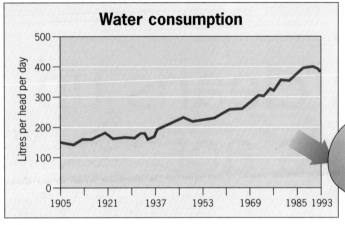

Water consumption

Litres per head per day

1905   1921   1937   1953   1969   1985 1993

There were, according to Bensted, several key reasons why the ring was necessary.

Demand

Water consumption per capita has risen from 120 litres a day in 1905 to nearly 400 litres now. Consumption is expected to rise 13% between now and 2011 as living standards improve and people bathe more often, own more dishwashers and washing machines, and have more time to wash cars and water gardens. The ring main will carry the bulk of London's water supply — about 1,300m litres a day, or enough to fill the Albert Hall eight times.

Pressure

Many existing mains water supplies, typically built a metre below the surface of London's roads, date back to the 19th century. To cope with greater demand, water pressures have had to be increased dramatically and many of the older mains pipes were being run at beyond their maximum pressure. This has led to frequent burst pipes, interrupting water supplies, disrupting road traffic and often electricity and gas supplies too. The ring means these pressures can be substantially reduced, avoiding the problems and prolonging the life of the existing infrastructure. Reducing pressure also reduces leakage which, before the ring began operations, accounted for as much as 20% of all the water passing through the system.

Cost

More than 100 jobs have been cut as 15 control stations have been reduced to three. Staff numbers at treatment works have also been cut. Only three people operate the ring-main control centre at Hampton, southwest London, and more than £1m was saved in pumping costs last year as the first phase came into operation.

Environment

As the ring main enables transfers of large amounts of water between rivers it raises ground water levels so that rivers such as the Darent, in Kent, which dried up in 1990 and 1991, should never dry up again.

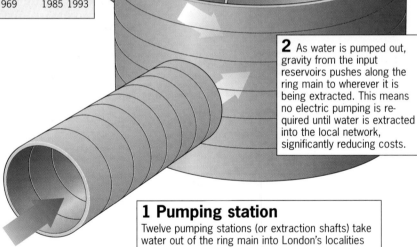

3 Water from the extraction shaft feeds into local water network. Pressure in the older long distance pipes beneath London's roads is thus reduced, cutting down on burst pipes. This avoids flooding and traffic congestion as well as disruption to telephone, electricity and gas supplies.

2 As water is pumped out, gravity from the input reservoirs pushes along the ring main to wherever it is being extracted. This means no electric pumping is required until water is extracted into the local network, significantly reducing costs.

1 Pumping station
Twelve pumping stations (or extraction shafts) take water out of the ring main into London's localities

Many water supply systems are old and still rely on relatively primitive methods and equipment. Today, however, technological advance enables the installation of storage and delivery systems which are more efficient mechanically, economically and environmentally. Yet critical factors in putting in these new technologies are their huge costs, the engineering problems in built-up areas and the long time-scale involved. None the less, London, where such factors are at their most acute, has succeeded, with the opening in 1994 of the Thames Water Ring Main system (Fig. 8.31).

?

20 Explain briefly how the Ring Main storage and supply system works.

21 Why is the Ring Main regarded as so necessary and important?

22 List any economic and environmental advantages and disadvantages of the scheme, indicated in the extract.

?

23 Outline the difficulties likely to arise if a water company decides to change from a single quality to a variable water quality recycling policy.

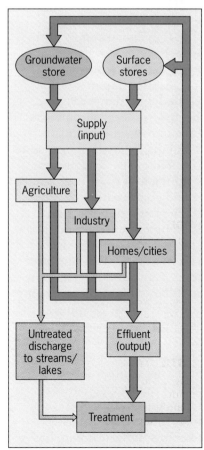

Figure 8.32 The 'single quality level' system

8.4 Considering the conservation and recycling option

Water management policies in most countries are today organised as integrated systems, based upon a balanced use of both surface and groundwater stores. This is especially true in densely populated and industrialised countries which have experienced the consequences of relying on either one or the other. The Beijing case study (see pages 134–6) shows how an uncontrolled development of groundwater resources led to extensive land subsidence – without being able to satisfy demand. In the USA, the enormous investments in surface storage projects in the Colorado and Mississippi basins have caused severe environmental impacts, and again, these projects have been unable to keep pace with expanding demand. A policy which integrates both surface and subsurface stores is likely to be more economic in cost, more reliable and more environmentally friendly.

Yet all countries must face the inevitable: first, water resource capacity is finite – there are limits; second, ensuring reliable water supplies is expensive; third, supply becomes increasingly costly as demand continues to grow. These realities are focusing the attention of governments and water managers on water conservation. Two key understandings which underpin conservation strategies are first, that water can be used more than once, i.e. it can be recycled, and second, that different uses need different water qualities.

There are three main categories of water users: human populations, agriculture, and industry. Water used in our homes needs to be potable (of drinkable quality). Once it leaves our homes it requires expensive treatment before it can be released into streams and water bodies and made available for human use once more (Fig. 8.32).

Agriculture and industry, however, are able to use water of lower quality. Even in our homes, water used for flushing toilets need not be of the same quality as that which flows from our taps. This understanding leads to the idea that water can be recycled for certain uses by minimal treatment, at reduced cost. The potential of the recycling and variable quality options is being considered and taken up in a number of countries. For example, in England, Thames Water plc, the company that supplies London, claims that about 10 per cent of its effluent water is reused. Water used upstream of London is treated and released back in the River Thames where it may be reused downstream. The following case study of Japan illustrates how continuing water scarcity is focusing attention on the recycling option across the world.

143

Changing water supply policies in Japan

During the summer of 1994, much of western Japan (Fig. 8.33) endured a long dry spell, and meteorologists claim that such droughts are becoming more frequent. However, since 1965 demand has trebled and during the 1994 drought, which reduced Japan's water reserves by one-third, many cities experienced water rationing. Factories, including steel mills and car plants, were shut down. This crisis has increased pressure for a rethink of Japan's water supply policies.

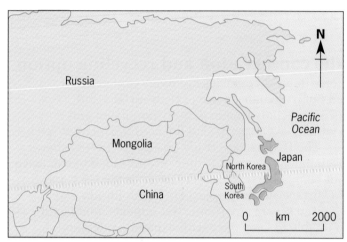

Figure 8.33 Japan

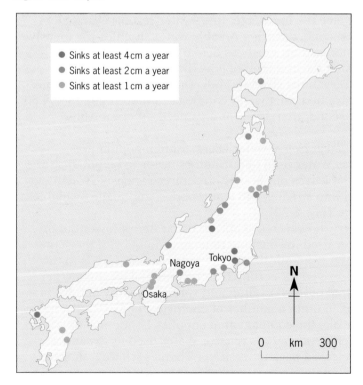

Figure 8.34 Land subsidence in Japan, 1991 (*Source*: Pearce, 1994)

Water policies

Several policy phases can be identified. Between 1950 and 1970 the additional supply came mainly from aquifers, and many thousands of wells were sunk, most below the expanding industrial cities. Abstractions (output) from the groundwater stores severely exceeded recharge (input), and water tables fell dramatically. By the early 1970s, widespread and severe subsidence, caused by this depletion of the groundwater, was occurring. Cities such as Tokyo and Osaka responded by banning the pumping of groundwater. This has allowed recharge of the aquifers, and by the early 1990s subsidence was much reduced, although not stopped (Fig. 8.34). To replace the dependency upon groundwater, during the 1970s the government launched a massive dam-building programme. Thus, since 1980, Japan's cities and industries have been supplied mostly from surface water stores.

Then came the summer drought of 1994; reservoirs and rivers proved inadequate; groundwater abstraction was largely banned. The government response to the water crisis and to the public outcry has been to propose a new programme of dam construction, i.e. to attempt to balance supply and demand by increasing surface water storage capacity (Fig. 8.35). This has enraged many scientists and environmentalists, who protest that Japan's mountains are already 'stuffed with dams' (Pearce, 1994). They claim that the government is influenced by the powerful lobby of the construction industry.

Teruyuki Shimazi, a distinguished hydrologist, sums up the views of the environmentalists: 'The present level of water [supply] is sufficient for our use. What's needed is more recycling and conservation of water' (quoted by Pearce, 1994). The potential of water conservation strategies is being largely ignored. For instance, Tokyo (population over 10 million) draws most of its waters from reservoirs in the basins of three major rivers, the Tone, Tama and Sagami. The effluent is then treated in 10 large plants before being discharged into streams or Tokyo Bay. Despite a massive campaign to clean up Tokyo since 1990, only one per cent of Tokyo's water is recycled, i.e. reused. Yet there are examples of recycling in operation. Sumida ward, in Tokyo itself, was vulnerable to flooding. So it built a series of underwater storage tanks for rainwater, and uses this natural and untreated water for flushing toilets and watering parks. Elsewhere, Fukuoka, in southern Japan, has installed a similar recycling system and now uses 20 per cent less water per person than Tokyo. A planner

Figure 8.35 Kurobe Dam, North Alps, Japan

in the Tokyo Sewage Bureau admits that much treated water which enters the streams of the Tokyo region is not fit for human use. But he also admits that little attempt is at present made to use it in industry or agriculture.

Equally worrying is the lifting of the ban on groundwater pumping in some districts. Although the government has promised to develop a national water policy, this is a long-term project. Meanwhile, cities and rural areas turn to short-term solutions such as the reopening of wells, even though this could trigger further land subsidence.

?

24a The systems diagram of Figure 8.32 summarises the water supply system in a 'single quality level' policy. Construct a similar diagram for a 'variable quality level' policy.
b In what ways do the recycling and variable quality approaches assist the development of water conservation policies?

Summary

- Groundwater makes up at least 90 per cent of the world's accessible reserve of freshwater.
- Each soil and rock type has a distinctive capacity to store and transmit water down to a certain depth.
- The groundwater store functions as an open system, and has a measurable water budget which determines its capacity for exploitation.
- Water-bearing strata are known as aquifers. There are three main types: confined, unconfined and perched. They may be 'live' or 'fossil' depending on whether they are currently being replenished.
- Water resource managers organise supply by drawing on surface water stores and subsurface stores. Attempts to maintain supply often result in a variety of water management schemes.
- As water demands continue to rise, managers are increasingly turning to the examination of policies for recycling and two-level-quality supplies.

9 Water resource issues in the UK

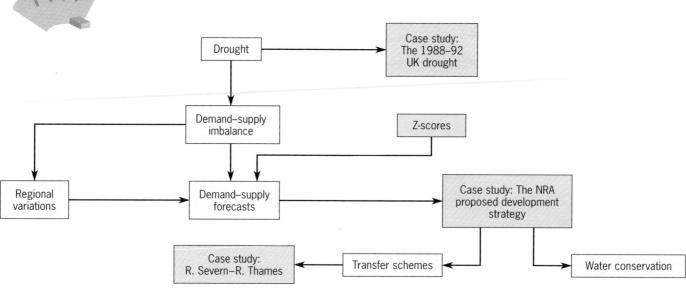

9.1 Introduction

A basic goal for water resource managers is to 'balance the budget' of an **aquifer**. If their policies are to be for **sustainable** yield, then over time, water **abstractions** must be matched by water inputs. Fluctuations in precipitation from year to year make it difficult to maintain this balance. The case study of the London Basin in Chapter 8 illustrates this struggle.

9.2 The dilemma for eastern and southern England

Throughout eastern and southern England – the most densely populated, yet driest, part of the UK – the **groundwater** resource is being used to its capacity. Further rises in demand and/or a fall in precipitation inputs will result in an increased dependence on surface water resources. However, existing rivers and reservoirs have little spare capacity. Therefore, despite integrated **conjunctive operation strategies** (see Section 8.2), the water companies of eastern and southern England face a dilemma (Fig. 9.1). Can they increase the yield of surface and groundwater stores within the region, or must they look to other parts of Britain; and what will such schemes cost?

It's all very confusing for consumers. A few days of sun and the hosepipe bans are back for 500 000 people after the wettest winter in years; yet more than 20 per cent of piped water leaks away; there are still hundreds of water pollution 'incidents' each year; water doesn't taste or look any better than anyone remembers; and many of Britain's rivers and beaches are still grim. And here they are paying a fortune.

Figure 9.1 Water supply in the UK (*Source: The Guardian, 28 July 1994*)

1 Look at Figure 9.1. What sorts of problems do both water companies and consumers face over the water supply in the UK?

The 1988–92 UK drought

The fragile margin between supply and shortage was harshly demonstrated by the so-called 'Great Drought' of 1988–92. Over extensive areas of the British Isles, these were four of the driest years of the past century (Table 9.1, Fig. 9.2). By 1992, serious deficiencies in precipitation inputs had accumulated (Fig. 9.3), causing the most severe drought in those regions where demand was greatest and supply reserves smallest.

Table 9.1 Rainfall, August 1988 to May 1992, as a percentage of the 1941–70 average (*Source*: Institute of Hydrology, 1994)

Region	Total rainfall over whole period (mm)	Percentage of average
Great Britain	4280	102
Scotland	6340	115
England and Wales	3080	95
Anglian region	1890	80

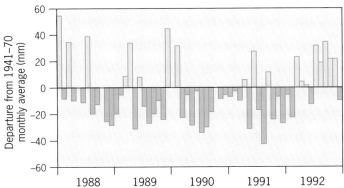

Figure 9.2 Monthly rainfall anomalies for the Anglian region, 1988–92 (*Source*: Marsh et al, 1994)

Drought conditions were intensified because 1988–92 was also the warmest five-year sequence in England in more than 300 years. The effectiveness of rainfall was thus reduced, because unusually high proportions of the moisture input were **evaporated**, rather than remaining to recharge streams and aquifers.

Streamflow

By late summer 1992, monthly flows in some eastern rivers had remained below average for nearly four years (Fig. 9.4). Despite rainfall totals only 20 per cent below average, the high evaporation rates and low soil moisture levels meant that runoff was reduced by 50 per cent in many areas (Fig. 9.5). Stream networks contracted as falling **water tables** caused **base flow**, fed by groundwater, to fail. The combination of drought and heavy water demands caused stretches of UK rivers to dry up for the first time this century (Fig. 9.6).

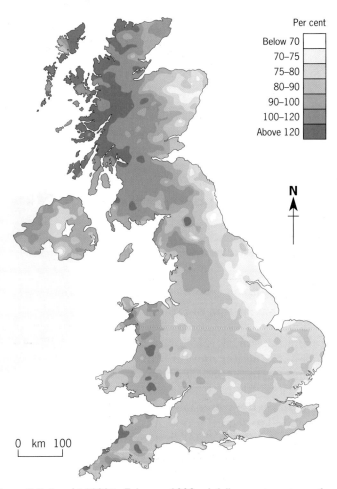

Figure 9.3 August 1988 to February 1992 rainfall as a percentage of the 1941–70 average (*Source*: Marsh et al, 1994)

Figure 9.4 Rainfall deficiency index for the South Dalton rain gauge, 1885–92 (*Source*: Marsh et al, 1994)

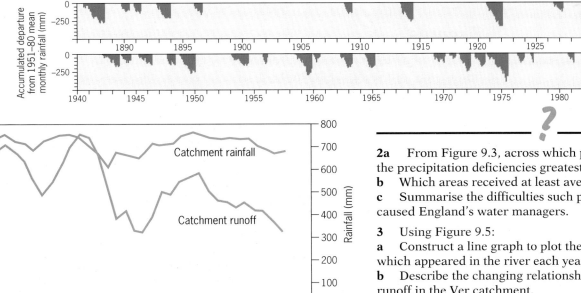

Figure 9.5 Rainfall–runoff relationships in the River Ver catchment, at Hansteads (*Source*: National Water Archive, Institute of Hydrology, 1994)

2a   From Figure 9.3, across which parts of England were the precipitation deficiencies greatest?
b   Which areas received at least average precipitation?
c   Summarise the difficulties such patterns may have caused England's water managers.

3   Using Figure 9.5:
a   Construct a line graph to plot the percentage of rainfall which appeared in the river each year, from 1960 to 1992.
b   Describe the changing relationship between rainfall and runoff in the Ver catchment.
c   In which years was the runoff percentage at its lowest?
d   Suggest reasons why the rainfall–runoff relationship has changed and, in particular, why the gap is growing wider.

The 1988–92 UK drought

Figure 9.6 The River Ver in Hertfordshire had dried up completely by May 1992

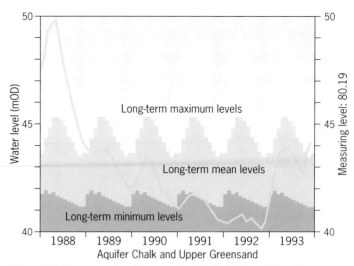

Aquifer Chalk and Upper Greensand

Figure 9.7 The water level in a well at Washpit Farm, Norfolk, 1988–93 (*Source:* Marsh et al, 1994)

Groundwater stores

The normal rhythm of groundwater stores across England is a draw-down, i.e. a fall of the water table, during the summer, followed by a recharge, i.e. rise, during the winter months. After several wet years during the mid 1980s, aquifers were well stocked by early 1988. Figure 9.7 records the impact of the drought on the water table over the next four years which fell to record levels. A report from the Institute of Hydrology concludes that 'in the summer of 1992, overall groundwater resources for England and Wales were at their lowest since at least the turn of the century' (Marsh et al, 1994).

4   From Figure 9.7:
a   Support the claim that groundwater levels follow a seasonal rhythm.
b   Describe what happened to the water table between 1988 and 1992.
c   What evidence is there that the 1988–92 drought caused the water table to fall more than ever before recorded?
d   During what period was the water table at Washpit Farm at a record low level?

5a   Calculate the *z* scores and probabilities for the River Lambourn (using Appendix A3 and Table 9.2) for March, June, September and December.
b   Plot the percentage probability scores on a reverse bar chart for 1990. Indicate which months were above and below the mean by using the *z* scores. A positive value indicates a wet month and a negative value indicates a relatively dry month.
c   Comment on the nature of the UK drought in 1990, using Table 9.2 and your graph.
d   Describe the likely groundwater levels between the beginning and the end of 1990.

Z scores

Z scores allow us to assess the probability of an occurrence of a stated rainfall amount using the formula:

$$z = \frac{x - \bar{x}}{\sigma}$$

Where:
x = stated value
$\bar{x}$ = mean
σ = standard deviation.

The mean rainfall and standard deviation for the years 1980–9 have been calculated for the River Lambourn (Table 9.2). This allows us to compare the 1990 data with the previous 10 years (although we should remember that the UK drought started in 1988). The annual rainfall total for 1990 was 563 mm and the *z* score indicates that there is only a one per cent chance of this rainfall occurring, i.e. the total rainfall for 1990 has a probability of occurring only once in a hundred years.

More detailed analysis of this data allows us to discover something of the complexity of the UK drought. For example, the February rainfall in 1990 was an extremely rare event in that it was very heavy.

Table 9.2 Monthly rainfall (mm) for the River Lambourn at Shaw

Date	Jan	Feb	Mar	Apr	May	Jun	Jul	Aug	Sep	Oct	Nov	Dec	Total
1980	46	53	89	19	31	86	58	87	62	94	55	52	732
1981	34	29	161	47	102	35	63	34	124	85	47	108	869
1982	49	38	97	34	33	78	18	55	61	126	103	81	773
1983	78	27	49	95	88	20	50	14	75	66	51	67	680
1984	136	42	60	3	91	30	18	28	105	58	127	79	777
1985	56	39	46	38	75	149	59	81	29	42	48	127	789
1986	93	12	63	61	83	24	38	111	40	73	108	95	801
1987	13	50	65	61	44	96	59	31	47	137	65	38	706
1988	133	49	65	22	38	55	100	67	49	78	34	14	704
1989	38	78	71	69	20	34	34	46	20	66	44	151	671
Mean 1980s	67.6	41.7	76.6	44.9	60.5	60.7	49.7	55.4	61.2	82.5	68.2	81.2	750.2
Standard deviation	39.55	16.88	31.86	25.94	28.58	39.16	23.11	29.13	30.96	28.10	30.57	39.14	59.21
1990 rainfall (mm)	103	126	17	34	8	44	19	35	26	50	27	74	563
Z scores	0.89	4.99	−1.87	−0.42	−1.84	−0.426	−1.33	−0.70	−1.14	−1.16	−1.35	−0.18	−3.16
% probability of 1990 figures	18.4	0	?	34.5	3.6	?	9.7	24.2	?	13.6	9.7	?	1.0

9.3 Crisis management

In developed countries, water arrives at our taps by five main routes (Fig. 9.8). The balance between the routes depends upon where we live, and the status of the reservoirs, river channels and the aquifer groundwater store (Table 9.3).

?

6 Using Table 9.3:
a Express the rainfall–runoff relationship in graphical form and summarise what your graph reveals. (Spearman rank correlation may also be useful.)
b To what extent does the data support the idea that the water supply problem varies according to where you live? Suggest reasons for this variation.

7a Explain why the balance between surface and groundwater supplies varies from region to region.
b Suggest how this might affect water resource management policies.

8a Which region in England and Wales has the most urgent water supply problem?
b Suggest why it might be particularly difficult to solve this water problem by using the region's resources alone.
c Outline the different schemes for restoring the rivers' flow.
d Consider the interests involved, and make your own recommendation for re-establishing adequate flows. Give your reasons.

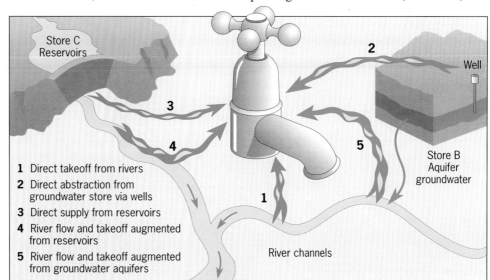

1 Direct takeoff from rivers
2 Direct abstraction from groundwater store via wells
3 Direct supply from reservoirs
4 River flow and takeoff augmented from reservoirs
5 River flow and takeoff augmented from groundwater aquifers

Figure 9.8 The five routes water takes to your tap, each including water treatment

Table 9.3 Water resources by NRA regions (*Source*: Institute of Hydrology, 1994)

Region	Mean annual rainfall (mm)	Mean annual runoff (mm)	Public water supply (1987–8) as percentage of runoff
Thames	704	240	47
Anglian	610	170	14
Southern	794	320	14
Severn-Trent	773	330	12
Yorkshire	833	420	9.1
Wessex	869	370	8.9
Northumbria	879	490	8.3
North West	1217	810	7.8
Welsh	1334	850	2.4
South West	1194	740	2.2

9 Read Figure 9.11.

a What are the differences in the five rivers named by the CPRE between the nineteenth century and the late twentieth century?

b List the reasons for these changes.

c Outline the different schemes for restoring the rivers' flow.

d Consider the interests involved, and make your own recommendation for re-establishing adequate flows. Give your reasons.

10 Outline the reasons why it is valuable to increase stream discharge during periods of very low flow.

Responding to drought in England and Wales

Over England and Wales as a whole, groundwater accounts for about one-third of the public water supply. However, in eastern and southern England more than one-half of the supply is drawn from the Chalk and upper Greensand aquifer. Each year approximately 25 per cent of the natural recharge to aquifers is abstracted for water supply and to sustain river flows. It is clear, therefore, that the reduced recharge of the aquifers from 1988 to 1992, over extensive areas less than 50 per cent of normal, affected water supplies significantly.

Private consumers, such as farmers, with their own shallow wells drilled mostly into chalk, are the first to suffer at times of drought. Water companies maintain river flows and water supplies by making increasing demands upon the surface reservoir stores. As inputs from runoff are reduced by drought, extra demand results in serious draw-down (Fig. 9.9).

During the 1988–92 drought, there was no surplus water for deliberate recharge of aquifers. By August 1990, 12.5 million customers were under a hosepipe ban, and 18 million had restricted water use. Yet the supply network held up remarkably well. None the less, the drought raised a number of issues for future management (Fig. 9.11).

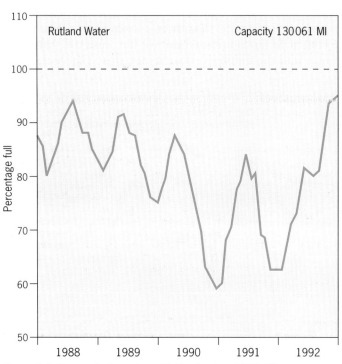

Figure 9.9 Reservoir draw-down: Rutland water, 1988–92

Figure 9.10 Algal blooms: Rutland Water

Environmental quality

Water managers have responsibilities for maintaining environmental quality. Thus, at periods of very low flow they conserve wetland and aquatic habitats by using water from reservoirs and groundwater stores to increase stream **discharge**. As drought progresses this becomes more difficult. For instance, if too much water is drawn from reservoirs, **algal blooms** can spread in warm weather, as occurred on Rutland Water (Fig 9.10). In consequence, managers may apply for a 'Drought Order' from the National Rivers Authority and the Department of the Environment. This allows the water company to abstract more than the agreed volume of water from rivers to help replenish the reservoir.

Diminishing return

Jim Manson on the rivers that are water starved

FROM the gloom among the weeping willows and the tangle of reeds, a swan slips out from the shallows, skimming across glistening wavelets, towards the deeper mid-stream.

The pastoral study comes courtesy of a turn-of-the-century picture postcard of the lake at Great Missenden Abbey Park in Buckinghamshire. A photograph taken in the same place in 1981 shows a rather different scene: the water level appears alarmingly low; a thick cover of river weed threatens to choke the life out of what remains of the lake. In another photograph, taken in 1987, the water in the lake has completely vanished: on its steep banks, a once stately oak stands forlorn.

The Lake at Great Missenden is fed by the River Misbourne. The water-starved Misbourne is suffering the dramatic effects of over-abstraction of ground — or underground — water.

One of the effects of soaring water treatment costs has been the increasing reliance by the water industry on groundwater, as distinct from reservoir and river sources, which requires minimal, if any, treatment. By chance, the areas which have traditionally relied on groundwater abstraction — in some parts of the country it provides up to 74 per cent of the water supply — are those like Buckinghamshire, where the demand for water is increasing fastest. The problem is that as more and more boreholes are sunk, the rate of abstraction threatens to exceed the rate of replenishment, causing the underground springs and rivers to run dry.

The National Rivers Authority (NRA) says it is adopting a 'softly, softly' approach to the issue. A spokesman insisted that 'there is nothing that can be done to increase river flows in the short term,' adding that the reviewing of abstraction licences was 'a long-term measure and one that is unlikely to alter significantly overall abstraction levels.' NRA officials have admitted privately that the chances of revoking these licences — which, once granted, are generally accepted to be permanent — are almost out of the question.

Five rivers were named last summer by the CPRE: the Pang, the Misbourne, the Ver, the Darent, the Wey and Letcombe Brook. Each has been affected differently according to the environment of the surrounding area. For example, the perennial heads of the rivers Pang, Ver and Misbourne have all shifted — the Misbourne by 5 km — while chalk-bedded rivers like the Darent in Kent have insufficient flow because of the combined effect of over-abstraction and leakage through the river bed.

In 1986 Thames Water commissioned Sir William Halcrow & Partners to examine the environmental problems arising from over-abstraction of these rivers and to recommend methods of alleviating them by re-establishing 'adequate flows' — everyone seems to rule out the prospect that the rivers will be restored to their proper natural flows. It was an attempt to establish roughly what were the natural, pre-abstraction, flows of the five rivers that led the consultants to museum records and, most helpfully, Victorian picture postcards.

In its report, Halcrow noted that abstraction has had a severe effect on the rivers. They often dry up in summer, river channels are no longer managed for land drainage purposes, the general appearance of the rivers has deteriorated and trout have almost disappeared.

In setting new flow targets Halcrow had to 'balance the requirements of water supply and the protection of the environment'. In other words, on cost grounds, the company was to rule out the possibility of reducing abstraction. Here then, as the Government's policies on water come into direct conflict with pressure on the water companies to keep operating costs down, the politically sensitive nature of the abstraction issue becomes clear. But Halcrow also rejected a controversial water industry proposal, to increase flows through the use of sewage effluents, due to water quality problems.

The favoured approach was to put in the new boreholes to abstract water from the aquifers and then to pump water into the rivers at certain times of the year at selected points. Existing boreholes are close to springs and rivers, in valley bottoms. Consequently, abstraction tends to dry up the river sources. Halcrow proposes that new boreholes be sunk at around 3km distance from the river to draw water which has collected underground during winter and pump it through pipelines during the summer. The company also recommends that lining work be carried out to prevent leakage and to create narrower river beds to help maintain flows.

The CPRE argues that this sort of remedial action is insufficient to restore the river environment to an acceptable condition.

Figure 9.11 Water-starved rivers (*Source: Guardian*, 20 July 1990)

The 1994 NRA Development Strategy

Response to the 1988–92 UK drought

The government body responsible for water resource management in England and Wales is the National Rivers Authority (NRA). The NRA was set up in 1989, at the same time as the 10 regional water authorities which supplied our water were privatised. One of the NRA's functions is to set the overall water policy. In 1994, in response to the issues raised by the 1988–92 UK drought, the NRA published its Development Strategy for water supply for the period until the year 2021. The full title of the report, *Water: nature's precious resource. An environmentally sustainable water resources development strategy for England and Wales*, sums up the NRA approach. Water is seen as 'precious', that is scarce, finite and to be used efficiently; and management is to be based on concern for the environment and sustainability. It is important for us to understand that it is, in reality, a discussion document rather than a formal plan. It sets out preferred options and implications based on several demand forecasts. It does not indicate which, if any, of the options will be followed.

NRA Strategy

Principles of the strategy

The NRA addressed four questions in their analysis:
1 What is the existing supply-demand relationship, nationally and regionally?
2 What is likely to be the future demand for public water supply, industry and agriculture?
3 How can river flows be protected from the effects of excessive abstraction?
4 What are the options for balancing demand and supply?

From this analysis, the NRA raised proposals based upon the three principles of sustainability, caution and conservation (Table 9.4). Future water supply needs are based upon forecasts of low, medium and high rates of growth in demand. The figures in Table 9.5 support the NRA's claim that, 'Currently there is a surplus in water supply resources. However, in 30 years' time ... a supply deficit could occur in most areas' (NRA, 1994).

The NRA conclude that, first, total supply must be increased, and second, regions in the north and west with potential surplus resources must increasingly be the source of supply for shortage regions in the east and south. Existing surface and groundwater stores in eastern and southern regions are already exploited to capacity.

Table 9.4 The NRA's three principles

Principle		Example
Sustainable development	There should be no long-term systematic environmental deterioration due to water resource development and water use. Long-term groundwater abstraction should be less than the average recharge.	The water table in the Chalk and Upper Greensand aquifer must be maintained at agreed levels over time. Allowing for normal seasonal variation, these levels must be high enough to supply springs and allow recharge to streams in order to sustain healthy aquatic communities.
Precautionary principle	Where significant environmental damage may occur, but knowledge on the matter is incomplete, decisions made and measures implemented should err on the side of caution.	If there is any uncertainty about the environmental impacts of the building of a dam and resevoir complex then the development should not go ahead until this uncertainty is removed.
Demand management	Management measures to control waste and consumption.	The installation of water meters in homes and charging by the litre for water used. This encourages families to use water more carefully.

Table 9.5 Demand–supply relationships for the medium growth rate scenario (*Source:* NRA, 1994)

NRA region	Demand increase (% of 1991 demand)	Supply shortfall if no new supplies are made available (million litres per day)
Northumbria	10	0
Yorkshire	8	29
North West	0	0
Severn–Trent	12	182
Anglian	27	100
Southern	15	57
Thames	7	270
Wessex	15	58
South West	27	40
Welsh	5	38

?

11 Essay: Study Table 9.5. To what extent is it true to say that, by the year 2021, the largest shortfall in water supply will be in those regions with the most rapid growth in demand if no new resources are made available? Use appropriate graphical and statistical techniques to support your answer. Justify your choice of techniques.

Development options

The NRA's strategy is to have three basic components:
1 Surface storage schemes (reservoirs) in the north and west, including Wales, are to be upgraded and enlarged.
2 Inter-basin water transfers will deliver additional water to rivers, reservoirs and aquifers in the east and south (Fig. 9.12).
3 The introduction of strengthened demand control measures, such as metering and pricing, will encourage consumers to use water more efficiently (Figs 9.13–15).

A number of storage and transfer schemes have been suggested and evaluated, primarily in terms of cost. For example, the existing Kielder Water Reservoir in Northumberland will continue to have a surplus capacity of up to 500 million litres a day for the needs of north-east England. The NRA accepts the technical feasibility of transfer schemes running south, but has rejected them for the present as being too costly. In contrast, the eastward transfer of water to the upper Thames basin from upgraded Welsh storage schemes is likely to be less expensive, and is therefore recommended by the NRA.

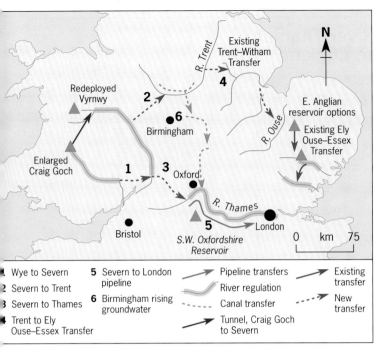

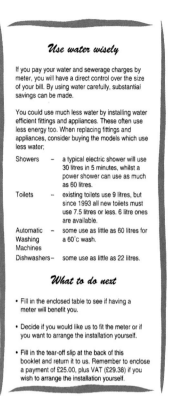

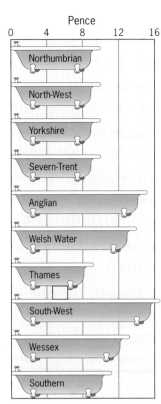

Figure 9.12 Proposed inter-basin water transfers in the south-east of the UK (*Source*: NRA, 1994)

1 Wye to Severn
2 Severn to Trent
3 Severn to Thames
4 Trent to Ely Ouse–Essex Transfer
5 Severn to London pipeline
6 Birmingham rising groundwater

Pipeline transfers
River regulation
Canal transfer
Tunnel, Craig Goch to Severn
Existing transfer
New transfer

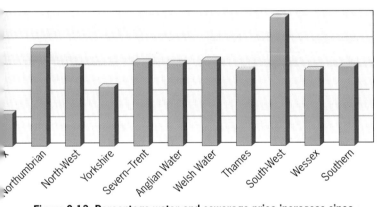

Figure 9.13 Percentage water and sewerage price increases since privatisation in 1990 (*Source*: CRI, 1994–5)

Use water wisely

If you pay your water and sewerage charges by meter, you will have a direct control over the size of your bill. By using water carefully, substantial savings can be made.

You could use much less water by installing water efficient fittings and appliances. These often use less energy too. When replacing fittings and appliances, consider buying the models which use less water;

Showers – a typical electric shower will use 30 litres in 5 minutes, whilst a power shower can use as much as 60 litres.

Toilets – existing toilets use 9 litres, but since 1993 all new toilets must use 7.5 litres or less. 6 litre ones are available.

Automatic Washing Machines – some use as little as 60 litres for a 60°C wash.

Dishwashers – some use as little as 22 litres.

What to do next

- Fill in the enclosed table to see if having a meter will benefit you.
- Decide if you would like us to fit the meter or if you want to arrange the installation yourself.
- Fill in the tear-off slip at the back of this booklet and return it to us. Remember to enclose a payment of £25.00, plus VAT (£29.38) if you wish to arrange the installation yourself.

Figure 9.14 Promoting the benefits of water meters (*Source*: Thames Water Utilities, 1994)

Figure 9.15 What it costs to fill your bath (*Source*: The Guardian, 28 July 1994)

Environmental considerations

The NRA is committed to environmental quality. For example, they feel that impacts from existing water transfer schemes in the Lake District and the Peak District National Parks have already reached acceptable limits (Fig. 9.16). Therefore, they do not propose increasing supply from these sources.

?

12 Once water has been transferred into a drainage basin it can be used in four ways:
a directly by consumers;
b to enlarge river discharge;
c to increase existing reservoirs and supply new reservoirs;
d to recharge aquifers.
Look again at Figure 9.8. Discuss how these external inputs affect this delivery system.

13 Consider the NRA's development options. Assess the impact of these schemes by drawing a matrix to show their advantages and disadvantages for: • the NRA, • the consumer.

Figure 9.16 Haweswater, Lake District National Park. This reservoir flooded a farming valley and settlement in the 1920s, resulting in a significant change of environmental character

River Severn – River Thames water transfer, England

The basic scheme

The basic Severn–Thames water transfer scheme involves abstracting water from the lower River Severn near Deerhurst and discharging it into the upper River Thames at Buscot (Fig. 9.17). This would resurrect a similar proposal made over a century ago. The Thames would then convey water downstream for final transfer into existing reservoirs near London. To avoid the potential environmental problems of mixing 'foreign' water with the Thames water, a possible option would be a 90 km pipeline from Deerhurst direct to the London reservoirs. This would cost at least £117 million.

Some storage space would be required at Deerhurst to allow for sediment to settle. At the Thames end, further storage would be needed for blending and control functions, but disused gravel pits in the Thames Valley are likely to be available. The Thames–Severn Canal, if refurbished, could also be incorporated.

In this basic scheme 'abstractions could be made at times of higher flows in the River Severn. This option provides only limited additional resources, but could be a relatively low-cost solution to slowly increasing demand. The reliable yield could be up to 146 million litres per day and the capital cost would be £5.7 million' (NRA, 1994).

Enhanced scheme

Enlarging the Craig Goch reservoir

The Craig Goch reservoir is one of several in the Elan Valley, part of the River Wye catchment. There are two suggestions for its enlargement:

1 The present **dam** could be raised by 49 m. Then, if a tunnel were cut northwards to the upper Severn at Llanidloes, the extra water stored could be used to regulate the low flows. The reliable yield would be 775 million litres per day. The scheme would cost £105 million.
2 A tunnel could be cut to the upper Wye at Nannerth, near Rhayader. The increased Wye flow would then provide for an abstraction near Ross-on-Wye, from which a pipeline would cross the Severn at Deerhurst and follow the line to the River Thames described above. This scheme would cost £72 million.

Changing the use of the Vyrnwy Reservoir

This reservoir in the upper Severn catchment currently supplies water directly by gravity to Liverpool along the Vyrnwy Aqueduct. While maintaining a minimum flow along this aqueduct of 60 million litres per day, up to 147 million litres per

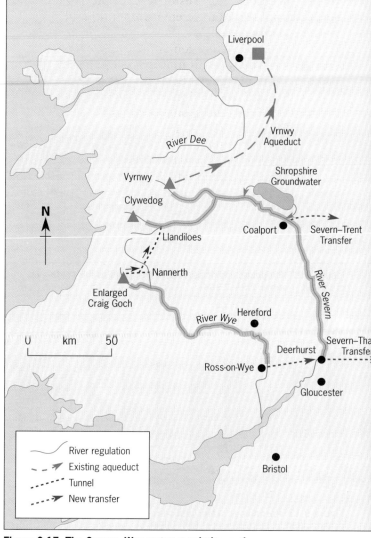

Figure 9.17 The Severn–Wye water regulation options (*Source*: NRA, 1994)

day could be made available for regulation and supply along the River Severn. Costs would be £42 million, spent on upgrading outlet facilities at Vyrnwy and replacing the supplies lost to the Liverpool area, e.g. by abstracting and treating water from the River Dee.

Environmental issues

1 Water quality and biological impacts of transferring water from the lower Severn into the upper Thames – the **hydrochemistry** and therefore the aquatic ecosystems are different.
2 The effects on salmon migration along the Severn and Wye rivers. Ecologists believe a minimum prescribed flow (PF), with artificial pulses of higher flows to trigger salmon runs, must be maintained in the River Severn if the salmon migration is to be

safeguarded. Fishing is an important recreational and economic activity along both rivers.

3 Pipeline routes must take into account conservation and archaeological sites. These are also possibilities for enhancements, e.g. restoration of the Thames and Severn canal would have environmental and recreational benefits.

4 Impacts of dam enlargement. Developments at Craig Goch would result in impacts upon the Eleynydd Site of Special Scientific Interest (SSSI) and other areas of conservation value. Such impacts would be 'of particular concern for the Countryside Council for Wales' (NRA, 1994). If the option to use the Wye as the regulator is taken, this would raise 'a number of concerns since the whole river, including the riparian (bank) habitats, has been classified as an SSSI and as such is of national value' (NRA, 1994).

Furthermore, the Wye is an important salmon river and flow levels are crucial.

5 The Vyrnwy options would affect the flora and fauna along the River Vyrnwy, again including salmon stocks. Water quality and temperature impacts, resulting from drawing off water from deeper in the reservoir, could be reduced by modifying levels of outlets from the dam.

14a List the costs and benefits of the Severn–Thames water transfer scheme.
b Evaluate the scheme according to your lists.
c State whether you agree with the scheme, giving your reasons.

Summary

- The National Rivers Authority (NRA) is the body responsible for water resource management in England and Wales. It is not itself a supplier, this being the duty of the water companies.

- Approximately one-third of all UK water supplies is abstracted from groundwater stores (aquifers), and in eastern and southern England this source exceeds 50 per cent.

- The 1988–92 drought, which was particularly severe in the east and south of England, caused a re-think of water supply strategies in the UK.

- The NRA have produced a development strategy for the period 1991 to 2021. The strategy accepts the need for additional water supplies but bases its plan on sustainability, the precautionary principle and demand management in order to stress economical use and environmental quality. The NRA's preferred strategy is for large-scale water transfers from the west, where there is a surplus, to the east and south, where untapped reserves are lowest and shortages imminent.

- UK trends in future demand are uncertain but increases are most likely in public water supply.

10 Water quality and pollution

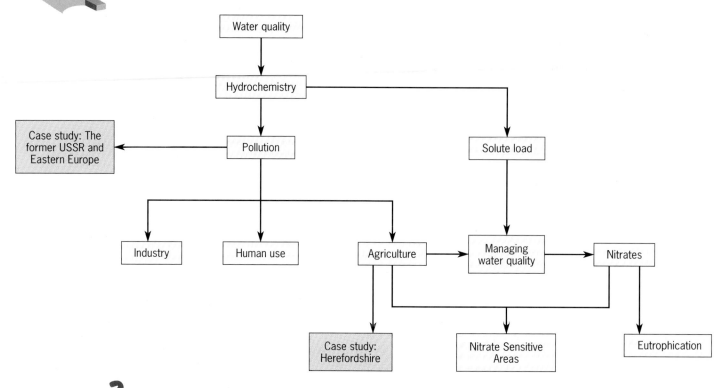

?

1a Draw an annotated systems diagram to summarise the pollution issue described in Figure 10.1.
b List the 'interested parties' and their positions in the issue.
c In what ways does this example illustrate the complexity of water pollution issues and why they are so often very difficult to deal with?

10.1 Introduction

Water quality has become a global environmental issue, as important as water quantity and distribution. For instance, the Rwandan refugee tragedy of 1994 was intensified by the spread of water-borne diseases such as cholera, when the only sources of water for more than one million people were severely polluted. However, the water quality issue is not restricted to the economically developing countries. For example, in 1990, over 190 water **abstraction** sources in England and Wales exceeded the European Community's (EC) nitrate directive limit of 50 milligrams per litre (mg/l) of nitrate (NO_3) for drinking water (Fig. 10.1).

10.2 Water quality

Water quality sounds straightforward, but in reality it is complex. 'Pure' water is made up of hydrogen and oxygen (H_2O), but all water in the environment contains other constituents. Measures of water quality are based upon these chemicals, that is the **hydrochemistry** of the water. Water quality, therefore, refers to the properties of the water. However, 'quality' is assessed with reference to the job water is doing or the way in which it is to be used. For example, the water quality, in terms of its hydrochemistry, required to support a vigorous aquatic ecosystem in a river is quite different from that delivered to our taps for us to drink. Water abstracted from rivers or **aquifers** for drinking purposes undergoes considerable treatment before its quality is tested. In this chapter we will explore the idea that 'quality' is a relative or comparative concept.

Cancer linked to river pollution

Polly Ghazi
Environment Correspondent

UNTIL recently, the picturesque village of Buckfastleigh in south Devon was renowned only for its ancient abbey, in an idyllic setting on the banks of the River Dart.

But in the past few weeks it has become the focus of a major health scare as officials investigate possible links between cancer clusters in nearby Torbay and chemicals pumped into the Dart's shallow waters.

One of England's best salmon and trout rivers, with its pristine source in the remote wilds of Dartmoor, the Dart is an unlikely possible culprit for a pollution blackspot. But Buckfastleigh's main employers, two wool processing factories, one owned by the Axminster Carpet Company, have pumped hundreds of thousands of tonnes of industrial waste, via sewage works, into the river for the past two decades.

Public health officials believe that industrial detergents discharged after being used to clean sheep fleeces may be partly to blame for the high number of women dying from breast cancer in south Devon.

Tap water supplied from the Dart to Torquay, Brixham and Paignton, the popular coastal resorts of Torbay, is being tested for traces of the suspect chemicals.

The investigation, launched by three district councils, represents a national test case into the public health risk from old-fashioned 'non-ionic' detergents pumped into rivers via sewage works. The detergents are known to be toxic to river life and are being phased out by many users.

There are no national standards setting safe levels of factory discharges of non-ionic industrial detergents, 18 000 tons of which are used in Britain every year. But a spokesman for the National Rivers Authority said spot checks in the Dart had found only 'very low traces' of nonylphenols, the main breakdown product under suspicion.

Only one of the companies discharging trade waste into the Dart, Devonia Products, still uses non-ionic detergents and a spokesman said alternatives were being urgently discussed.

A South-West Water spokesman said tests at its Torbay drinking water treatment plant over the past fortnight had found no traces of the suspect chemicals. 'Torbay's drinking water is safe and meets all the UK and European standards,' he said.

Figure 10.1 River Dart, Devon – cancer clusters cause health scare (Source: The Observer, 21 August 1994)

Water quality management

Water quality management is complex because the water abstracted from a stream or a **groundwater store** is the output from several processes operating through the **drainage basin** (Fig. 2.6). Remember that much water has arrived in the river channel not from **quickflow** runoff, but via **slowflow** routes through the soil and groundwater stores (see Chapters 2 and 8). This journey may have taken several decades. Thus, geology, climate, vegetation and land use all interact to influence the properties of stream water, groundwater and consequently tap water (Fig. 10.2). In general, the more intensive and varied the human activities in a drainage basin, the more difficult is water quality management.

Figure 10.2 Nitrate concentrations at boreholes under a limestone aquifer and a sandstone aquifer (Source: MAFF, 1993)

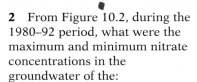

2 From Figure 10.2, during the 1980–92 period, what were the maximum and minimum nitrate concentrations in the groundwater of the:
a limestone,
b sandstone aquifer?

3 Groundwater will eventually enter into streams. Describe the seasonal patterns of nitrate concentration in a stream whose basin is underlain by:
a limestone,
b sandstone.

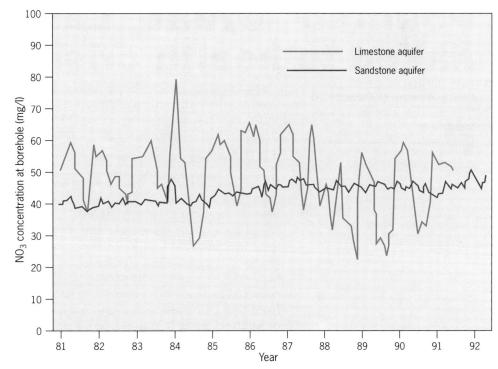

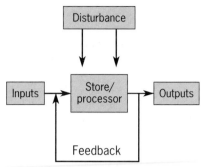

Figure 10.3 Pollution disturbs the in-stream purification process

10.3 The pollution of rivers, lakes and seas

In this section we shall focus mainly on river water **pollution**, but similar factors affect groundwater, and we must remember that there is a close two-way relationship between stream water and groundwater.

Definitions

Rivers have their own in-built 'purification power', i.e. processes which work to absorb and control the effects of the introduced materials. This is called the **assimilation capacity** of the river and is an example of **negative feedback**. Each river has its own unique assimilation capacity, and within a river there will be variations over time. Some researchers claim that 'it is upon the in-stream processes of purification that we depend across the world when using rivers as conveyor belts for the waste products of housing, farming and industry' (Newson, 1992).

None the less, waters do become polluted, so what do we mean by 'water pollution'? A simple definition is 'the introduction of damaging loads or concentrations of material or compounds' (Newson, 1992). Notice the word 'damaging'. This refers to the impacts on living organisms in the river (the biotic community) and to effects on users of water abstracted from the river. This is distinct from **contamination**, which is a general term used to refer to 'the introduction of new material and compounds to the system' (Newson, 1992), i.e. not necessarily at damaging levels. Pollution disturbs the water system, causing a change in hydrochemistry and in water quality (Fig. 10.3).

Inputs of contaminants and pollutants come from two types of source:

1 **Point sources**: discharges into a river at a specific location, e.g. sewage effluent from a pipe; irrigation ditch return flow.

2 **Diffuse sources**: inputs are from an area rather than a point and often arrive in the channel via bed and banks after soil water and groundwater **percolation**, e.g. nitrate and phosphate excesses from agricultural fertiliser; acid rain.

Figure 10.4 Water quality issues for Canada and the USA in the Great Lakes (*Source*: The *Guardian*, 18 February 1994)

Polluted Great Lakes linked to health crisis

Claire Trevena in Toronto

POLLUTION in the Great Lakes is being linked to a spread in cancer, damage to human reproductive systems, and developmental problems in children.

A report yesterday by the International Joint Commission, the water quality watchdog for the five lakes, called on the US and Canadian governments and industry to halt the discharge of chemical waste into the lakes because it was ending up in the food chain.

Efforts to control the discharge of toxic compounds had failed and substances which were supposed to be banned were being released into the environment.

Canada and the US signed a water quality agreement in 1972 to try to improve the quality of the Great Lakes. But the commission said governments and industry did not realise how great the problem still was.

Among the commission's recommendations was that the chemical industry find a way to halt the use of chlorine in manufacturing.

But it has wider goals, and called on the Canadian and US governments to find out what pollutants were being released, and establish a timetable for them to be banned.

The commission admitted that these recommendations had been around since the agency was formed 22 years ago; now the evidence of a threat to human health was greater.

While the report was welcomed by environmental groups, the chemical industry said there was still not enough evidence to support a ban on certain compounds.

?

4 Study Figure 10.4.
a What are the pollutants and where do they come from? You may find it useful to base your answer on a systems diagram.
b What effects do these pollutants have?
c What evidence is given which suggests that pollution is difficult to control?
d Why do you think this pollution is proving so difficult to control?

Clearly, diffuse sources of pollution are more difficult than point sources to identify, monitor and control in both rivers and aquifers.

Water pollution of rivers and lakes is a global problem reflecting three main causal factors: changes in agricultural techniques; growth of urban populations and their wastes; the advance of industrial technology. Even where the sources and causes are known, and when action has been taken, pollution is proving very difficult to control (Fig. 10.4). In densely populated, industrialised regions, such as the Great Lakes of North America, or the UK, the difficulties are perhaps not surprising. In the UK alone, there are more than 12 000 licensed discharge points along our rivers and lakes (Fig. 10.1).

Across extensive areas of the economically developing world, people take drinking water directly from rivers and shallow wells without further treatment. Also, there are widespread inputs of untreated sewage and industrial effluents into these same streams and aquifers. This situation clearly produces a pollution hazard, although populations exposed regularly to such conditions develop a degree of resistance.

Industrial pollution sources

In Europe, as in North America, water pollution control is a complex and slow process, partly because it is often an international problem and because the range and source of pollutants are so varied (Table 10.1).

As long ago as 1974, the countries surrounding the North Sea, including the UK, signed an agreement known as the Paris Convention. The aim was to reduce industrial discharges of heavy metals into rivers. (Seas and oceans are the sinks into which rivers dump their pollutant loads.) In 1990, in response to growing public concern, another agreement was signed. This aimed to reduce discharges of 38 poisonous substances by 50 per cent by 1995.

Within the UK, industrial pollution of rivers affects both river life and water supplies (Fig. 10.5). For instance, for several days in April 1994 approximately 100 000 people in the Worcester area of the Severn Valley were unable to use their tap water. The river which supplied their water was

Figure 10.5 The River Tyne: an ecological disaster zone? (*Source: Environment Guardian*, 16 March 1990)

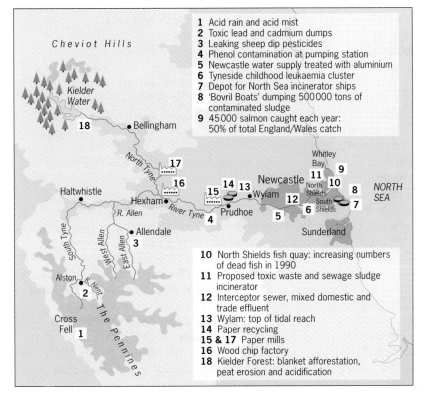

1 Acid rain and acid mist
2 Toxic lead and cadmium dumps
3 Leaking sheep dip pesticides
4 Phenol contamination at pumping station
5 Newcastle water supply treated with aluminium
6 Tyneside childhood leukaemia cluster
7 Depot for North Sea incinerator ships
8 'Bovril Boats' dumping 500 000 tons of contaminated sludge
9 45 000 salmon caught each year: 50% of total England/Wales catch
10 North Shields fish quay: increasing numbers of dead fish in 1990
11 Proposed toxic waste and sewage sludge incinerator
12 Interceptor sewer, mixed domestic and trade effluent
13 Wylam: top of tidal reach
14 Paper recycling
15 & 17 Paper mills
16 Wood chip factory
18 Kielder Forest: blanket afforestation, peat erosion and acidification

Table 10.1 Sources of water pollution (*Source:* Newson, 1992)

Type	Factors influencing
Domestic sewage	BOD; suspended solids; ammonia; nitrate; phosphate
Chemical industry	BOD; ammonia; phenols; non-biodegradable organics; heat
Iron and steel manufacturers	Cyanide; phenols; pH; ammonia; sulphides
Coal mining	Suspended solids; iron; pH; dissolved solids
Metal finishing	Cyanide; copper; cadmium; nickel; pH
Dairy products	BOD; pH
Oil refineries	Heat; ammonia; phenols; oil; sulphide
Power generation	Heat

Note: BOD = the biological oxygen demand, a common measure of organic pollution. It represents the amount of biochemically degradable substances in the water or effluent sample. A test sample is stored in darkness for five days at 20°C and the amount of oxygen taken up by the micro-organisms present is measured in grams per cubic metre. A clean mountain stream will have a value in the region of 0.05 mg/l.

?

5 Study Figure 10.6.
a What has caused the pollution?
b What are the effects?
c What are issues involved in solving the problem?
d What do you think should be done, who should pay and who should be responsible? Give reasons for your answer.

6 From Figures 10.7 and 10.8, compare and contrast the character of water pollution in England and Wales with that of Scotland. Suggest possible reasons for any differences you identify.

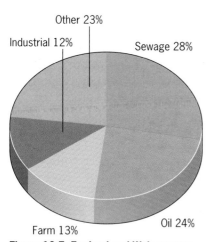

Figure 10.7 England and Wales: water pollution incidents reported by source of pollution, 1991 (*Source:* Institute of Hydrology, 1993)

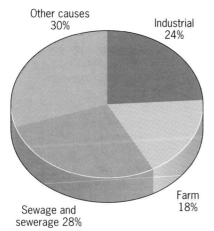

Figure 10.8 Scotland: water pollution incidents reported by source of pollution, 1991 (*Source:* Institute of Hydrology, 1993)

Acid water in old mine shafts 'damages the balance of life'

WHERE coalfields have been closed, as in County Durham, contamination of rivers and drinking water becomes a serious risk as mines, once kept dry by pumping, fill and overflow.

Northumbria Water, which extracts large quantities of drinking water from the River Wear, has expressed serious concern about the overflow. The acid water from mine shafts would damage the balance of life in the river and, according to the National Rivers Authority, kill most of the fish.

Some water tables in mining areas have been controlled for centuries by pumping from old shafts. Otherwise acid water percolates through, picking up heavy metals and other pollutants before overflowing into rivers. British Coal is keeping some pumps going in the Durham coalfield to prevent ecological damage, but maintaining them will cost several million pounds a year. The Government has yet to decide who will pay after BC is privatised.

Any proposal to turn pumps off has to be backed up by a detailed justification by BC. There is no proposal at present to do so in the sensitive southwest area of the Durham coalfield at Vinovium, Page Bank and Ushaw Moor.

At Westoe, near Wearmouth, pumps have been turned off, but pumping will restart from new submersible pumps in three to six months.

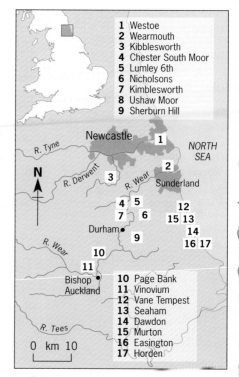

Figure 10.6 Water pollution from old mines (*Source:* The *Guardian*, 15 April 1994)

polluted by a point source chemical discharge from a factory further upstream at Wem, in Shropshire. Not all such problems arise from present-day industry, as earlier industries can leave problems behind. Who is responsible, who should pay and how control can be achieved, have become important issues as mining declines extensively across the UK (Fig. 10.6).

Urban sources of pollution

Despite the high profile some incidents achieve, industry is not the major source of river pollution in the UK (Figs 10.7 and 10.8). Sewage, largely from urban areas, is the main source, accounting for more than one-quarter of all pollution. This is despite huge expenditure on treatment plants and strict regulations, such as the 1993 EC Urban Waste Water Treatment Directive. Treatment plants remove about 95 per cent of the polluting load of sewage before the water is discharged into inland rivers. The water service companies responsible for sewage treatment and disposal in England and Wales (in Scotland and Northern Ireland there are Regional Councils) must obtain formal consents from the NRA to discharge treated sewage. Consent conditions vary according to the assimilative capacity of the receiving waters, but this does not account for the wide regional variations in standards recorded (Fig. 10.9). Yet incident levels are falling. In the early 1990s, less than 10 per cent of sewage treatment works were below the required standard, compared with 23 per cent in 1986.

?

7 Incidents of water pollution by industry tend to receive higher media profiles than do sewage pollution incidents. Suggest reasons for this.

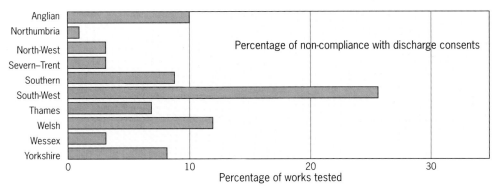

Percentage of non-compliance with discharge consents

Anglian
Northumbria
North-West
Severn–Trent
Southern
South-West
Thames
Welsh
Wessex
Yorkshire

Percentage of works tested

Figure 10.9 England and Wales: river and canal quality, 1980, 1985 and 1990 (Source: Institute of Hydrology, 1993)

Water pollution in the former USSR and Eastern Europe

Water pollution is a problem not only in capitalist systems. Since the communist regimes of Eastern Europe and the USSR collapsed at the end of the 1980s, the environmental impacts of their centralised command economies and the consequences of more than four decades of over-investment in heavy and heavily pollutant industry have been revealed. Across the vast expanses of the former USSR, all major rivers are polluted (Fig. 10.10). Throughout Eastern Europe, water pollution is a major problem: from the Baltic to the Black Sea and along the main arteries of the rivers Vistula, Oder and Danube we see closed beaches, decimated fish stocks and hazardous drinking water (Fig. 10.11). In trying to achieve rapid industrial growth, environmental controls were often neglected.

By 1994 in the former USSR, waste from Moscow included 15 tonnes of metals daily to four massive sewage plants. At least three tonnes of this passes into the Moscow River and on to the Volga. Further east, environmentalists have become increasingly concerned over Lake Baikal. It is the world's deepest lake, and one of the purest, but by the late 1980s, parts were classified as 'severely polluted'. The main sources of the pollution are the huge Baikalsk pulp and paper mills near Irkutsk on the lake's southern shore. Yet, as the figures of Table 10.2 show, by 1990 the Russians had responded to the ecological threat by improving the treatment of wastes. Indeed, in 1992, the Russian government promised to close the mills, but by 1994 they were still open.

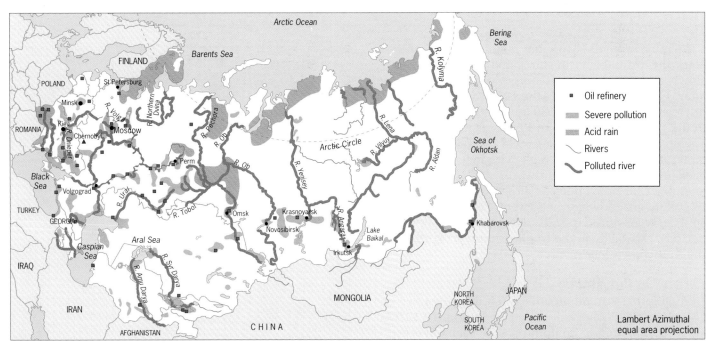

Figure 10.10 A universe of pollution (Source: Institute of Geography, Russian Academy of Sciences; Natural Resources Defence Council, Washington DC)

Figure 10.11 Water problems in Eastern Europe

Czech Republic
70% of rivers are polluted by mining wastes, nitrates, liquid manure and oil. 40% of all sewage is untreated. 50% of all drinking water is contaminated.

Former East Germany
66% of rivers and 23% of standing water bodies need cleaning. Noxious emissions from power stations are uncontrolled. Organic waste is responsible for 80% of the pollution and metals for 3%.

Baltic Sea
Greenpeace has labelled the Gulf of Gdańsk 'an ecological disaster zone'.

River Danube
Because the Danube serves as a border between countries, it is used as a convenient dumping place. It has attracted a wide variety of polluting industries from its source in Germany to its mouth in Romania, including chemicals, iron and steel, paper and petroleum.

Poland
50% (6 billion m3) of industrial and municipal effluent is dumped into Poland's rivers every year. The Vistula, from Warsaw to the sea at Gdańsk, is too polluted to be used even in industry. 95% of the river water is unfit for drinking.

Hungary
Adequate sewerage systems exist for only 46% of the population. Almost 800 towns and villages use water thought to be unfit for consumption. Over 100000 tonnes of nitrogen seeps into groundwater supplies annually.

Romania
85% of Romania's main rivers contain water unfit for drinking. Pollution of the River Tisza, which flows into Hungary, is causing concern to the Hungarian government.

Bulgaria
Experts forecast that by the year 2000 the Black Sea will be dead if pollution rates continue.

Table 10.2 Quality of treated water released by Baikalsk Mills (*Source: George, 1994*)

Year	Prime pulp (tonnes/year)	Fresh water flow (m3/y)	Sewage water flow (m3/y)	pH	BOD (mg/l)	Suspended substances (mg/l)	Mineral substances (mg/l)	Oxygen (mg/l)	Sulphur organics (mg/l)	Phenols (mg/l)	Chlorides (mg/l)	Sulphates (mg/l)
1985	215.005	116.688	674	6.4	4.5	9.3	618	7.1	0.13	0.011	93	307
1986	224.000	110.160	629	6.4	2.5	6.4	606	7.3	0.17	0.011	105	301
1987	219.000	106.910	599	6.4	1.7	3.2	568	7.8	0.15	0.011	101	250
1988	217.790	89.805	587	6.4	1.4	2.3	521	7.7	0.16	0.009	97.3	234
1989	213.869	83.285	587	6.4	1.8	2.7	485	–	0.16	0.009	93.8	230.4
1990	191.141	81.376	575	6.3	1.3	3.0	448	7.5	0.16	0.008	91	211

We must remember too that pollutants, once they enter the drainage basin stores, may be released slowly and delivered to streams and lakes many years later. For example, during the 1950s and 1960s, a nuclear military complex 80 km north of Chelyabinsk, in the Ural Mountains, poured wastes into the River Techa. A reporter writing in 1994 claimed, 'river banks and **sediment** still tingle with long-lived caesium and strontium' (Edwards, 1994). The fallout from the Chernobyl nuclear disaster of 1987 continues to pollute groundwater and rivers. Pollution from oil spills may be stored in soils and streams for long periods, especially in the fragile tundra **ecosystems** of the Arctic northlands.

Oil spill in the Arctic
In August 1994 an oil pipeline burst near the town of Usinsk, in the Pechora drainage basin (Fig. 10.12). An earthen dam built to contain the spill then burst in September after heavy rain. An area of more than 67 km2 was covered by a slick 10 cm deep.

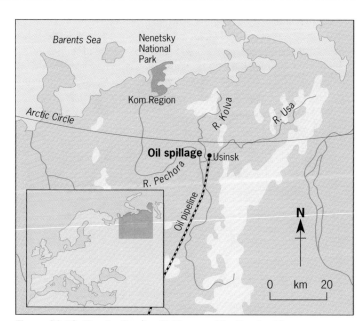

Figure 10.12 The Arctic oil spill (*Source: The Sunday Times*, 30 October 1994) © Times Newspapers Ltd 1994

Close to the Arctic Circle, this region has a fragile tundra ecosystem underlain by a deep zone of permafrost. During the summer and autumn of 1994 there was much secrecy and uncertainty about the oil spill. As late as November figures varying from 14 000 tonnes to 60 000 tonnes of oil spillage were still being claimed. Yet three things were indisputable:

1 Large quantites of heavy crude oil had spread on to the tundra and into rivers.

2 The pollution had moved down the Pechora River into the Barents Sea.

3 Clean-up efforts were inadequate.

Figure 10.13 Burning oil lake following the oil spill, Usinsk

This disaster was waiting to happen. The pipeline is 20 years old and it's been leaking, on and off, since 1988. We're worried that the hot oil will enter the permafrost and remain there for generations. We shall be sending experts to advise on the spill.

US government official

We realise that we originally underestimated the size of the spill. This is a dangerous ecological situation and we will continue to work through the winter to clear the oil. Freezing temperatures will turn the oil into a slow-moving sludge which will be easier to clean.

Spokesperson for the Russian government

This is not an ecological disaster. Nothing or no one has suffered. About 14 000 tonnes of boiling oil has escaped, but the spill has been contained. Most of the oil has been cleaned up, but the temperature has now dropped to -10°C and further work will have to wait until spring. I doubt that the oil will have a dangerous effect on the tundra.

Komineft oil company executive

I haven't read that much about the spill. It hasn't really been in the news. Perhaps it's because few people live in that part of the country. Anyway, the oil will end up in the Arctic, not Moscow.

Architect in Moscow

Our river water is contaminated with oil and the snow on the river banks is a grey sludge. The fish smell of oil and are inedible.

Villager living 300 km downstream of the Pechora River

This is the largest spill since the 1989 Exxon Valdez disaster in Alaska. About 60 000 tonnes of oil have been spilt.

We fear that the oil will flow down the Pechora River and into the Barents Sea. Precious tundra wildlife such as Arctic foxes, lemmings, snowy owls and reindeer will be affected. Thousands of migratory birds, some rare, such as the Bewick swan, will arrive in spring. The Pechora is also Europe's richest salmon river, where thousands of salmon come to spawn in spring. If oil has been slowly leaking over time, effects are already likely to have accumulated in other fish.

During the warmer summer months the oil will become vaporous and spread more widely through the tundra region.

Environmentalist

Figure 10.14 The ecological impact of the oil spill (*After: The Guardian*, 26 October 1994 and *The Sunday Times*, 30 October 1994)

?

8 Draw an annotated systems diagram (inputs–stores–throughputs–outputs) to explain why stream pollution may continue long after the initial input of oil has stopped.

9 Read Figure 10.14.

a Outline what happened in the Usinsk oil spill.

b In what ways do the long cold winter and the frozen environment influence the impact of the pollutants?

c Why do you think the various interested parties have such contrasting understandings and opinions of the event and its consequences?

Agricultural sources of pollution

In addition to artificial fertiliser residues, farms generate several forms of effluent which can cause pollution. First, the rigorous cleansing process on dairy farms produces large volumes of water which contain impurities. Secondly, there is slurry or animal waste. This is commonly spread thinly and irregularly across fields and, once there, causes few problems unless flushed into rivers by heavy rain. However, if it is left in high concentrations in farmyards or on fields near streams, it can be dangerous – undiluted slurry is 100 times more polluting than domestic sewage. Thirdly, there is silage. This is cut grass which is allowed to ferment in the absence of air to produce an animal feed rich in sugars. Unlike hay, the grass for silage does not need drying and, because it is easy to store and handle with modern equipment, silage production in England and Wales tripled between 1976 and 1986. Unfortunately, the silage process produces a liquid effluent with a polluting power higher than animal waste. It is very acid (has a low pH) and has a very high **biological oxygen demand** (BOD). Consequently, once it reaches streams, it has a disastrous effect upon aquatic life.

Where slurry and silage effluent are allowed to leak from the farm storage areas, impacts can be rapid and severe. Pollution occurs because bacteria use oxygen in the water to break down the high organic content. This results in deoxygenation of the water, which quickly kills fish and other aquatic life.

Waste and silage effluent leakage make up a large proportion of all farm incidents in England and Wales (Fig. 10.15), and their number more than doubled during the 1980s to over 3500. The reasons for this are mixed (Fig 10.16).

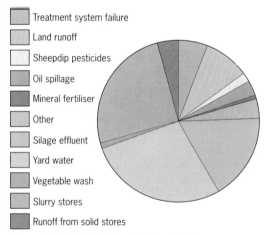

- Treatment system failure
- Land runoff
- Sheepdip pesticides
- Oil spillage
- Mineral fertiliser
- Other
- Silage effluent
- Yard water
- Vegetable wash
- Slurry stores
- Runoff from solid stores

Figure 10.15 England and Wales: total farm pollution incidents by cause, 1986 (*Source*: Water Authorities Association, 1987)

'The main causes of [river] deterioration are sewage effluents and agricultural practices with a few localised problems due to sewerage problems ... of particular concern is the impact of repeated pollution incidents in rural areas. Silage liquors and animal wastes are so polluting that even small quantities can be sufficient to affect water quality'.

Figure 10.16 Reasons for waste and sewage leakage (*Source:* HMSO, 1986)

In the early 1990s there were signs that the increases in UK river pollution had been stopped. Less intensive agriculture, the introduction of stricter building, storage and handling regulations from 1991 and firmer prosecutions all helped. The Government, too, has introduced positive schemes to encourage farmers to improve river water quality. For instance, in May 1994 a 'water fringe habitat scheme' was launched in six pilot areas (Fig. 10.17). The aim is to encourage farmers to stop applying fertiliser or pesticide across a 20 m wide fringe either side of a stream. This will protect the water from pollution, allow the growth of plants as a buffer zone from agriculture, and improve the stream's in-built 'purification power'. The fringes will also act as wildlife habitats and corridors for movement and colonisation. In 1994 the grants payable to farmers joining this scheme were £240–360 per ha.

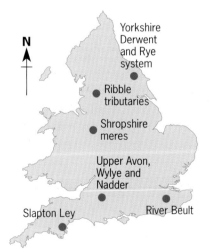

N

Yorkshire Derwent and Rye system

Ribble tributaries

Shropshire meres

Upper Avon, Wylye and Nadder

Slapton Ley

River Beult

Figure 10.17 Proposed water fringe areas, 1994 (*Source*: The *Guardian*, 16 May 1994)

A Herefordshire farming incident, England

A change in farming practice

Land on a farm in North Herefordshire slopes gently northwards towards a stream which flows into the River Teme (Fig. 10.18). In 1984 the farmer decided to intensify his animal-rearing enterprise. In order to be able to keep more cattle, he built a new shed (at A) to house 80 animals through the winter. To increase the feed supply, he changed his feeding regime from mainly hay to silage and so dug a long silage pit (at B). During the winter, when the ground is generally too wet to allow animal waste to be spread on the fields, the waste was cleared from the shed and piled outside (at C).

The consequences

In the wet spring of 1988, water pollution was recorded 4 km downstream in the River Teme. The source of the pollution was traced back to the farm. Slurry from the shed and manure piles, and silage from the pit had reached the field ditches by surface runoff and ground seepage. This had then been transported by the local stream to the River Teme.

The solution

The farmer was taken to court and fined. He was given advice on the storage and handling of the wastes and silage, and was required to upgrade his buildings and change the farm layout. He received a grant to help with the cost of these changes. First he relocated his silage pit (at D) further from the field ditches. Next he laid a leakage-free waste yard (at E) outside his animal shed and reorganised the drainage from the shed to lead into this yard. Since completion in 1991, there has been no further evidence of water pollution.

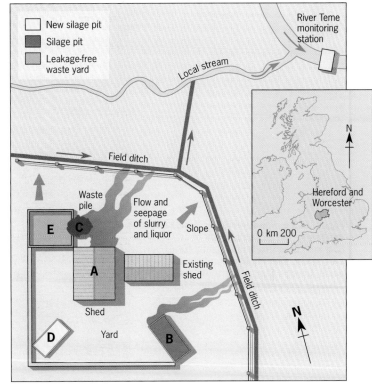

Figure 10.18 Managing a farm pollution source

?

10   Explain the role played by changing farming practice in causing pollution.

11   Explain why the changes made since the court case have reduced the risk of stream pollution.

10.4 The solute load of rivers

Most of the pollutants we have discussed are found in water in their dissolved state. They become part of the **solute load** of a river. However, we must not forget that all rivers have a hydrochemistry. In the environment there is no stream which consists of 'pure ' H_2O. It is normal for streams to carry and transfer a solute load. In this section we explore what we mean by 'normal'. By focusing on the nitrate content of our water, we shall examine how these 'normal' conditions are altered.

From Table 10.3 we can see the major properties of water in the River Stour (Fig. 10.19). The table shows the main constituents of the solute load of this river and summarises the river's hydrochemistry. The details are complicated, but we can pick out three basic understandings:
• There is a wide variety of dissolved materials in the river.
• The solute load shows year-to-year variation.
• There is a range of values for all constituents of the solute load within a particular year.

Table 10.3 River Stour at Langham, Essex: water quality

	Year 1989			Year 1992			Years 1974–91
	Mean	Max	Min	Mean	Max	Min	Average
Temperature (°C)	11.7	21.5	2.0	12.1	23.5	3.0	11.3
pH	8.3	9.0	7.8	8.4	9.1	8.0	8.2
Conductivity (yS/cm)	871	1011	716	942	1280	799	914
BOD (mg/l O)	2.6	7.8	0.7	3.0	10.4	1.0	3.2
Nitrate (mg/l N)	6.33	15.10	0.50	7.49	19.96	1.30	7.80
Chloride (mg/l Cl)	72.0	293.0	35.5	78.4	180.0	48.5	68.9
Total alkalinity (mg/l $CaCO_3$)	253.0	285.0	295.0	242.7	280.0	219.0	246.2
Silica (mg/l SiO_2)	10.57	46.10	3.70	8.53	13.83	0.32	7.72
Sulphate (mg/l SO_4)	90.7	119.0	71.6	194.4	191.3	69.9	104.1
Calcium (mg/l Ca)	128.8	145.0	108.0	137.8	171.0	108.0	134.4
Magnesium (mg/l Mg)	8.3	11.8	6.2	7.41	10.70	5.70	8.80
Potassium (mg/l K)	8.6	12.7	5.6	7.43	9.60	4.60	7.60
Sodium (mg/l Na)	47.5	67.0	31.0	40.3	56.0	24.1	43.9
Suspended solids (mg/l)	11.6	122.0	0.5	22.6	166.0	2.5	16.1

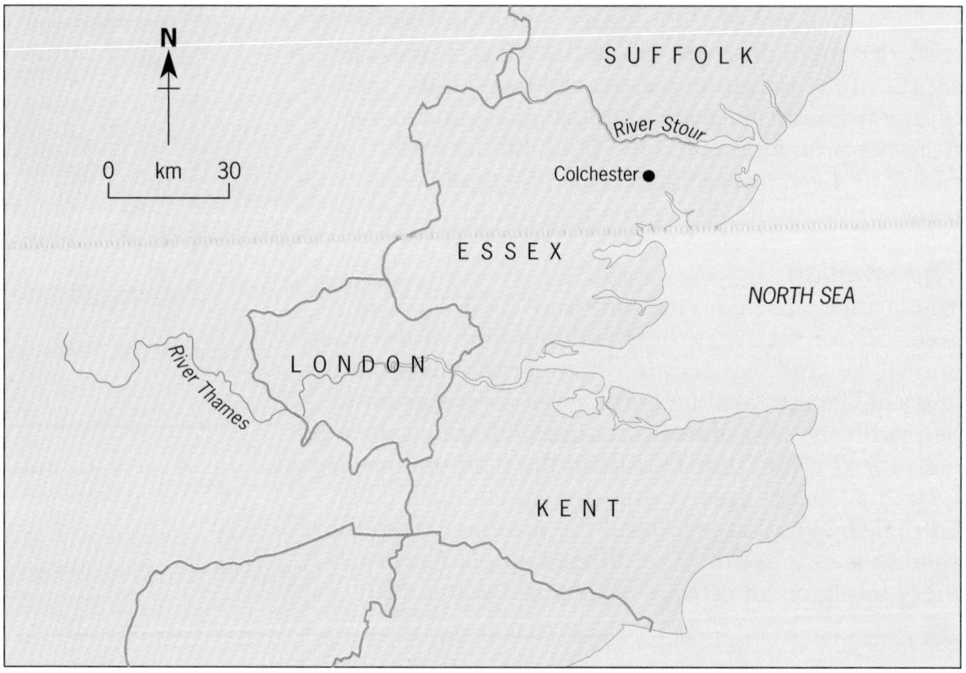

Figure 10.19 The River Stour drains an intensively farmed catchment of 578 km² in Essex. It is a mainly rural catchment, with chalk outcrops in the north, London Clay in the south and a cover of semi-pervious Boulder Clay

Table 10.4 Mean solute load concentrations in the world's rivers (*Source*: Newson, 1992)

Solute	Average load (mg/l)
Calcium (Ca^{2+})	13.5
Magnesium (Mg^{2+})	3.6
Sodium (Na^+)	7.4
Potassium (K^+)	1.35
Chlorine (Ci^-)	9.6
Sulphate (SO_4^{2-})	8.7
Hydrogen carbonate (HCO_3^-)	52.0
Silicon oxide (SiO_2)	10.4
Total all solutes	106.6

?

12 Study Tables 10.3 and 10.4. Compare the River Stour's hydrochemistry with the world averages.

The River Stour is affected by human activities. **Streamflow** is increased by intermittent pumping from an Ely–Ouse water transfer scheme and occasional borehole pumping. It is also influenced by groundwater abstraction and recharge. Water is abstracted for industrial, agricultural and public use. However, the River Stour's solute composition is not unusual, nor is it an especially polluted river. In the 1990 National River Quality Survey (see Fig. 10.23), it is listed in Class 2, which indicates a 'fair' water quality.

All rivers, therefore, carry varied solute loads. This load, that is the stream's hydrochemistry, is influenced by **discharge**, water temperatures and the pathways that water takes to reach the channel (Fig. 10.20). For example, in the Peak District of the southern Pennines, streams with headwaters on Carboniferous Limestones have a different chemical make-up from streams which originate on Millstone Grits. So, we talk of 'hard' or 'soft' water from our taps. Streams from acid peat moorlands differ from streams within deciduous woodlands, and so on. The mean pH of stream water is approximately 4.6, but commonly ranges from 4.0 to 5.0.

Figure 10.20 Sources of solutes to streams (*Source*: Newson, 1992).

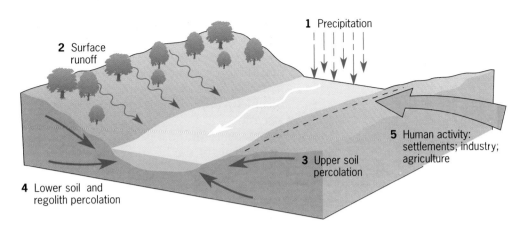

1 Precipitation

2 Surface runoff

3 Upper soil percolation

4 Lower soil and regolith percolation

5 Human activity: settlements; industry; agriculture

?

13 From Figure 10.20, suggest three of the effects that increased human activities could have upon the other solute sources to streams.

Relationships between discharge and solute load

We can measure the quantity of the solute load, i.e. how much there is, or its concentration, i.e. how much there is per unit volume. Hydrologists usually use concentration levels, e.g. milligrams of solute per litre of water. Thus, if discharge doubles while the amount of a particular mineral remains constant, then the concentration will be halved.

Dilution and pumping effects

The relationship between river flow and its solute concentration is complex. In some situations, concentration decreases as flow increases. This is known as the **dilution effect**. In other situations, concentration may increase as flow increases. This is known as the **pumping effect**. We can illustrate both effects by studying nitrate concentrations.

In a mainly rural catchment, such as the River Leach in the Cotswolds, nitrate levels in streams may rise as flow increases after a rainstorm, shown by three storm hydrograph peaks, A, B and C (Fig. 10.21). This is caused by surface runoff and soil water flow 'flushing' nitrates from the fields, i.e. a pumping effect. In a mainly urban catchment, on the other hand, sewage effluent may constitute a high proportion of the low flow. At high flows the nitrate may become diluted, so that nitrate concentration decreases as flow increases, i.e. the dilution effect.

In densely occupied countries such as the UK, most river basins include both urban and rural land uses. As a result, their hydrochemistry exhibits what is called mixed mechanism responses to fluctuations in discharge.

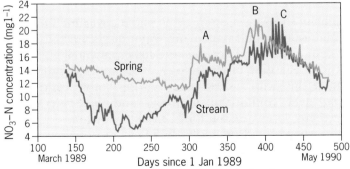

Figure 10.21(a) River Leach: seasonal changes in the nitrate concentration of the channel and nearby spring (*Source*: Burt and Haycock, 1992)

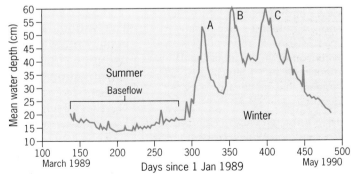

Figure 10.21(b) River Leach: stream discharge hydrograph (*Source*: Burt and Haycock, 1992)

Variations in solute load character

We should also understand that each of the water input sources shown in Figure 10.20 will have a distinctive hydrochemistry. Thus, when discharge consists entirely of the **base flow** component, the regolith and groundwater stores are the main sources of water, and the solute composition will depend heavily upon the nature of the bedrocks. Following a storm, surface runoff and soil water from the upper horizons increase, flushing solutes from organic sources and, in farming areas, chemicals such as nitrates. Thus, hydrologists need to distinguish between base flows and storm flows, and to be able to assess the contribution of each to the total solute load carried by a stream.

A measure of the base flow/storm or runoff flow is the **base flow index (BFI)**. This is 'the fraction of streamflow over a given period which is base flow' (Institute of Hydrology, 1992). In 1985, for the Kirkton Burn hydrograph at Balquhidder the BFI was 0.35, i.e. 35 per cent of the total flow in that year was base flow (Fig. 10.22).

Figure 10.22 Kirkton Burn at Balquhidder: hydrograph with separated flow, 1985 (*Source:* Littlewood, 1992)

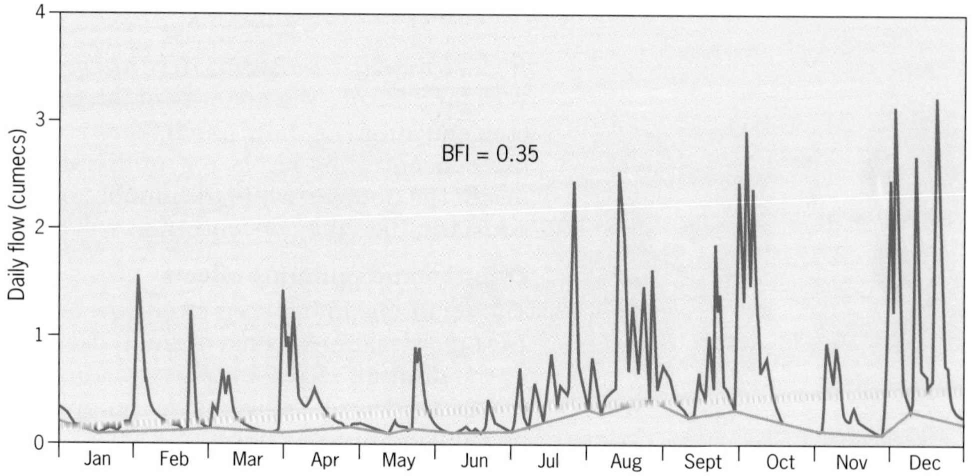

It is important for water quality managers to distinguish between solutes with a natural origin and those resulting from human activities (anthropogenic). The outcome of the complex ways in which these variables interact is that it is very difficult to measure, explain and therefore forecast the solute load of rivers. Even after a five-year national study of UK rivers, the Institute of Hydrology has concluded, 'The detailed nature of the links and interactions between natural hydrochemical processes, anthropogenic processes and the dynamics of stream chemistry is not yet fully understood' (Littlewood, 1992).

10.5 Managing water quality in UK rivers

The National Rivers Authority (NRA), set up in 1989, is the government agency responsible 'for maintaining and improving water quality and for pollution control, water resources, flood defence and fisheries, navigation, conservation and recreation' (Institute of Hydrology, 1993) in England and Wales. There are separate bodies with similar functions in Scotland and Northern Ireland. They regularly conduct river surveys, and place rivers in four classes according to their water quality (Fig. 10.23).

In the 1992 water quality survey for England and Wales, approximately 90 per cent of the total length of rivers was of Class 1, 'good' or Class 2, 'fair' quality. This was approximately the same as in 1980. In contrast, 99 per cent of the length of the rivers and lochs in Scotland was of Class 1 or 2 quality, a significant improvement since 1980. In Northern Ireland, the figure was 95 per cent, a slight improvement on earlier surveys. Alongside these water quality surveys, there is the Harmonised Monitoring Scheme (HMS) which is establishing a national database. A further 220 monitoring stations send in regular sample records to be added to the HMS database.

?

14 Make a list of factors which might influence the quality of river water. Identify 'natural' and 'human' factors separately.

15 From Figure 10.23, select *two* rivers in different regions which show significant stretches of 'poor' (Class 3) and 'bad' (Class 4) water quality. Use atlases and other reference material to suggest reasons for this poor quality.

16 Of the ten water regions of England and Wales, Northumbria shows the lowest proportion of polluted rivers. Less than three per cent are 'poor' or 'bad'. The highest pollution proportions are recorded for the North-West and South-West, both with 19 per cent classed as 'poor' or 'bad'. Suggest reasons for these characteristics.

**Figure 10.23 Quality of river water,
England and Wales, 1985
(*Source: HMSO, 1986*)**

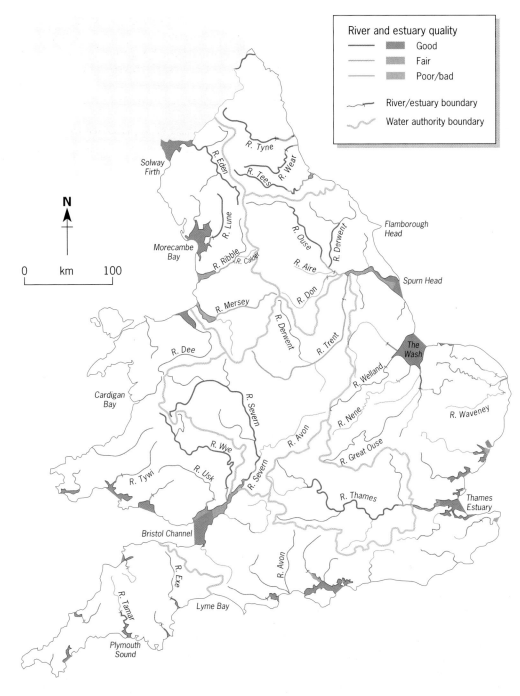

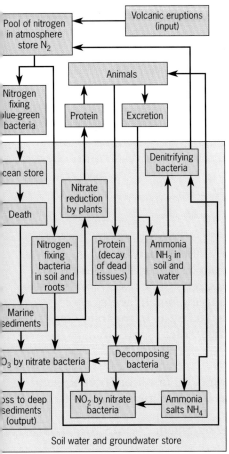

Figure 10.24 The nitrogen cycle

10.6 Water quality and the nitrate issue

Natural processes ensure that all streams contain nitrogen (N), most
commonly in nitrate form (as NO_3). For example decomposition of organic
matter in the surface litter layer and the soil horizons releases nitrogen as
soluble nitrate. Nitrogen is an essential element in all living matter, and is
recycled through the nitrogen cycle (Fig. 10.24). During photosynthesis,
plants such as cereal crops use about 30 kg of nitrogen to form one hectare
of green plant surface. Yet concern is growing that human activities – urban
and rural – are causing nitrogen and nitrate levels to rise dangerously in
many rivers and aquifers. For example, nitrate levels in the river water of
several regions exceed the EC prescribed limit of 50 mg/l (Figs 10.25 and
10.26).

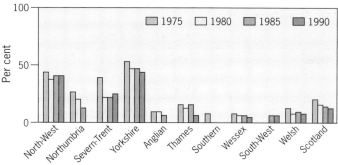

Figure 10.25 Mean percentage of sampling points where ammoniacal nitrogen exceeded 0.5 mg/l N, 1974–5

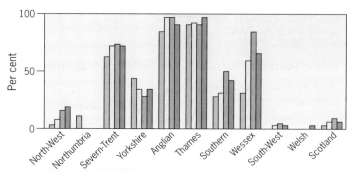

Figure 10.26 Mean percentage of sampling points where nitrate exceeded 5 mg/l N, 1974–5

?

17 Use the data of Figures 10.25 and 10.26 to assess the accuracy of the statement that nitrate levels in rivers have been rising over the past 20 years.

Excess nitrate can become a health hazard and, when in conjunction with phosphate, can lead to **eutrophication** of surface waters. Thus it has become a high-profile environmental issue.

Eutrophication

Pollution can be caused by the presence of too little or too much of specific solutes. Eutrophication means 'excessive enrichment', that is, too much, in this case of nitrogen and phosphorus. The normally low concentrations of nitrogen and phosphorus in water bodies control the growth of organisms, including phytoplankton and algae. However, if concentrations increase, these elements can become pollutants by making water unfit for human consumption or by encouraging **algal blooms**. Excess nitrates, mainly from inefficient application of artificial fertiliser on farmland, lead to the growth of green algae. The main sources of excess phosphates are farm wastes and treated urban sewage effluents. These generate blue-green algae.

Algal blooms, seen as surface blankets across the water, are most common on lakes, reservoirs and ponds, especially during warm, dry spells (Fig. 9.10). At such times water flow and movement is minimal. The growth of such blooms is a steady process whereby oxygen availability gradually decreases (Fig. 10.27). Eventually everything in the food chain is affected. During the 1988–92 UK drought, algal blooms became particularly widespread (see Chapter 9) as water bodies shrank and **throughflow** was reduced. Water supplies from some reservoirs were threatened and water-based recreational activities suspended. For example, the large Rutland Water reservoir in the East Midlands was seriously affected and closed for water sports over several periods during the 1990–2 summers.

The issue

In the UK, agriculture is most frequently blamed for high nitrate concentrations in river water. However, the relationship between agricultural practices and nitrate levels is not simple, and so the solution will not be easy. Two scientists wrote in 1992: 'The popular misconception is that the nitrate problem is caused by farmers applying too much fertiliser to crops so that the surplus left after harvest is leached away in the following winter; this is too simplistic' (Burt and Haycock, 1992).

Nitrates in the farm system

There are six sources of nitrate in the farm system (Table 10.5). Three aspects of farming practices influence how much of these nitrate inputs are 'lost', i.e. leached, to streams and aquifers:
1 the amount of organic and inorganic fertilisers applied;
2 the timing of the applications;
3 the crop and animal feeding patterns adopted.

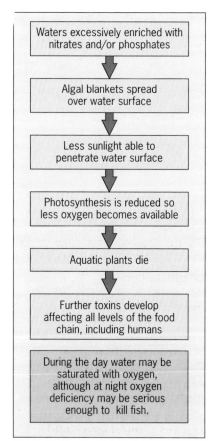

Figure 10.27 The development of algal blooms

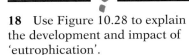

18 Use Figure 10.28 to explain the development and impact of 'eutrophication'.

19 Explain why eutrophication is more common on standing water bodies than in streams.

20 Suggest ways of reducing eutrophication.

Table 10.5 Sources of nitrate in the farm system

Input	Nitrogen (kg/ha/y)
1 Mineralisation of soil organic matter	50–100
2 Effects of cultivation, released by ploughing of a 3-year ley (rotation grass)	100–200
3 Mineralisation of organic nitrogen from crop residues	Variable according to crop patterns
4 Fertiliser residues	5–50 (cereals low, potatoes high)
5 Organic manures	Very variable according to animal densities
6 Atmospheric inputs (dissolved in rain)	40–50

In this system (Fig. 10.28) the aim of the farmer and the hydrologist is to match the nitrate input to crop needs and so maximise the proportion which is output as products rather than lost to streams and aquifers. The efficiency of the system will be affected by three variables: the crop yield per hectare; how much nitrate is already stored in the soil; and the loss of available nitrogen before the crop takes it up.

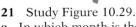

21 Study Figure 10.29.
a In which month is the soil nitrogen contrast greatest between early- and late-sown fields?
b Why might the timing of this maximum contrast have a particularly strong impact upon stream hydrochemistry?
c Suggest reasons why soil nitrogen concentration in fields with late sowing falls so rapidly during March.

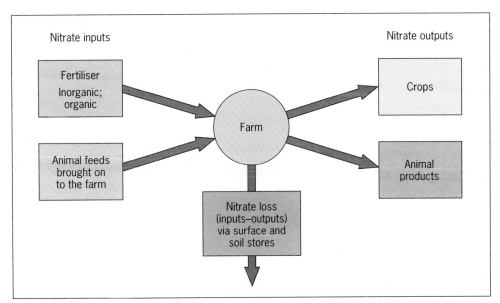

Figure 10.28 Nitrates in the farm system

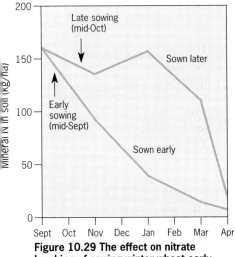

Figure 10.29 The effect on nitrate leaching of sowing winter wheat early or late (*Source*: MAFF, 1993)

These decisions interact with climatic rhythms and hydrological processes (Fig. 10.21). For example, in the UK stream and groundwater flows are lowest during the summer months. In this season, too, nitrogen take-up by plants is greatest. Consequently, from late spring through summer, leaching of nitrates is at a minimum. During the late autumn and winter months, heavier rainfall inputs, lower water take-up by plants, and reduced **evapotranspiration** cause soil and groundwater stores to become **saturated**. Runoff, **infiltration**, deep percolation and stream recharge combine to increase **leaching**.

Influence of farming practices
Farming practices can accelerate or slow down the leaching process. For instance, autumn ploughing triggers a surge of nitrate release and an increase in leaching. This can be particularly severe where the land is left bare until spring planting. For this reason the MAFF strongly advises farmers to plant as early in the autumn as possible. This gives ground cover and allows the young plants to take up nitrogen, and so reduces winter leaching (Fig. 10.29). It is worth noting that conservationists are concerned about this

trend to autumn planting. These crops, e.g. winter wheat and barley, may be harvested too early in the following summer for many ground-nesting birds and other field animals to complete their nesting and rearing cycles. This early harvest, and the increased early mowing of meadows for silage, are significant factors in the reduction in numbers of many species of farmland birds.

Government responses

Because of the impact of nitrate levels on aquatic ecosystems and upon public water supplies, the UK government introduced in 1990 the Pilot Nitrate Scheme to run for five years. Its aim is to reduce nitrate inputs to the groundwater store from farmland. The main strategy has been to designate ten Nitrate Sensitive Areas (NSAs), within which 'voluntary but substantial agricultural restrictions' were introduced (Fig. 10.30). In return for joining the scheme, farmers are compensated for loss of profits resulting from the changes in farming practice. (In 1993, compensation could be as high as £380 per ha.)

The scheme has four main requirements for the farmer:

1 Application of the correct (economic optimum) amount of nitrogen fertiliser to each field, with reductions in fertiliser input for winter cereals and oilseed rape;

2 a limit of 170 kg N/ha/y as livestock manure;

3 a ban on the autumn application of slurry or poultry manure;

4 use of cover crops where land would otherwise be bare during autumn and winter.

The farmer is also advised against grassland ploughing, especially in autumn.

In addition there are nine Nitrate Advisory Areas (NAAs) where advisory campaigns are run to encourage farmers to adopt good practice (Fig. 10.30). Seven of the nine NAAs are mainly groundwater catchments.

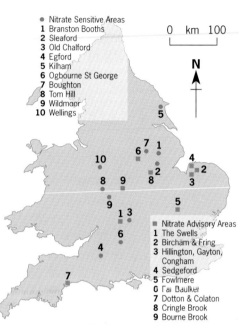

● Nitrate Sensitive Areas
1 Branston Booths
2 Sleaford
3 Old Chalford
4 Egford
5 Kilham
6 Ogbourne St George
7 Boughton
8 Tom Hill
9 Wildmoor
10 Wellings

■ Nitrate Advisory Areas
1 The Swells
2 Bircham & Fring
3 Hillington, Gayton, Congham
4 Sedgeford
5 Fowlmere
6 Tai Baulker
7 Dotton & Colaton
8 Cringle Brook
9 Bourne Brook

0 km 100

N

Figure 10.30 Location of NSAs and NAAs (*Source:* MAFF, 1993)

Summary

- All rivers and water bodies contain solute loads – the water's hydrochemistry. This is determined by a range of environmental variables. It is most commonly measured in terms of the concentration, i.e. the amount of a constituent per unit volume.

- The hydrochemistry of a river changes over time, especially in relation to discharge.

- Streams contain their own in-built 'purification power'. An important strategy for water managers is to sustain this power.

- People can alter the hydrochemistry and quality of river water, intentionally and accidentally.

- Water managers need to be able to distinguish between natural and anthropogenic components of the river's hydrochemistry.

- Water quality management involves two key dimensions: the maintenance of healthy biotic communities and the provision of potable (drinkable) water supplies.

- Water pollution results from the introduction of material and compounds at damaging levels of concentration.

- Point and diffuse pollution from human activities are caused by: agriculture, e.g. nitrates, farm wastes; cities, e.g. domestic wastes; industry, e.g. process effluents.

- Bodies such as the NRA in the UK and agencies of the EU are setting increasingly rigorous water control standards. However, consistent water quality maintenance is proving very difficult to achieve.

11 Bangladesh: water resource management

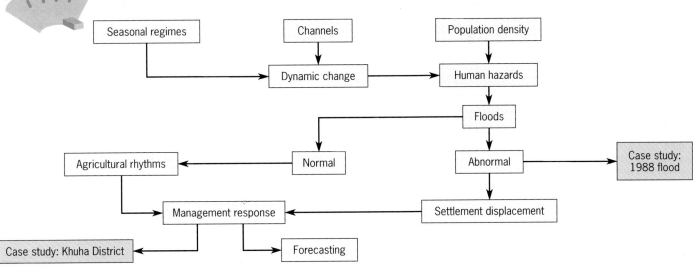

```
Seasonal regimes        Channels            Population density
                           │                      │
                           ▼                      ▼
            ──────▶ Dynamic change ──────▶ Human hazards
                                                  │
                                                  ▼
                                               Floods
                                      ┌───────────┴───────────┐
                                      ▼                       ▼
Agricultural rhythms ◀──────  Normal              Abnormal ──────▶ Case study:
        │                                             │               1988 flood
        │                                             ▼
        ▼                                       Settlement displacement
Management response ◀───────────────────────────────┘
        │        │
        ▼        ▼
Case study: Khuha District    Forecasting
```

11.1 Introduction

This chapter focuses on a single geographical unit: the nation-state of Bangladesh. It brings together the various aspects of rivers, **drainage basins**, and hydrological processes covered in previous chapters, and allows you to review your understanding by applying them to a specific situation.

11.2 Sediment, landforms and floods

The physical environment
Bangladesh lies in the lower **floodplain** and **delta** formed where three great rivers, the Ganges, Brahmaputra, and Meghna converge (Fig. 11.2). The delta is the output store of the drainage basin **sediment** transfer system, and owes its existence to the two billion tonnes of sediment delivered by the rivers each year.

Dhaka
23°46'N, 90°23'E

Figure 11.1 Climate graph for Dhaka, Bangladesh

The catchment basin of the three rivers covers almost 2 million km². Only 7.5% of this catchment area lies within Bangladesh.

Note: The Brahmaputra river is called the Jamuna in Bangladesh.

Figure 11.2 Bangladesh: catchment area of rivers entering Bangladesh

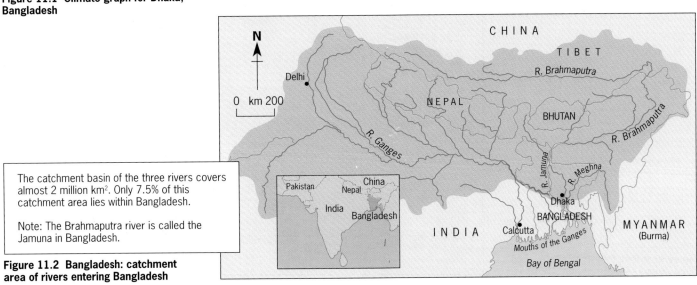

11

Table 11.1 Discharge data for Bangladesh's three major rivers (*Source*: Bramner, 1990)

Parameter (m³/s)	Ganges (Harding Bridge) (m³/s)	Brahmaputra (Bahadurabad) (m³/s)	Meghna (Bhairab Bazar) (m³/s)
Mean low flow	790*	37 550	1 332
Mean peak flow	51 625	65 491	14 047
Highest peak flow	76 000	98 600	19 800
Mean annual flow	8 544	19 557	6 748

*Mean for 1975–88 since operation of the Farakka barrage
Mean for 1934–74 was 1806 **(m³/s)**

Figure 11.3 Bangladesh is essentially a low-lying fluvial environment, with more than 80 per cent of the land lying less than 6 m above mean sea level

Like all active deltas, this is a dynamic and constantly changing environment, part water and part land (Fig. 11.3). The landscape is not merely 'flat', but shows a complexity (Fig. 11.4) which has important implications for water and flood management policy. The rivers all have strongly seasonal **regimes,** controlled by summer monsoon rains and snowmelt patterns in the Himalayan mountain catchments.

The main river channels are huge – up to 20 km wide in places – but have strong seasonal variations in **discharge** and sediment load (see Table 5.1). As is typical in deltas, channels are unstable, showing both **braided** and **meandering** forms. The meanders shift laterally, and the braided networks change constantly, reworking and relocating the sediment store of the delta surfaces. Lateral bank erosion rates of up to 860 m in a year have been

?

1a Use Figures 11.2, 11.4 and Table 11.1 to describe and explain the variation in discharge for the three major rivers of Bangladesh.
b Suggest what natural processes could affect these regimes.

Only 17 per cent of Bangladesh lies above normal flood levels.

Up to 40 per cent of the country experiences floods reaching 400 mm in depth.

Two per cent is covered by over 3 metres of water.

Figure 11.4 Bangladesh: landforms and flood areas (*After*: Bramner, 1990)

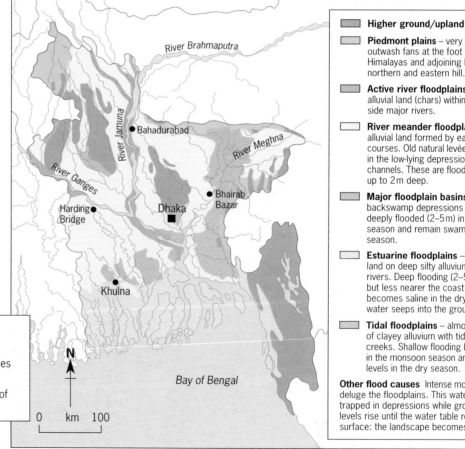

Higher ground/upland

Piedmont plains – very gently sloping outwash fans at the foot of the Himalayas and adjoining Bangladesh's northern and eastern hill.

Active river floodplains – ephemeral alluvial land (chars) within and alongside major rivers.

River meander floodplains – older alluvial land formed by earlier river courses. Old natural levées form ridges in the low-lying depressions and old channels. These are flooded seasonally up to 2 m deep.

Major floodplain basins – large old backswamp depressions which are deeply flooded (2–5 m) in the monsoon season and remain swampy in the dry season.

Estuarine floodplains – almost level land on deep silty alluvium with few rivers. Deep flooding (2–5 m) inland but less nearer the coast. The area becomes saline in the dry season as water seeps into the groundwater.

Tidal floodplains – almost level land of clayey alluvium with tidal rivers and creeks. Shallow flooding by river water in the monsoon season and at high tide levels in the dry season.

Other flood causes Intense monsoon rains deluge the floodplains. This water lies trapped in depressions while groundwater levels rise until the water table reaches the surface: the landscape becomes saturated.

?

2 What physical factors contribute to the seasonal flooding in Bangladesh? Consider the following in your answer and suggest their significance in extreme events:
- seasonal rainfall;
- seasonal flow regimes;
- snowmelt in the Himalayas;
- steep slopes and thin soils in an area of high structural instability (Himalayas);
- groundwater levels.

3 Produce an annotated sketch map to show the landforms in Bangladesh. Add notes on how these landforms develop and the nature of the rivers in the country.

recorded. Deposition in the channel bed creates large bedforms up to 15 m high and 100 m long which move downstream during floods at rates of up to 600 m a day. It is the combination of sheer scale and the constant and unpredictable fluctuations in channels, sediment and energy which make river management especially problematic.

Humans and hazards

This fragile and shifting environment is crowded (Table 11.2). It is therefore not surprising that people continue to move to hazardous, low-lying areas. The fresh silts, rich with organic and chemical nutrients, along with the year-round warmth and available water, permit two and even three crops a year.

Each year in May and June, the surge of high volume discharge fed by snowmelt in the Himalayan headwater catchments across India and Nepal moves down the tributaries and main channels of the three great rivers. By July, this surge is reaching Bangladesh and is further increased by the arrival of the summer monsoon rains on the mountains and the plains (Fig. 11.2). The result is that from July, about 25 per cent of Bangladesh is covered by up to one metre of water. Farmers plant rice and other crops as the water levels in their fields begin to fall from August onwards.

Even in normal years, the flood season brings significant changes to the landscape (Fig. 11.4). Consequently, thousands of people are forced to move each year and relocate on a new **char** or river bank (Fig. 11.6). A traditional Bengali folk song sums it up: 'The river wanders this way and breaks that way – that is the river's play'. Fatalism and an acceptance of risk is part of local culture.

Figure 11.5 A traveller crossing the region in August made these observations (*Source*: Cobb, 1993)

'Roads and rice fields were underwater. Here and there clusters of small huts huddled on tiny patches of high ground.... All day I had been travelling across flooded rice fields, and in my mind that added up to catastrophe, disaster. But to Rajendra, a local fisherman who had joined us, the flood meant good things: the chance to use his boat to visit neighbouring villages: an abundance of fish: and sediments left behind that makes the land bountiful and gives him the chance to grow his own rice.'

Table 11.2 Human aspects of Bangladesh

- Densely populated: over 888 people per km²
- Population (116.5 million in 1994) doubles every 30 years at present growth rates
- One of the most intensively farmed countries in the world
- Eighty-two per cent of population are farmers
- Twelve people per hectare of arable land
- Average per capita income in 1992 only US $200
- Sixty per cent of population are landless

Figure 11.6 These families, who have already moved four or five times, will be made homeless again at the first flood

11.3 Normal and abnormal flooding

The lives and livelihood of millions of people depend upon the annual floods, and yet they are also put at risk by them. This is where the distinction between 'normal' and 'abnormal' floods becomes crucial.

In some years, the floods are 'abnormal': 1954, 1955, 1974, 1977, 1985, 1987 and 1988. An extra metre of flood height is disastrous in this low-lying landscape and the increased energy available in the abnormal flood surge can be used not only to carry more sediment to the delta, but also to erode extensive areas of the existing land. Remember that the cities also occupy low, flat sites. It is against these unusually high-energy events that the Bangladeshi government and local communities have developed management strategies.

Management policies

India and Pakistan became independent countries in 1947. At that time, Pakistan consisted of two parts, East and West Pakistan. In 1971, they separated and East Pakistan became Bangladesh. As a response to the serious floods of 1954 and 1955, the Government established the East Pakistan Water and Power Development Authority (EPWAPDA) in 1959. With the assistance of a United Nations consultants' report, the Authority produced a national Master Plan in 1964. This emphasised the 'hard' engineering approach of embankments, channel improvement by dredging, river training and meander cut-offs, and the construction of bypasses or floodways (Chapter 6). One example is the Meghna–Dhonagoda Irrigation Project (Fig. 11.7), built between 1964 and 1970 along the east bank of the River Meghna, south-east of Dhaka. About US $50 million were spent to build high embankments around a 207 km² area and to criss-cross the enclosed land with a network of irrigation channels. Yet in years of abnormal floods the waters still eroded and penetrated the area. During the 1980s, therefore, new embankments were built 3 km back from the main river as an extra line of defence.

Figure 11.7 'Hard' engineering: the Meghna–Dhonagoda Irrigation Project

The 1988 flood disaster

But then came 1988! During the floods which peaked in early September, at least 50 per cent of Bangladesh was under water (Fig. 11.8). Despite 30 years of construction and vast expenditure by this poor nation, disaster could still strike.

Table 11.3 Damage due to abnormal floods 1971–88

Year	Loss of human life	Loss of livestock (000)	Loss of rice production (000 tonnes)	Houses totally/partially damaged (000)
1971	120	2	285	229
1974*	1987	46	800	6165
1975	15	n/a	93	19
1976	54	n/a	682	89
1984*	553	76	2147	536
1987*	1657	65	2036	2536
1988*	2379	172	2922	7179

*Catastrophic flood years   n/a = not applicable.

What caused the disaster?

Proposition A: deforestation in the mountain catchment areas

Research indicates that Bangladesh floods result primarily from snowmelt and runoff from the Himalayas in the spring and early summer, topped up by direct precipitation across the floodplain. International development agencies (e.g. the World Bank and the UN Development Programme (UNDP)) claim that severe deforestation across these mountain catchments, especially in Nepal, is accelerating runoff and increasing erosion rates (Fig. 11.9). Other hydrologists, however, dispute this as the prime cause of the 1988 disaster. They accept that deforestation inevitably has an effect on runoff, erosion, and sediment supply and transport, but they question its degree.

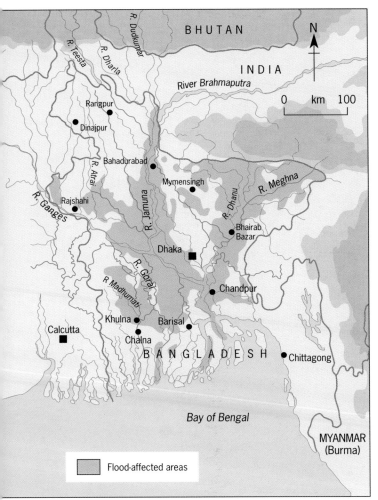

Figure 11.8 Major areas affected by the 1988 flood (*Source*: Haque and Zaman, 1993)

Proposition B: timing of the flood surge

The Bangladesh floodplain and delta collect water from several river basins spread across a huge area. All endure some of the highest rainfall totals in the world, and at greater altitudes accumulate large snowpacks. In most years, i.e. 'normal' flood years, the timing of the rains and snowmelt vary from catchment to catchment. Also the distance the floodwater surge has to travel varies from one basin to another (see Fig. 4.14). Hence the flood surges moving down the three great rivers arrive in Bangladesh at different times. In years of 'normal' floods the Brahmaputra discharge peaks about a month before the Ganges. In 1988, however, the flood surges coincided.

None the less, timing alone does not account for the severity of the flooding: first, the summer discharges along the Brahmaputra were 50 per cent greater than the previous year, which itself was an above-average year. Second, there were unusually heavy rainstorms over the lower river basins, i.e. over Bangladesh, which poured yet more water on to the already overwhelmed floodplain. Third, the peak discharges coincided with the days of the highest tides in the Bay of Bengal, which caused the ponding back of the arriving floodwaters. Thus, as with many extreme events which turn into 'disasters', it was the coming together of several influential variables, rather than one unusual input, which proved crucial.

Proposition C: throughput and storage changes caused by flood control structures

Some hydrologists blame the embankments, **levées**, barrages, **dams** and other 'hard' engineering structures placed along the upstream reaches of rivers. These structures channel the discharge more directly and reduce the flood storage role of the middle and upper sections of the river basins (see Chapters 6 and 7). Thus a higher proportion of the flood discharge is passed quickly downstream to overwhelm the channels in the delta.

Opponents of the 'hard' structures claim that they merely shift the location of the floods to other areas. Such floods may then become more severe because of the more rapid arrival of the water, and, when embankments do fail, the waters burst on to the once-protected fields and villages with increased vigour.

?

4 The 1988 flood affected 45 million people, destroyed 900 bridges and culverts at a cost of over US $2 billion. Use Table 11.3 to outline the impact of the 1988 flood compared with other recent floods in Bangladesh.

5 Some hydrologists believe that deforestation in the headwaters, e.g. Nepal, is a cause of the flooding. Construct a block diagram to show why they think this. Include detailed annotation of the hydrological processes involved.

Figure 11.9 Deforestation: the impact on flooding

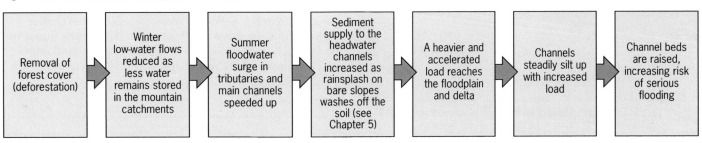

The 1988 flood disaster

Although the available storage space across the floodplain and delta surface has been reduced, the floodwater still seeks its 'natural' outlet – to spill over the floodplain.

Additionally, the operation of dams can raise delicate **hydropolitical** issues when downstream countries are affected. For example, controversy surrounds the Farakka Dam on the Ganges, 25 km upstream of the Indian–Bangladeshi border (Fig. 11.10).

With Bangladesh's severe flood problems, it seems ironic that there is a water shortage in the dry season. River water is used to irrigate crops in Bangladesh and is a vital source of water for the upstream countries as well. Since 1982, however, India has taken more and more water from the Ganges.

As controls for the barrage lie mostly in India, Bangladesh has little influence over water storage and release policies for those sections of the river basins. The vulnerability of Bangladesh's downstream location causes major disagreements with India and was an important contributor to the 1988 flood.

At that time, some Bangladeshi politicians blamed the Indian government for allowing water managers

> The Indian government uses the Farakka Dam to divert water from the Ganges through a feeder canal in order to flush silt (see Chapter 5) from the Hooghly River. This improves navigation in Calcutta and provides irrigation water. The Ganges dry season flow at Farakka is about 2400m³/s, but in the 1993 dry season the Indian intervention meant that only 255m³/s of Ganges streamflow entered Bangladesh.

Figure 11.10 The Farakka Diversion Barrage (*Source: Barrow, 1987*)

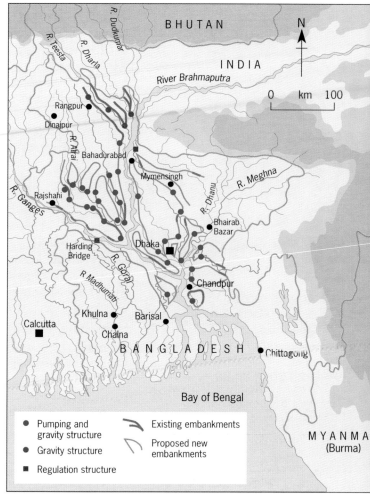

Figure 11.11 Existing and proposed embankments (*Source: Geographical Magazine*, August 1992)

to open the sluice gates of the Farakka Dam on the Ganges at the height of the monsoon flow. This allowed a further flood surge to enter the Bangladesh channel network. The Indian government claim they had to open the sluice gates to prevent flooding further downstream in Calcutta.

?

6 Trace Figure 11.11 and overlay it on Figure 11.8 to assess the effectiveness of existing embankments during the 1988 floods.

7 The drainage basin is an integrated system. In order to understand the causes of, and solutions to flooding, a whole-basin approach is needed. Produce an annotated sketch map to show the three possible causes of the 1988 floods in Bangladesh. Include details about the international issues and the nature of the whole drainage basin system

8 Explain why it is so difficult to be sure of a single cause of the 1988 floods.

11.4 Future plans

Just as there is no single cause of the floods in Bangladesh, so there is no single answer. Effective management strategies must be based on:
- Flood control rather than total flood prevention.
- A combination of 'hard' and 'soft' approaches (see Chapter 7).
- The adoption of a whole-basin approach and taking into account, wherever possible, natural rhythms and processes.
- International co-operation involving delicate hydropolitical issues.
- The acceptance of the enormous cost and long timescales involved.

The 'hard' approach

So far, management strategies have focused on structural, 'hard' engineering solutions such as dams and embankments. The first aims to reduce the volume of water entering the Bangladesh channels at any given time, by providing additional surface and groundwater storage capacity elsewhere in the drainage basins. This would involve building dams and reservoirs in the mountain catchments in collaboration with other upper basin countries , especially Nepal. The space demands, the huge costs, Nepal's own need to use, as well as store, the water, and hence the complex hydropolitics, combine to limit the potential of this approach.

Dams

Dams are 'hard' engineering structures which have significant environmental impact downstream (Chapters 4, 5 and 7). The operation of dams can raise delicate hydropolitical issues when downstream countries are affected, for example, the Farakka Dam (Fig. 11.10).

Embankments

The second component of the 'hard' approach is the construction of embankments along channels, to prevent, divert and regulate flood waters once they enter Bangladesh. This preventative approach has been the most favoured to date (Fig. 11.11). The 1964 Master Plan foresaw the eventual elimination of floods through the construction of embankments along all the main channels. A 1992 estimate of the cost by a consortium of French engineers totalled US $10 billion to build and up to US $600 million a year to maintain for over 3350 km of high embankments.

Combining 'hard' and 'soft' approaches

Some engineers doubt whether floods would be eliminated even after the building of continuous embankments (Fig. 11.11). This controversy has led to the emergence of a more realistic corrective or control approach. This adopts elements of both 'hard' and 'soft' strategies. Hard structures are built to protect densely populated and intensively farmed areas. Floodplain and delta surfaces with lower population densities are identified as flood storage areas. This compartmentalisation allows controlled flooding to 'normal' levels by the use of regulators and sluices within embankments. This 'soft' approach imitates natural floodplain processes and their benefits, e.g. maintenance of soil fertility, fish production, groundwater recharge. During exceptional floods, compartments can be more deeply flooded as emergency stores (see Chapter 9 – the Mississippi case study).

Once again, like all structural techniques, this needs careful apraisal. There remains the 'knock-on' effect: the Brahmaputra Right Bank Protection Embankment is a 217-km-long structure, but is causing the main Brahmaputra-Jamuna channel to migrate rapidly westwards by increased erosion of the unprotected right, i.e. western, bank, thus displacing many thousands of families.

9 Using Figure 11.11 as a base map, draw an annotated sketch map to show the social, economic and environmental impacts of the Farakka Dam downstream in Bangladesh.

'For many Bangladeshis, the only safe high-ground they could find was on what some environmentalists and hydrologists believe to be one of the major causes of the flood problem – the man-made embankments lining the rivers. Time and time again, this expensive form of flood prevention has proved futile and in many cases has only aggravated the situation downstream, in less protected areas.

Perhaps it is time that the Bangladeshi authorities and their foreign advisers realise that they cannot control the country's river system. As Philip Williams says: "You can never control floods, you simply try to reduce the risk to lives and property to acceptable levels." '

Figure 11.12 Embankments – one of the causes of the problem? (*Source: Geographical Magazine*, July 1994)

Table 11.4 How communities cope

	(% of respondents)
Adjustment measures	
Sold land	2
Sold livestock	17
Sold belongings	26
Mortgaged land	4
Took down housing structure	39
Borrowed money	39
Spent savings	24
Moved to new area	66
Sources of help	
Relatives	79
Other villagers	33
Local government	7
National government	4
Relief agencies	51

10a Present the data in Table 11.4 graphically.

b Suggest ways in which government and international aid could help people cope with extreme events.

11 Study the Flood Action Plan proposals for Bangladesh (Table 11.5). Divide the list of proposals and supporting activities into the following groups (See Chapter 9 – floods) and calculate the money spent in each.

a Structural control measures, i.e. hard engineering (e.g. embankments and dams).

b Flood warnings and other non-structural control measures.

c Water and land use control measures (include compartmentalisation in here).

d Research and information-gathering.

Comment on the appropriateness of the groups of proposals for Bangladesh.

12 Why is upstream storage an unlikely option for Bangladesh?

Notes:
Item 14. Part of this study will investigate floodplain zoning possibilities
Items 12, 13, 14, 19, 25 will investigate closer involvement of the public in decision-making and management, e.g. of embankments.
Items 20, 21 will investigate the confinement impacts of embankments on river levels and velocities.
Item 21 will investigate measures to improve the physical and social security of people occupying active floodplains.
Item 22 studies measures to improve the resistance of rural and urban infrastructure, farming, fisheries etc. to floods.

Hazards and coping stratagies

There is growing acceptance that flood prevention is an unrealistic dream, and a progressive shift towards the 'soft' non-structural approach to flood mitigation. As it becomes accepted that extreme discharge events will continue to result in floods, so modern management programmes are coming to focus more on flood forecasting and warning systems, flood insurance, and flood relief and rehabilitation; warn people → move people → help people. Equally important is the growing awareness of the experience and resourcefulness of local communities. The Bangladeshi people have lived all their lives with the flood hazard, and have evolved sophisticated systems of coping stagies, e.g. building houses on natural or built levées, raising houses on stilts. The attitude to flooding is more fatalistic than 'western' views of flooding and people are more likely to view them as 'Acts of God'. However, the impacts are severe and flood management projects should be tailored to local conditions and involve local communities in the decision-making process, while setting such projects within a regional and national context. Table 11.4 summarises the results of a survey of 280 families in the Munshigania District of the delta after the 1988 flood.

Planning the future

The Bangladesh government is basing its long-term policies upon the 1989 Flood Action Plan (FAP) (Table 11.5). The FAP is an integrated programme which attemps to reconcile the various approaches to flood management.

The huge costs involved are being helped by 15 donor countries with the World Bank acting as co-ordinator. However, part of the vast cost must be met by Bangladesh, and this will be at the expense of other development plans, for example, clean drinking water (see below), irrigation projects and agricultural expansion. This is the **opportunity cost** of FAP. The issues of the most appropriate way forward for Bangladesh, and the large costs involved in the long-term maintenance of any hard engineering structures, are still to be addressed.

Table 11.5 Flood Action Plan components and supporting activities

Components	Cost (million US$)	Supporting activities	Cost (million US$)
1 Brahmaputra right embankment strengthening	0.7	12 Flood control, drainage and irrigation projects, agricultural study	0.6
2 Brahmaputra right bank North-west drainage study North-west diversion drain North-west interceptor drain	2.8	13 Operation and maintenance study	0.3
		14 Socio-economic studies	0.7
		15 Environment study	0.2
3 Brahmaputra left bank North-central regional study Brahmaputra left embankment Brahmaputra left bank compartment	4.6	16 Fisheries study	3.1
		17 Topographic mapping	3.9
		18 Geographic information system	5.1
4 Ganges right bank South-west regional study Gorai intake and Ganges right embankment South-west and south-central drainage study	3.9	19 Compartmentalisation pilot project	10.8
		20 Bank protection pilot project	29.3
		21 River training and active floodplain management pilot project	6.0
5 Meghna left bank South-east regional study Gumti and south-east drainage study	2.9	22 Flood-proofing pilot project	5.0
		23 River survey programme	17.3
6 North-east region North-east regional study North-east rehabilitation project	3.6	24 Flood modelling/management	2.5
		25 Institutional development programme	2.6
Cyclone protection project	2.0		
8 Dhaka town protection	4.0		
9 Other towns protection	3.5	**Total**	**146.3**
10 Flood forecasting and early warning	24.7		
11 Flood preparedness	6.2		

Opposing views

There is a philosophy of risk aversion. Farmers and others are simply not prepared to put their assets at stake. While total elimination of the annual floods is neither possible nor desirable, Bangladesh must protect itself from the worst effects of exceptional floods.

Figure 11.13 Response to flooding: comments of M H Siddique, chief engineer of the Flood Action Plan Co-ordination Office (*Source: Geographical Magazine*, August 1992)

Overall, it is evident that, in the context of the rural habitat and agriculture of Bangladesh, flooding is a vital agent to its resources. Although some extreme events turn out to be a serious threat to local resources and human lives, traditional wisdom suggests that devastating floods occur once in every five to ten years. Floods comparable to the 1988 one are rare. There is evidence that floods of this magnitude have not previously been recorded in the country. Frequency of these rare events is measured in the range of the 50 to 100-year event. The floodplain inhabitants would gain little from prevention of such rare events.

Figure 11.14 Response to flooding (*Source:* Haque and Zaman, 1993)

13 Figures 11.13 and 11.14 show evidence of disagreement on the way forward for Bangladesh. Using all the evidence available, evaluate the validity of each of these statements.

14 Produce your own flood action plan for Bangladesh using both information from this chapter, and relevant material from other chapters in this book.

11.5 Water resource management at the local scale

In a country with high annual rainfall and recurring flood problems, it is ironic that 85 per cent of the population have no access to 'clean' drinking water, i.e. water of a 'potable' standard. Problems are especially serious at times of flood and during the dry season. A village household has three possible sources of water:

1 Surface water, mainly river water;
2 **Groundwater**, obtained via shallow tubewells;
3 Direct storage of rainwater.

   Most villagers rely on a combination of all three, and when possible, favour fresh rainwater.

Self-help in Khuha District

A 1992 survey of 36 households in 12 villages in the Khuha district of south-west Bangladesh reveals the problems and resourcefulness of the villagers in providing drinking water (Fig. 11.15). As the district lies near to the ocean, surface and groundwater sources are often saline.

   The area has 53 tubewells, but only 27 were in working order at the time of the survey. Eleven of these were not used by villagers because the water was too salty. Despite efforts by the Department of Public Health (DPHE) and UNICEF to provide better-quality drinking water, nearly half of the DPHE–UNICEF sand-filtered facilities were not used. This is because the groundwater was too salty. Rainwater is used for drinking, cooking, bathing and washing clothes. The taste of rainwater was preferred for cooking and making tea.

Water collection and storage

Collection of water is considered a woman's job – usually involving a long walk with an earthen container called a *kalshi*. During the rainy season, the villagers collect the rainwater for storage.

   'Rainwater harvesting' is when water is collected from roof tops or directly as falling rain. The method

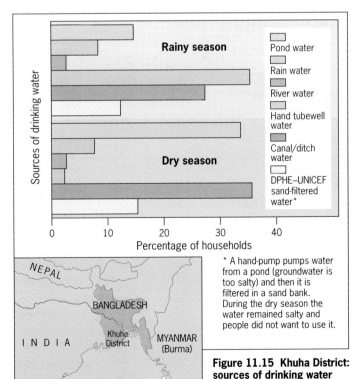

* A hand-pump pumps water from a pond (groundwater is too salty) and then it is filtered in a sand bank. During the dry season the water remained salty and people did not want to use it.

Figure 11.15 Khuha District: sources of drinking water during the wet and dry seasons

Kuha District

Table 11.6 Rainwater collection and storage in Dacope village (*Source: Waterlines*, 1992)

Total rainwater storage capacity for drinking purposes only

Number of households (persons)	For rainy season use (litres)	Also for off-season use (litres)	Type and number of storage facilities (type/number)	Method of rainwater collection (type)
6	90	–	A – 5	I
9	–	5376	D – 4 C – 8	I
6	–	4224	D – 6	I
5	96	–	A – 6	I
8	64	–	A – 4	I
22	640	–	C – 2	I
6	192	–	B – 1 A – 5	I
5	128	–	B – 1 A – 1	V
12	576	–	C – 1 B – 2	I
5	128	–	B – 1 A – 1	IV
5	32	–	A – 2	II
16	960	–	C – 3	I
7	288	–	B – 2 A – 3	III
6	724	–	C – 2 A – 4	I
20	384	–	B – 3 A – 2	V
9		1280	C – 4 A – 2	I
7	80	–	A – 5	II

Storage facilities
Type A = a *Kalshi* of 16 litres
Type B = a *Motka* of 120 litres
Type C = a *Motka* of 350 litres
Type D = a *Motka* of 750 litres

Method of rainwater collection
Type I = roof discharge through CI sheet
Type II = roof discharge through tiles
Type III = roof discharge through straw
Type IV = polythene paper under open sky
Type V = bedsheet/sari under open sky

used depends on the type of house in which people live (Table 11.6). The water is then stored in either a *kalshi* or large earthen vessels called *motkas*. The motkas, especially the larger ones, are used by richer people for long-term storage of water into the dry season.

It is difficult to store rainwater and maintain its quality. Mosquito larvae and other insects tend to be found within two weeks in stored rainwater. Some villagers add fish to eat the larvae, but the fish excreta again reduces water quality. This improper storage means villagers find frogs, toads, dead rodents, lizards and cockroaches in their water supply. Some families simply filter the water before drinking, and a few use chemicals to sterilise the water.

Which way forward?

The survey showed that most villagers (75 per cent) wanted to build better and larger rainwater storage for their families to use. Only rich households with farms of over two hectares were in a position to do this, though. People thought it was the Government's responsibility to provide pure water for them. The poorer farmers with less than half a hectare of land preferred the provision of community-shared facilities as a way forward.

15 Compare drinking water sources for the wet and dry seasons (Fig. 11.15).

16a Using Table 11.6, what is the main method of rainwater collection used by villagers?
b What evidence is there from Table 11.6 that only rich people have large motkas for long-term storage?

17 Why was the DHPE–UNICEF sand-filtering scheme unsuccessful in this area?

18 Identify the priorities for government action regarding water storage and quality in Khuha.

Summary

- Bangladesh displays all the various aspects of rivers. It consists of a drainage basin system which functions as an integrated whole.
- The delta environment is dynamic and constantly changing.
- People are forced to live in low-lying areas where they are both dependent on and at danger from floods.
- Irregular, abnormal floods have important implications for water and flood management policy.
- Management strategies include a variety of hard and soft options.
- The causes and management of abnormal floods involve delicate hydropolitical aspects.

Appendices

A1 Spearman's rank correlation coefficient

The Spearman rank correlation coefficient uses data measured on an ordinal or rank scale, and is particularly useful in surveys of attitudes or decision-making, where respondents are often asked to rank their preferences.

n = number of pairs
d = difference in rank of each pair of values

Spearman rank correlation coefficient $(r_s) = 1 - \left[\dfrac{6\Sigma d^2}{n^3 - n} \right]$

When you have calculated r_s, you need to find its statistical significance. This enables you to discover whether or not r_s is the result of a chance association. To do this, you need to consult a significance table.

The critical values of r_s for $n = 4$ to $n = 30$ are at the 0.05 and 0.01 levels of significance. The larger the value of r_s, the more significant the result. For numbers of pairs greater than $n = 30$, the value of r_s changes very little.

Significance level (one-tailed test)
(*Source*: Siegel (1956) after Olds (1938 and 1949))

n	0.05	0.01
4	1.000	
5	0.900	1.000
6	0.829	0.943
7	0.714	0.893
8	0.643	0.833
9	0.600	0.783
10	0.564	0.746
12	0.506	0.712
14	0.456	0.645
16	0.425	0.601
18	0.399	0.564
20	0.377	0.534
22	0.359	0.508
24	0.343	0.485
26	0.329	0.465
28	0.317	0.448
30	0.306	0.432

A2 The National Water Archive

Both the scientific understanding of hydrological processes and the assessment and management of water resources depends, to a considerable degree, on the ready availability of relevant hydrological data. The increasing number of people at risk from floods and drought around the world, and the recent evidence of the continuing vulnerability of the United Kingdom to the impact of unusual climatic conditions, underline the need for appropriate data on all elements of the hydrological cycle to strengthen the foundations upon which improved water management procedures are based.

A significant proportion of the UK data presented in this book derives from the National Water Archive (NWA) maintained by the Institute of Hydrology (IH) at Wallingford. The NWA is one of the Natural Environment Research Council's six Designated Data Centres, the purpose of which is to fully exploit – and improve accessibility to – the enormous volumes of environmental data currently being collected.

The Institute of Hydrology has been a natural focus for the acquisition and exploitation of major hydrological databases for many years: long-running experimental catchments in central Wales and in Scotland have furnished a wealth of data on hydrological processes, and since 1982 management of the National River Flow and National Groundwater Level Archives has been undertaken by IH and the British Geological Survey (BGS) respectively (BGS is also part of NERC and shares the Wallingford site with IH). These databases form the kernel of the National Water Archive, but a broad range of hydrological and related data sets have been absorbed into the co-ordinated management that it provides. Data holdings range from the catchment scale to national and, in the case of the Worlds Flood Archive, global scales. The value of the basic data is increased by the availability of interrelated spatial information: for example, detailed computerised representations of the UK river network and UK soil maps.

To make the archived data available to a large number of users a comprehensive suite of retrievals has been developed. Examples appear throughout this volume and descriptions of the retrieval services appear in the Hydrological Data UK publications, a series of yearbooks and reports dealing with nationally archived data and significant hydrological events. The yearbooks bring together the principal data sets relating to catchment rainfall, river flow and groundwater levels for the UK; water quality data are also featured for a representative network of monitoring sites.

Access arrangements vary between data sets held under the NWA umbrella, but for busy river flow and groundwater level data a modest handling charge is made; there is a 50 per cent reduction for educational usage, and charges may be waived for bona fide research investigations. Charging policies are currently under review.

Individuals or organisations wishing to use the National Water Archive retrieval services, or to enquire about the range of data sets available, should contact:

The National Water Archive Office
Institute of Hydrology
Maclean Building
Wallingford
Oxfordshire OX10 8BB

Tel: 01491 838800   Facsimile: 01491 83225

A3 Table of z scores

	Column A	Column B	Column C
z	p	p_1	p_2
0.0	0.000	0.500	1.000
0.1	0.040	0.460	0.920
0.2	0.079	0.421	0.841
0.3	0.118	0.382	0.764
0.4	0.155	0.345	0.689
0.5	0.191	0.309	0.617
0.6	0.226	0.274	0.549
0.7	0.258	0.242	0.484
0.8	0.288	0.212	0.424
0.9	0.316	0.184	0.368
1.0	0.341	0.159	0.317
1.1	0.364	0.136	0.271
1.2	0.385	0.115	0.230
1.3	0.403	0.097	0.193
1.4	0.419	0.081	0.162
1.5	0.433	0.067	0.134
1.6	0.445	0.055	0.110
1.7	0.455	0.045	0.089
1.8	0.464	0.036	0.072
1.9	0.471	0.029	0.057
*1.96	0.475	0.025	0.050
2.0	0.477	0.023	0.046
2.1	0.482	0.018	0.036
2.2	0.486	0.014	0.028
2.3	0.489	0.011	0.021
2.4	0.492	0.008	0.016
2.5	0.494	0.006	0.012
*2.28	0.495	0.005	0.010
2.6	0.495	0.005	0.009
2.7	0.496	0.004	0.007
2.8	0.497	0.003	0.005
2.9	0.498	0.002	0.004
3.0	0.499	0.001	0.003
3.1	0.499	0.001	0.002
3.2	0.499	0.001	0.001
3.3	0.499	0.001	0.001
3.4	0.500	0.000	0.001
3.5	0.500	0.000	0.000

Note:
Col A: p = the probability of a value lying between the mean and the corresponding value of z.
Col B: p_1 = the probability of a value exceeding the given value of z (a one-tailed probability).
Col C: p_2 = the probability of a value exceeding either $+ z$ or $- z$ (a two-tailed probability).
*Critical care values of z corresponding to the 0.05 and 0.01 levels (two-tailed) have been given to two decimal places.
After Lindley and Miller (1953).

A4 MAFF guidelines for choosing a flood defence strategy

A. Preliminary thinking
Are people and/or built or natural assets at risk?
How urgent is it?
What options are available?
What are the likely environmental consequences?

B. Developing and appraising the options
There are four flood defence options:
1. **Do nothing.**
2. **Reduce** – maintain flood defences at a lower standard of protection in the future If maintenance of existing levels is difficult to justify.
3. **Sustain** – present standards of flood defence are sustained by maintenance work.
4. **Improve** – the standards of flood defences are improved beyond the current design level or by new projects.

C. Choose the preferred option
This choice is made from the short list of alternatives which are environmentally, technically and economically acceptable. Options are ranked by cost–benefit ratio and by an Environmental Impact Assessment if environmental impacts have not been given monetary values and included in the cost–benefit analysis.

D. Design of the preferred option in detail

E. Operational phase, i.e. construction and maintenance

F. Post-project appraisal
This is an important step, since it allows evaluation of the project's effectiveness in environmental and engineering terms. This information can then be used in deciding upon future flood management strategies.

Flood defence schemes are subject to the normal planning procedures in England and Wales, and local councils and other organisations are involved in the process. Some schemes are discussed by public inquiry. New flood defence works generally require planning permission.

A5 Environmental Impact Assessment

Environmental Impact Assessments (EIAs) were introduced in the 1988 Town and Country Planning Regulations. The aim of an EIA is to discover the likely environmental impacts of a planning proposal such as a flood alleviation scheme. The environmental impacts and issues raised by an EIA form an environmental statement which then becomes part of the decision-making and planning process, along with economic and technical factors.

At Ashby Folville, the NRA was involved in consultations with several agencies as part of the EIA, such as the County Council and the Director of Museums. The issues highlighted were: 1) The village is a conservation area; 2) The area is one of archaeological importance; 3) The stream channel was of ecological significance; 4) Public rights of way were involved.

Schemes such as the flood alleviation proposal of Ashby Folville (see the example below) always require planning permission from the Local Authority and, despite the EIA, there is no guarantee that there will be no environmental damage.

FLOOD DEFENCE CAPITAL WORKS – ENVIRONMENTAL IMPACT ASSESSMENT FORM

Watercourse ..... *Twyford Brook* .... LTS/LTN   Location ..... *Ashby Folville* ....

From NGR .... To NGR .... FDC Prog. no ....

Start date .... Completion date ....

FDC Project Officer ....

Under Section 16 of the Water Resources Act 1991 it is a legal requirement to ensure that all operational activities are assessed for their impact on the environment.

Environmental aspects	Yes/No
Visual amenity	Yes
National Parks/Area of Outstanding Natural Beauty	No
Conservation area	Yes
High visual amenity area	–
Requires enhancement	–

Historic	
Scheduled ancient monuments	No
Area of archaeological imp. (County Site)	Yes
Listed buildings and structures	?
Registered historic gardens	–
Other interesting features	–

Natural history	
SSSI/NNR	No
Geological SSSI	No
Local nature reserve	No
County sites/prime sites	No
County Trust Reserve	No
T.P.O.	?
Fisheries	Yes

Recreation	
Public footpath/bridleway	Yes
Angling	No
Watersport/recreation	No
Other bankside recreation	No

Other

References

Barrow, C (1987) *Water resources and agricultural development in the Tropics*, Longman Scientific and Technical.

Barry, R G and Chorley, R J (1982), *Atmosphere, weather and climate*, Methuen and Coltel.

Benn and Erskine (1994).

Beven, K and Carling, P (1992) in Carling and Petts (eds), *Lowland floodplain rivers*, Wiley.

Boon, PJ et al. (1992), *River conservation and management*, Wiley.

Bramner, H (1990), 'Floods in Bangladesh. Geographical background to the 1987–8 floods', *The Geographical Journal*, 156, 1, Royal Geographical Society.

Briggs, D and Smithson, P (1989), *Fundamentals of physical geography*, Routledge.

Brookes, A (1985a), 'River channelisation in progress', *Progress in physical geography*, 9.

Brookes, A (1985b), 'Downstream morphological consequences of river channelisation in England and Wales', *Geographical Journal*, 151, 1, Royal Geographical Society.

Brown, A (1992), *The UK environment*, Department of the Environment, HMSO.

Burt, T (1987), 'Measuring infiltration capacity', *Geography Review*, 1, 2, Philip Allan Publishers.

Burt, T H and Haycock, N E (1992), 'Catchment planning and the nitrate issue: a UK perspective', *Progress in Physical Geography*, 16, 4.

Carling, P A and Petts, G E (eds) (1992), *Lowland floodplain rivers: geomorphological perspectives*, Wiley.

Centre for the Study of Regulated Industries (1994–5), The UK water industry, CIPFA.

Clowes, A and Comfort, P (1987), 'Process and landform, conceptual frameworks', *Geography*, Oliver and Boyd.

Cobb, C E (1993), 'Bangladesh: when the water comes', *National Geographic*, 183, 6.

Cooke, R U and Doornkamp, J C (1990), *Geomorphology in environmental management*, Oxford University Press.

Department of the Environment, Environmental Protection Statistics Division, Room A105, Romney House, 43 Marsham Street, London SW1P 3PY.

Disler (1985), in Carling, P A and Petts, G E (eds) (1992) *Lowland floodplain rivers: geomorphological perspectives*, Wiley.

Ericksen, N J (1986), 'Creating flood disasters', *Water and soil*, NWASCA, New Zealand.

Falkenmark, M (1977), 'Water and mankind – a complex system of mutual interaction', *AMBIO*, 6, 1.

George, R (1994), 'Lake Baikal, Siberia', *Wideworld*, September.

Goudie, A (1990a), *The human impact on the natural environment*, Blackwell.

Goudie, A (1990b), *The Landforms of England and Wales*, Blackwell.

Gregory, K J and Walling, D E (1973), *Drainage basin form and process: a geomorphological approach*, Edward Arnold.

Hanwell, J D and Newson, M D (1973), *Techniques in physical geography*, Macmillan Education.

Harris, G L (1992), 'Influence of farm management and drainage on leaching of nitrate from former floodlands in a lowland clay catchment', in Carling and Petts, *Lowland floodplain rivers*.

Haque, C E and Zaman, M Q (1993), 'Human responses to riverine hazards in Bangladesh: a proposal for sustainable floodplain development', *World Development*, 21, 1, Pergamon Press.

Hilton, K (1979), *Process and pattern in physical geography*, Collins Educational.

Hilton, K (1985), *Patterns in physical geography*, Bell and Hyman.

Hollis, G E (1977), 'Canon's Brook catchment', *Hydrological Sciences Bulletin*, XXII.

Hollis, G E (1988), 'Rain, roads, roofs and runoff: hydrology in cities', *Geography*, 73, 1, The Geographical Association.

Howell, P P and Allen, J A (eds), 1990 *The Nile: resource evaluation, resource management, hydropolitics and legal issues*, conference proceedings, Royal Geographical Society and School of Oriental and African Studies, London.

HMSO (1986), Department of the Environment, *River quality in England and Wales*, 1985.

Hussain, M D and Ziauddin, A T M, (1992), 'Rainwater harvesting and storage techniques from Bangladesh', *Waterlines*, 10, 3.

Kern, K (1992), 'Restoration of lowland rivers: the German experience', in Carling and Petts, *Lowland floodplain rivers*.

Kesel, R H et al. (1992), 'An approximation of the sediment budget of the Lower Mississippi River prior to major human modification', *Earth Surface Processes and Landforms*, 17, 7.

Knapp, B and Child, S (1979), 'Updating geomorphology: hydrological effects of man's activities', *Teaching Geography*, 5, 2, The Geographical Association.

Knapp, B et al. (1989), *The challenge of the natural environment*, Longman.

Kwebenah Acheampong, P (1988). 'Water balance analysis for Ghana', *Geography*, 73, 2, The Geographical Association.

Lajczak, A and Jansson, M B (1993), 'Suspended sediment yield in the Baltic drainage basin', *Nordic Hydrology*, 24.

Lewis, G and Williams, G (1984), *Rivers and wildlife handbook*, RSPB/RSNC.

Lvovitch, M I (1973), *Transactions of American Geophysical Union*, 54, p.34, Fig 1. ©1973 American Geophysical Union.

Marsh, T J et al, (1994), *The 1988–92 UK drought*, Institute of Hydrology.

Marsh, T J and Davies, P A (1983), 'The decline and partial recovery of groundwater levels below London', *Proceedings of the Institute of Civil Engineers*, 74, 1.

Marsh, T J and MacRuairi, R E (1993), '1988–92: a demonstration of the United Kingdom's vulnerability to drought', *BHS Fourth National Hydrology Symposium*, Cardiff.

McDonald, A T and Kay, D (1988), *Water resources: issues and strategies*, Longman Scientific and Technical.

Ministry of Agriculture, Fisheries and Food (1993), *Solving the nitrate problem*, HMSO.

Ministry of Agriculture, Fisheries and Food (1994), *Flood and coastal defence: project appraisal guidance notes*, HMSO.

National Rivers Authority (1994), *Water: nature's precious resource*, HMSO.

Newson, M (1979), 'Up and down and seldom average: streamflow variability with time', *Teaching Geography*, 4, 3, Longman.

Newson, M (1992), *Land, water and development*, Routledge.

Oliver, H R and Oliver, S A (1988), *Geography Review*, 1, 3, Philip Allan Publishers.

Park, C (1983), *Environmental hazards*, 'Aspects of Geography' series, Macmillan Education.

Pearce, F (1993), *New Scientist*, 18 September.

Pearce, F (1994), *New Scientist*, 20 August.

Penning-Rowsell, E C and Handmer, J W (1988), 'Flood management in Britain: a changing scene', *Geographical Journal*, 154, 2, Royal Geographical Society.

Raabe (1968), *Deutscher Rat fur Landespflege*, Bonn.

Roberts, C R (1989), 'Flood frequency and urban-induced channel change: some British examples', in Beven, K and Carlos, P (eds) *Floods: hydrological, sedimentological and geomorphological implications*, Wiley.

Ross, S M et al. (1990), 'Soil hydrology, nutrient and erosional response to the clearance of terra firma forest, Maraca Island, Roraima, northern Brazil', *Geographical Journal*, 156, 3, Royal Geographical Society.

Severn–Trent Water Authority (1978), *River Soar basin report*, Corporate Planning Department.

Smith, K (1993), 'Riverine flood hazard', *Geography*, 78, 2, The Geographical Association.

Sutcliffe and Lazenby (1990), in Howell and Allen, *The Nile*.

Tivy, J and O'Hare, G (1981), *Human impact on the ecosystem*, Oliver and Boyd.

Thames Water Utilities Ltd (1994) 'Optional metering scheme: Will I benefit from paying by meter?', Thames Water plc.

Thoms, M C and Walker, K F (1992), 'Channel changes related to low-level weirs on the River Murray, South Australia', in Carling and Petts, *Lowland floodplain rivers*.

Thornes, C R (1992), *River meanders: nature's answer to the straight line*, inaugural lecture, University of Nottingham.

Thornes, C R et al. (1993), Natural and engineered channels, University of Nottingham.

UNEP (1993), *Environmental data report*, 1991–92, UNEP/Blackwell.

Volker, A and Henry, J C (1988), *Side effects of water resources management*, IAHS.

Walker, K F et al. (1992), 'Effects of weirs on the littoral environment of the River Murray, S. Australia', in Boon et al, *River conservation and management*.

Ward, R C (1981) in Ward, R C and Robinson, M (1990), *Principles of hydrology*, McGraw-Hill International (UK).

Water Authorities Association (1987), in *Data support for education – water pollution*, Nature Conservancy Council (1988).

Weyman, D and Wilson, C (1975), 'Hydrology for schools', *Teaching Geography*, Occasional Paper, 5, 25, The Geographical Association.

Wheeler, D A (1988), 'Water resource problems in Catalonia', *Geography*, 73, 1, The Geographical Association.

White, I D et al. (1986), *Environmental systems*, Allen and Unwin.

Witherick, M and Carr, M (1993), *The changing face of Japan*, Hodder and Stoughton.

Glossary

Abstraction Removal of water from rivers, lakes, etc. or from groundwater for human use.

Actual evapotranspiration (AET) See **Evapotranspiration.**

Aggradation The building-up of the land surface or river bed by deposition of sediment.

Algal bloom A huge growth of algae in a water body due to overfeeding by water pollutants (see Eutrophication).

Alluvial fan A cone-shaped depositional landform, formed by water in semi-arid or arid seas.

Alluvial morphology The shape of landforms produced by alluvium (a sedimentary deposit made by a river).

Aquifer A permeable rock, such as limestone, which is capable of holding and transmitting groundwater. In a **confined aquifer** the upper boundary of the water body is formed by an overlying aquitard (less permeable bed). In an **unconfined aquifer** groundwater is not confined by an aquitard and the top surface is the water table where porewater pressure is equal to atmospheric pressure. In a **perched aquifer** the underlying impermeable bed is not continuous over a large area but is sufficient to support an unconfined aquifer above the main groundwater body.

Aquitard A less permeable rock in a sequence of permeable rocks which may be able to transmit water, but not in economic quantities.

Artesian basin A basin structure containing water under hydrostatic pressure in an aquifer.

Artesian well Well dug into water existing under hydrostatic pressure.

Assimilation capacity The ability of natural processes in the river ecosystem to absorb and control the effects of introduced materials such as pollutants.

Bankfull discharge The state of a river's flow, at which the channel is completely filled from the top of one bank into another. Beyond this point, overbank flow occurs.

Base flow The flow of water in a river which is produced by subsurface processes, especially groundwater flow.

Base flow index (BFI) The fraction of streamflow over a given period which occurs as baseflow, i.e. fed by slow throughflow and groundwater flow rather than from faster stormflow processes.

Bed armouring The lining of a river bed with coarse debris as a result of the selective removal of fine material. This sediment 'armour' can protect the bed from erosion.

Bifurcation ratio (Rb) The ratio of the number of streams of a particular order to the number of streams of the next highest order within a drainage basin. Most values lie between ratios of 2:5 and 3:5.

Biological oxygen demand (BOD) Used as a measure of organic pollution in water. It represents the amount of biochemically degradable substances in the water or effluent sample. A test sample is stored in darkness for five days at 20°C and the amount of oxygen taken up by the micro-organisms present is measured in grams per cubic metre.

Braided channel A river channel which divides and rejoins around piles of larger sediment. Associated with seasonal regimes.

Capacity (stream) The total sediment load of a river at a particular time or location.

Capillary action Surface tension and adsorptive forces which allow water to rise or move. The mechanism by which water moves upwards through part of the regolith known as the capillary fringe.

Catchment area The area of land which water drains into a river or stream.

Channelisation Modification of river channels for flood control, navigation, etc.

Char A depositional feature in a river formed when deposits build up above water level. These islands are mobile and temporary.

Clear water erosion Increased erosion downstream of dams which occurs as a result of the rescued sediment load. The river has increased energy to erode its bed.

Competence The size of the largest sediment particle that can be carried by a river at a particular place/time.

Cones of depression The area below and around a well, where the water table has been lowered as a result of water abstraction via the well.

Confined aquifer See **Aquifer**

Conjunctive operation strategy A policy in which several sources of supply are combined.

Contamination Introduction of a foreign substance to an environment, which is capable of causing pollution.

Corrasion Another name for abrasion, i.e. erosion by rock hitting rock, e.g. by sediment in a stream striking the bed and banks as it is transported.

Cost–benefit ratio The ratio of the costs and benefits of a proposed scheme, such as a flood control measure. For the scheme to be economically viable, the benefits must be higher than the costs, i.e. greater than 1:1.

Critical erosion velocity The stream velocity which is able to entrain sediment.

Culvert A subsurface pipe inserted to transfer water, e.g. beneath a road.

Dam A barrier built across a river to create a body of water.

Delta The deposition of sediment at the mouth of a river.

Depression storage Storage of water in hollows and holes in the ground surface.

Diffuse source See Pollution.

Dilution effect The process by which concentration of a solute decreases as discharge increases.

Discharge Water flowing past a gauging station within a given period. Usually expressed in cumecs: cubic metres per second.

Drainage basin The area of land drained by a river and its tributaries. Bordered by higher land or watershed.

Dual regime See Regime.

Dynamic equilibrium A state of balance which is constantly adjusting to changing conditions.

Ecosystem A self-regulating biological community in which living things interact with the environment. Ecosystems can be small or large, e.g. a tree, a tropical rainforest, depending on the interests of the person who defines the ecosystem.

Ephemeral channel Channel which only contains water after intermittent downpours of rain, separated by longer periods when the channel is dry.

Eutrophication The process by which excess nutrients are added to streams and standing water bodies, causing rapid expansion of aquatic plants and animal life, which in turn reduces oxygen supply in the water.

Evaporation The process by which water is changed to water vapour (gas) by molecular transfer.

Evapotranspiration The loss of moisture to the atmosphere by the combined processes of evaporation and transpiration. **Actual evapotranspiration (AET)** takes into account atmospheric, soil moisture and plant characteristics. **Potential evapotranspiration (PET)** is the amount of evapotranspiration which would occur if enough water was available.

Field capacity The amount of water remaining in a freely drained soil after all gravity water has been removed.

Flashy hydrograph See **Hydrograph.**

Floodplain Land over which a river spreads during seasonal or short-term floods. It is modified by shifts of the river's course.

Floodway A channel designed and located to transfer floodwaters.

Flow duration curve A graph which plots the frequency distribution of mean daily flow of a river at a particular gauging station. It indicates the percentage of time during which particular discharge rates are equalled or exceeded.

Fluvial system The interrelated parts of a river/water system.

Gauging station A site where river flow is measured using continuous readings over time or at a specific point in time. River discharge is most commonly measured.

Graded profile The long profile of a stream where erosion, transport and deposition are in a state of equilibrium. Discharge and available energy are in balance with available load.

Groundwater store The water held below the water table in aquifers. Groundwater flow describes the movement of water below the regolith.

Groyne An artificial construction built out from a shoreline or river bank to collect material and to inhibit erosion.

Horton's law of stream numbers The inverse relationship between the stream order and the number of streams of that order in a drainage basin.

Hydraulic action The force exerted by moving water on the bed and bank materials of a channel.

Hydraulic radius (HR) The cross-section of water flowing through a channel divided by the wetted perimeter of the channel. Also known as hydraulic mean depth.

Hydrochemistry The chemical make-up of the solute load of a stream.

Hydrograph Graph of water flow in a river channel over time. The **storm hydrograph** records the surge of discharge past a stream gauge which is the result of a single rainstorm. A river which responds quickly to a rainfall input, giving a high peak and rapid rise on the graph, is described as giving a **flashy hydrograph.**

Hydrological cycle The movement of water through the set of environment stores and pathways.

Hydropolitics The politics of water management issues which involve interstate or international discussion/agreement.

Hydrostatic pressure The fluid pressure exerted by the underlying column of water in a body of water when at rest.

Infiltration The movement of water, from rainfall or snowmelt, into the soil. **Infiltration capacity** is the maximum rate at which water can enter the soil in a particular case. **Infiltration rate** refers to how much water is passing through in a certain time.

Interception loss The process whereby a proportion of the precipitation input is caught and held by vegetation.

Intermittent stream Stream which flows seasonally.

Knickpoint A break of slope in the long profile of a stream. Often the upper limit along the stream to which downcutting triggered by rejuvenation has reached.

Laminar streamflow See **Streamflow.**

Leaching The removal of dissolved chemicals from the soil as precipitation drains down.

Levée A bank of sediment along the edge of the river channel, deposited naturally with floodwaters. Natural levées are often raised and strengthened artificially to contain floodwaters.

Long profile A longitudinal section of a stream channel drawn from source to mouth along the thalweg. Usually expressed graphically as a curve.

Manning's roughness coefficient A measure of the resistance of the channel to river flow. This depends upon the nature of the bed and bank material, vegetation cover and sinuosity of the channel.

Meander A pronounced bend in a river with a sinuosity ratio greater than 1:5.

Negative feedback The feedback mechanism in a system which keeps the system stable or in dynamic equilibrium. It decreases the amount of change by reducing some of the inputs.

Opportunity cost A measure of the return to be gained by using resources to produce a good or service as opposed to the return to be gained by using the same resources to produce an alternative good or service.

Overland flow The component of the precipitation input which is transferred to a stream channel by movement across the ground surface. **Saturated overland flow** occurs when excess water flows across the ground surface when the subsurface is saturated.

Perched aquifer See **Aquifer.**

Percolation The process by which water moves downwards

through rock. Often used for deeper movement below the water table.

Perennial stream Stream with permanent discharge.

Permeability The ability of rock, sediment or soil to permit water to flow through it.

Point bar Sediments laid down on the inside of a meander bend.

Point source See **Pollution.**

Pollution A condition which occurs when environmental features become adverse to the normal existence of living organisms. Pollution from a single entry point, e.g. a sewage outflow pipe, is called **point source** pollution. Pollution which has its source over a wide area, e.g. from agricultural fertilisers applied over several fields, is called **diffuse source** pollution.

Porosity The volume of water which can be held (stored) within a rock or soil.

Positive feedback The feedback mechanism in a system which causes the system to become unstable or break down. It increases the amount of change by raising some of the inputs.

Potential evapotranspiration (PET) See **Evapotranspiration.**

Potentiometric surface The level to which water will rise within an aquifer. Also known as the piezometric surface.

Precipitation The deposition of water in either liquid or solid form. It usually reaches the earth's surface from clouds in the atmosphere and includes rain, sleet, snow, hail, dew and frost.

Pumping effect The process whereby concentration of a solute increases with stream discharge.

Quickflow processes That component of the precipitation input which is delivered to the stream channel by overland flow, or rapid soil transfer.

Recurrence interval The length of time before a flood of a certain scale is likely to occur again. How often a storm and flood of a certain size is likely to occur, e.g. a 100-year flood.

Regime The seasonal discharge rhythm of a stream. A **dual regime** is when there are two seasonal peaks, while a **uniform regime** refers to a stream with a single seasonal peak.

Regolith The layer of broken material overlying bedrock.

Rejuvenation A renewal of available energy in a stream which permits accelerated erosion, entrainment and transportation. The stream has more energy and can do more work.

Revetments Artificial strengthening along a river bank to reduce erosion and control floods.

Runoff Water that moves across the surface of the land into streams rather than being absorbed by the soil.

Salinisation The build-up of salts in water and soils in arid and semi-arid areas.

Saturation The state when a parcel of air can hold (store) no additional moisture at that temperature and pressure.

Sediment Particles derived from rock material by weathering and erosion. **Sediment yield** is the amount of sediment output from a store, e.g. a slope, a stream bed, over a given period. Sedimentary deposits are areas of sediment which have been laid down by natural processes, e.g. by a river as it floods over its floodplain. Some **sedimentary deposits** form distinctive landforms.

Sinuosity The degree to which a river channel swings from side to side, usually expressed as a ratio between channel length and valley length.

Slowflow processes The hydrological processes which transmit water slowly to the river channel, e.g. slow throughflow and groundwater flow. These make up the baseflow of the river.

Soil moisture budget The balance between moisture inputs and outputs in a soil over time.

Soil moisture deficiency A condition in which more water is being lost from a soil (output) than is arriving into the soil (input).

Soil moisture recharge An increase in the water content stored in a soil.

Soil moisture surplus A condition in which there is more water entering and being stored in a soil (input and store) than is being lost or taken out (output).

Solute load That component of a stream's load which is held and transferred in the dissolved state.

Stemflow The components of precipitation input which, having been intercepted by vegetation, run down plant stems to the ground surface.

Storm hydrograph See **Hydrograph.**

Streamflow The movement of water in a stream channel. There are two main types of streamflow: (1) **Laminar streamflow** is the movement of stream water in a series of layers. Usually low velocity over a smooth surface. (2) **Turbulent streamflow** is the movement of stream water as a collection of swirling eddies. Associated with high velocities over rough surfaces.

Sustainable Which can be continued because it does not use resources faster than natural processes can replenish them.

Thalweg The long profile of a river which follows the line of maximum flow.

Throughfall Water which drips from leaves and stems to reach the ground surface.

Throughflow The downslope movement of water through the regolith.

Transpiration The process by which plants lose moisture as water vapour through their leaf stomata into the atmosphere.

Turbulent streamflow See **Streamflow**.

Unconfined aquifer See **Aquifer.**

Uniform regime See **Regime.**

Water budget/balance The balance between the inputs (precipitation) and outputs (runoff, evapotranspiration, soil and groundwater storage changes) of a drainage basin. We can show the relationship or balance between water inputs and outputs by a water budget graph.

Watershed The water-parting from which headstreams flow to separate drainage basins.

Water table The upper surface of the zone of saturation in a permeable rock. Rainwater percolates to the water table whenever precipitation exceeds evapotranspiration.

Wetted perimeter The line of contact between the water and the river channel.

Index

Published by Collins Educational
77-85 Fulham Palace Road
London W6 8JB

An imprint of HarperCollins *Publishers*

© 1995 Victoria Bishop and Robert Prosser

First published 1995
Reprinted 1996, 1997, 1998, 2000

ISBN 0 00 326684 2

Edited by Kate Hardcastle and Ron Hawkins
Designed by Wendi Watson
Outline design by Jacky Wedgwood
Picture research by Caroline Thompson
Artwork by Contour Publishing, Tom Cross, Joan Corlass, Jerry Fowler, Jeremy Glover, TTP International
Cover artwork by Jerry Fowler
Printed and bound in China

The authors and publishers are grateful to Richard Batchelor, and to Terry Marsh of the Institute of Hydrology, for their detailed comments on the typescript. They would also like to acknowledge the considerable help given by the Institute of Hydrology in providing data and visual resources for the book.

Acknowledgements

Every effort has been made to contact the holders of copyright material, but if any have been inadvertently overlooked the publishers will be pleased to make the necessary arrangements at the first opportunity.

Photographs
The publishers would like to thank the following for permission to reproduce photographs.
Patrick Bailey, Fig. 5.18;
Victoria Bishop, Figs 3.19, 3.20, 3.21, 6.6, 6.7, 6.10, 6.11;
City of Bristol Museum and Art Gallery/Bridgeman Art Library, London Fig. 7.3;
The Cheltenham Newspaper Co. Ltd, Fig. 7.1;
Altaf Hossain/DRIK, Fig. 11.3;
Paul Ferraby/Environmental Picture Library, Fig. 9.10;
Warford/Environmental Picture Library, Fig. 10.13;
Firo-Foto, Fig. 4.33;
Inga Spence/Holt Studios International, Fig. 8.1;
Institute of Hydrology, Figs. 3.2, 5.21, 6.5, 9.6;
Scot Rail/Institute of Hydrology, Fig. 7.13;
Fritz Hoffman/JB Pictures Ltd, Fig. 7.26;
London Aerial Photo Library, Figs 7.21, 8.23;
Fred Mayer/Magnum Photos, Fig. 4.36;
NASA, Fig. 4.40;
Stephen Dalton/NHPA, Fig. 6.8;
David Woodfall/NHPA, Fig. 6.23;
Bruce Paton/Panos Pictures, Figs 4.1, 4.2;
Ross Hughes/Panos Pictures, Fig. 11.7;
Robert Prosser, Figs 2.14, 2.20, 4.12, 4.13, 8.6, 8.19, 8.21, 9.16;
RGS London, Fig. 3.38;
Science Photo Library, Figs 1.2, 2.3;
Mark Edwards/Still Pictures, Fig. 3.29;
Daniel Dancer/Still Pictures, Fig. 5.7;
Paul Harrison/Still Pictures, Fig. 11.6;
Tony Stone Images, Fig. 8.35;
Thames Water, Fig. 9.14;
Caroline Thompson, Figs 3.45, 8.18;
Professor DE Walling, Fig. 5.1.

Cover picture
Uribante Caparo hydro-electric dam project, Andes, Venezuela.
Source: Tony Stone Images.

Map
Fig. 7.5, reproduced with the permission of the Controller of Her Majesty's Stationery Office, © Crown Copyright, from: Reading, Windsor and surrounding area 1994 1:50 000.